D0184873

The Official Introduction to the ITIL Service Lifecycle

London: TSO

Published by TSO (The Stationery Office) and available from:

Online
www.tsoshop.co.uk

Mail, Telephone, Fax & E-mail
TSO
PO Box 29, Norwich NR3 1GN
Telephone orders/General enquiries: 0870 600 5522
Fax orders: 0870 600 5533
E-mail: customer.services@tso.co.uk
Textphone: 0870 240 3701

TSO Shops
16 Arthur Street, Belfast BT1 4GD
028 9023 8451 Fax 028 9023 5401
71 Lothian Road, Edinburgh EH3 9AZ
0870 606 5566 Fax 0870 606 5588

TSO@Blackwell and other Accredited Agents

First published 2007

ISBN 9780113310616

Printed in the United Kingdom for The Stationery Office

N5635491 c60   08/07

Contents

List of figures

List of tables

OGC's foreword

As co-founder of the ITIL concept and leader of its early development, I'm delighted by the positive impact it has made on companies and organizations around the world. What began as a UK government initiative to set out an efficient, successful and reliable approach to service management is now a global endeavour, with publications, training and support tools available in various languages. Of course, successful growth doesn't happen by chance and ITIL has proven itself many times over through the benefits it brings to the businesses that embed its practices.

Since its creation in the late 1980s, ITIL has been developed to keep up to date with a constantly changing service management environment. Here in the latest version, I am pleased to see a top-quality product. Consultation with experts on a global scale brings you leading practices, identified through experience and brought together with the skills and expertise of our publishing partner, The Stationery Office (TSO).

I believe ITIL will continue to play an important role within government as an effective standard framework for delivery. However, the real value in ITIL is that its benefits are available to every organization, large or small, with a genuine desire to deliver a high-performing service provision. May your organization be one of those!

John Stewart
Office of Government Commerce

Chief Architect's foreword

This book is dedicated to the people who practise IT service management. Through their knowledge and experiences we have shaped the present and can see further toward the future along our journey to service excellence.

Over the past two decades the world of IT has changed dramatically. The IT Infrastructure Library framework has grown along with it and has shaped a community of practice that has spawned an entire industry. What hasn't changed in all that time is the need for us as practitioners of service management to learn how best practices evolve and how they support and influence the customer's successes or failures.

In a world of growing complexity, choice and globalization, ITIL has remained at the heart of the industry, growing and evolving to meet the needs of service providers. The current version of ITIL is a product of this evolution.

Within the pages of this book, we will introduce ITIL to the novice, further educate the practitioner and transform our understanding of IT service management best practices.

This book captures the basic concepts of the ITIL Service Lifecycle and its benefits. It serves as a reference to ITIL service management practices, but should not be considered a substitute for the ITIL core practice set.

It is from here we begin the journey into the ITIL service management practices.

Sharon Taylor
Chief Architect, ITIL Service Management Practices

Preface

Life-cycle (noun) – The various stages through which a living thing passes (*Kernerman English Multilingual Dictionary*)

The very term 'lifecycle' is used to describe the evolution of many living things in this world from their creation to expiration. The time between creation and expiration is the 'journey'.

We need only look at our own life journeys to see a living example.

Creation – the first part of our journey. As an embryo develops, its life blueprint is being established through the architecture of its DNA. The embryo's genetic structure will dictate its capability, propensity for immunity or vulnerability to disease, and certain personality characteristics it will carry throughout life.

Childhood – the formative stage. We are influenced by our exposure to the world around us and can influence our life blueprint in how we manifest and integrate ourselves with the world around us. Our understanding of our needs, both for growth and creativity, are our 'requirements' that allow us to create value for ourselves and those who come into contact with us.

Adulthood – where we hone our skills and perform within expected societal parameters. We strive to improve our capabilities continually and define our value. By this time, we have built a complex network of relationships and dependencies to others. The world we live in has become far more complex than in childhood and managing our lives more challenging.

If you replace the human metaphor above with the lifecycle of service management, you will see many similarities. This is because the ITIL Service Lifecycle represents the same evolution – from creation to expiration – and the stages in the ITIL Service Lifecycle are what fall in between.

We often forget that services are living things. They require sustenance to survive, they must continually adapt and evolve with changing needs of the business, and they will pass through various stages over their lifetime.

Services are constrained by their genetic blueprint – risks, financial investment, culture and economics – but should evolve to influence their value through interaction, evolution, dependencies and relationships, and to exploit these for positive outcomes.

This book will take you through these Service Lifecycle stages and show how to apply the knowledge contained in the ITIL core lifecycle publications.

Introduction

1

1 Introduction

1.1 A HISTORICAL PERSPECTIVE OF IT SERVICE MANAGEMENT AND ITIL

IT service management (ITSM) evolved naturally as services became underpinned in time by the developing technology. In its early years, IT was mainly focused on application development – all the new possibilities seeming to be ends in themselves. Harnessing the apparent benefits of these new technologies meant concentrating on delivering the created applications as a part of a larger service offering, supporting the business itself.

During the 1980s, as the practice of service management grew, so too did the dependency of the business. Meeting the business need called for a more radical refocus for an IT service approach and the 'IT help desk' emerged to deal with the frequency of issues suffered by those trying to use IT services in delivery of their business.

At the same time, the UK government, fuelled by a need for finding efficiencies, set out to document how the best and most successful organizations approached service management. By the late 1980s and early 1990s, they had produced a series of books documenting an approach to the IT service management needed to support business users. This library of practice was entitled the IT Infrastructure Library – ITIL to its friends.

The original Library grew to over 40 books, and started a chain reaction of interest in the UK IT service community. The term 'IT service management' had not been coined at this point, but became a common term around the mid 1990s as the popularity of ITIL grew. In 1991, a user forum, the IT Information Management Forum (ITIMF), was created to bring ITIL users together to exchange ideas and learn from each other, and would eventually change its name to the IT Service Management Forum (itSMF). Today,

the itSMF has members worldwide as ITIL's popularity continues to grow.

A formal standard for ITSM, The British Standard 15000, largely based on ITIL practices, was established and followed by various national standards in numerous countries. Since then the ISO 20000:2005 Standard was introduced and gained rapid recognition globally.

ITIL's next revision began in the mid 1990s, until 2004. Version 2 of ITIL, as it is commonly referred to, was a more targeted product – with nine books – explicitly bridging the gap between technology and business, and with guidance focused strongly on the processes required to deliver effective services to the business customer.

1.2 ITIL TODAY

In 2004, the OGC began the second major refresh initiative of ITIL, in recognition of the massive advancements in technology and emerging challenges for IT service providers. New technology architectures, virtualization and outsourcing became a mainstay of IT and the process-based approach of ITIL needed to be revamped to address service management challenges.

After twenty years ITIL remains the most recognized framework for ITSM in the world. While it has evolved and changed its breadth and depth, it preserves the fundamental concepts of leading practice.

1.2.1 Why is ITIL so successful?

ITIL is intentionally composed of a common sense approach to service management – do what works. And what works is adapting a common framework of practices that unite all areas of IT service provision toward a single aim – delivering value to the business. The following list defines the key characteristics of ITIL that contribute to its global success:

- **Non-proprietary** – ITIL service management practices are applicable in any IT organization because they are not based on any particular technology platform, or industry type. ITIL is owned by the UK government and not tied to any commercial proprietary practice or solution
- **Non-prescriptive** – ITIL offers robust, mature and time-tested practices that have applicability to all types of service organizations. It continues to be useful and relevant in public and private sectors, internal and external service providers, small, medium and large enterprise, and within any technical environment
- **Best practice** – ITIL service management practices represent the learning experiences and thought leadership of the world's best in class service providers
- **Good practice** – Not every practice in ITIL can be considered 'best practice', and for good reason. For many, a blend of common, good and best practices are what give meaning and achievability to ITSM. In some respects, best practices are the flavour of the day. All best practices become common practices over time, being replaced by new best practices.

1.3 THE ITIL VALUE PROPOSITION

All high-performing service providers share similar characteristics. This is not coincidence. There are specific capabilities inherent in their success that they demonstrate consistently. A core capability is their strategy. If you were to ask a high-achieving service provider what makes them distinctive from their competitors, they would tell you that it is their intrinsic understanding of how they provide value to their customers. They understand the customer's business objectives and the role they play in enabling those objectives to be met. A closer look would reveal that their ability to do this does not come from reacting to

customer needs, but from predicting them through preparation, analysis and examining customer usage patterns.

The next significant characteristic is the systematic use of service management practices that are responsive, consistent and measurable, and define the provider's quality in the eyes of their customers. These practices provide stability and predictability, and permeate the service provider's culture.

The final characteristic is the provider's ability to continuously analyse and fine tune service provision to maintain stable, reliable yet adaptive and responsive services that allow the customer to focus on their business without concern for IT service reliability.

In these situations you see a trusted partnership between the customer and the service provider. They share risk and reward and evolve together. Each knows they play a role in the success of the other.

As a service provider, this is what you want to achieve. As a customer, this is what you want in a service provider.

Take a moment look around at the industry high-performing service providers. You'll see that most use ITIL Service Management practices. This isn't coincidence at all.

1.4 THE ITIL SERVICE MANAGEMENT PRACTICES

When we turn on a water tap, we expect to see water flow from it. When we press down a light switch, we expect to see light fill the room. Not so many years ago these very basic things were not as reliable as they are today. We know instinctively that the advances in technology have made them reliable enough to be considered a utility. But it isn't just the technology that makes the services reliable. It is how they are managed. *This* is service management!

The use of IT today has become the utility of business. Simply having the best technology will not ensure it provides utility-like reliability. Professional, responsive, value-driven service management is what brings this quality of service to the business.

The objective of the ITIL Service Management practice framework is to provide services to business customers that are fit for purpose, stable and that are so reliable, the business views them as a trusted utility.

ITIL offers best practice guidance applicable to all types of organizations who provide services to a business. Each publication addresses capabilities having direct impact on a service provider's performance. The structure of the core practice takes form in a Service Lifecycle. It is iterative and multidimensional. It ensures organizations are set up to leverage capabilities in one area for learning and improvements in others. The core is expected to provide structure, stability and strength to service management capabilities with durable principles, methods and tools. This serves to protect investments and provide the necessary basis for measurement, learning and improvement.

The guidance in ITIL can be adapted for use in various business environments and organizational strategies. The complementary guidance provides flexibility to implement the core in a diverse range of environments. Practitioners can select complementary guidance as needed to provide traction for the core in a given business context, much like tyres are selected based on the type of automobile, purpose and road conditions. This is to increase the durability and portability of knowledge assets and to protect investments in service management capabilities.

1.5 WHAT IS A SERVICE?

Service management is more than just a set of capabilities. It is also a professional practice supported by an extensive body of knowledge, experience and skills. A global community of individuals and organizations in the public and private sectors fosters its growth and maturity. Formal schemes exist for the education, training and certification of practising organizations, and individuals influence its quality. Industry best practices, academic research and formal standards contribute to its intellectual capital and draw from it.

The origins of service management are in traditional service businesses such as airlines, banks, hotels and phone companies. Its practice has grown with the adoption by IT organizations of a service-oriented approach to managing IT applications, infrastructure and processes. Solutions to business problems and support for business models, strategies and operations are increasingly in the form of services. The popularity of shared services and outsourcing has contributed to the increase in the number of organizations who are service providers, including internal organizational units. This in turn has strengthened the practice of service management and at the same time imposed greater challenges upon it.

> **Definition of a service**
> A 'service' is a means of delivering value to customers by facilitating outcomes customers want to achieve without the ownership of specific costs and risks.
>
> There are a variety of contexts in which the definition of a service can be expanded upon, but as a basic concept, service is the means of delivering value, and no matter how your organization chooses to define a service, this must be at the heart of what defines a service.

1.6 NAVIGATING THE ITIL SERVICE MANAGEMENT LIFECYCLE

Before discussing the principles of ITIL service management practices, it is helpful to understand the overall content structure and how topics areas are organized within each of the books that together comprise the practices.

The ITIL service management practices are comprised of three main sets of products and services:

- ITIL service management practices – core guidance
- ITIL service management practices – complementary guidance
- ITIL web support services.

1.6.1 ITIL service management practices – core guidance

The core set consists of six publications:

- *Introduction to ITIL Service Management Practices* (this publication)
- *Service Strategy*
- *Service Design*
- *Service Transition*
- *Service Operation*
- *Continual Service Improvement*.

A common structure across all the core guidance publications helps to easily find references between volumes and where to look for similar guidance topics within each stage of the lifecycle:

Practice fundamentals

This section of each core publication sets out the business case argument of the need for viewing service management in a lifecycle context and an overview of the practices in that stage of the lifecycle that contributes to it. It briefly outlines the context for the practices that follow and how they contribute to business value.

Practice principles

Practice principles are the policies and governance aspects of that lifecycle stage that anchor the tactical processes and activities to achieving their objectives.

Lifecycle processes and activities

The Service Lifecycle stages rely on processes to execute each element of the practice in a consistent, measurable, repeatable way. Each core publication identifies the processes it makes use of, how they integrate with the other stages of the lifecycle, and the activities needed to carry them out.

Supporting organization structures and roles

Each publication identifies the organizational roles and responsibilities that should be considered to manage the Service Lifecycle. These roles are provided as a guideline and can be combined to fit into a variety of organization structures. Suggestions for optimal organization structures are also provided.

Technology considerations

ITIL service management practices gain momentum when the right type of technical automation is applied. Each lifecycle publication makes recommendations on the areas to focus technology automation on, and the basic requirements a service provider will want to consider when choosing service management tools.

Practice implementation

For organizations new to ITIL, or those wishing to improve their practice maturity and service capability, each publication outlines the best ways to implement the ITIL Service Lifecycle stage.

Challenges, risks and critical success factors

These are always present in any organization. Each publication highlights the common challenges, risks and success factors that most organizations experience and how to overcome them.

Complementary guidance

There are many external methods, practices and frameworks that align well to ITIL practices. Each publication provides a list of these and how they integrate into the ITIL Service Lifecycle, when they are useful and how.

Examples and templates

Each publication provides working templates and examples of how the practices can be applied. They are provided to help you capitalize on the industry experience and expertise already in use. Each can be adapted within your particular organizational context.

1.6.2 ITIL service management practices – complementary guidance

This is a living library of publications with guidance specific to industry sectors, organization types, operating models and technology architectures. Each publication supports and enhances the guidance in the ITIL core. Publications in this category will be continually added to the complementary library of practice and will contain contributions from the expert and user ITSM community. In this way, ITIL practices are illustrated in real-life situations and in a variety of contexts that add value and knowledge to your own ITIL practice.

1.6.3 ITIL web support services

These products are online, interactive services including a Glossary of Terms and Definitions, Interactive Service Management Model, online subscriber services, case studies, templates and ITIL Live® (www.itil-live-portal.com), an interactive expert knowledge centre where users can access time with ITSM experts to discuss questions and issues, and seek advice.

Core guidance topics 2

2   Core guidance topics

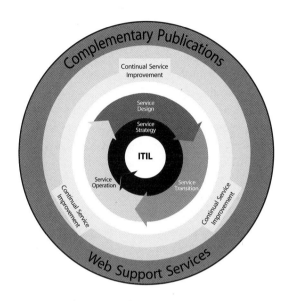

2.1   SERVICE STRATEGY

At the core of the Service Lifecycle is Service Strategy.

Service Strategy provides guidance on how to view service management not only as an organizational capability but as a strategic asset. Guidance is provided on the principles underpinning the practice of service management which are useful for developing service management policies, guidelines and processes across the ITIL Service Lifecycle.

Topics covered in Service Strategy include the development of service markets, characteristics of internal and external provider types, service assets, the service portfolio and implementation of strategy through the Service Lifecycle. Financial Management, Demand Management, Organizational Development and Strategic Risks are among other major topics.

Organizations should use Service Strategy guidance to set objectives and expectations of performance towards

serving customers and market spaces, and to identify, select and prioritize opportunities. Service Strategy is about ensuring that organizations are in position to handle the costs and risks associated with their service portfolios, and are set up not just for operational effectiveness but for distinctive performance.

Organizations already practicing ITIL use Service Strategy to guide a strategic review of their ITIL-based service management capabilities and to improve the alignment between those capabilities and their business strategies. This ITIL volume encourages readers to stop and think about why something is to be done before thinking of how.

2.2   SERVICE DESIGN

'If you build it, they will come' is a saying from a famous 1989 Hollywood movie, *Field of Dreams*. But if you build it and it doesn't provide value, they will soon leave!

For services to provide true value to the business, they must be designed with the business objectives in mind. Service Design is the stage in the lifecycle that turns Service Strategy into the blueprint for delivering the business objectives.

Service Design provides guidance for the design and development of services and service management practices. It covers design principles and methods for converting strategic objectives into portfolios of services and service assets. The scope of Service Design is not limited to new services. It includes the changes and improvements necessary to increase or maintain value to customers over the lifecycle of services, the continuity of services, achievement of service levels, and conformance to standards and regulations. It guides organizations on how to develop design capabilities for service management.

Among the key topics in Service Design are Service Catalogue, Availability, Capacity, Continuity and Service Level Management.

2.3 SERVICE TRANSITION

Transition [tran-zish-*uhn*] – Movement, passage, or change from one position, state, stage, subject, concept, etc., to another; change: the transition from adolescence to adulthood.

Service Transition provides guidance for the development and improvement of capabilities for transitioning new and changed services into live service operation. This publication provides guidance on how the requirements of Service Strategy encoded in Service Design are effectively realized in Service Operation while controlling the risks of failure and disruption.

The publication combines practices in Change, Configuration, Asset, Release and Deployment, Programme and Risk Management and places them in the practical context of service management. It provides guidance on managing the complexity related to changes to services and service management processes; preventing undesired consequences while allowing for innovation. Guidance is provided on transferring the control of services between customers and service providers.

Service Transition introduces the Service Knowledge Management System, which builds upon the current data and information within Configuration, Capacity, Known Error, Definitive Media and Assets systems and broadens the use of service information into knowledge capability for decision and management of services.

2.4 SERVICE OPERATION

Service Operation embodies practices in the management of the day-to-day operation of services. It includes guidance on achieving effectiveness and efficiency in the delivery and support of services to ensure value for the customer and the service provider. Strategic objectives are ultimately realized through Service Operation, therefore making it a critical capability. Guidance is provided on how to maintain stability in service operations, allowing for changes in design, scale, scope and service levels. Organizations are provided with detailed process guidelines, methods and tools for use in two major control perspectives: reactive and proactive. Managers and practitioners are provided with knowledge allowing them to make better decisions in areas such as managing the availability of services, controlling demand, optimizing capacity utilization, scheduling of operations and fixing problems. Guidance is provided on supporting operations through new models and architectures such as shared services, utility computing, web services and mobile commerce.

Among the topics in this book are Event, Incident, Problem, Request, Application and Technical Management practices. This book discusses some of the newer industry practices to manage virtual and service-oriented architectures.

2.5 CONTINUAL SERVICE IMPROVEMENT

Continual Service Improvement provides instrumental guidance in creating and maintaining value for customers through better design, transition and operation of services. It combines principles, practices and methods from quality management, change management and capability improvement. Organizations learn to realize incremental and large-scale improvements in service quality, operational efficiency and business continuity. Guidance is provided for linking improvement efforts and outcomes with service strategy, design and transition. A closed-loop feedback system, based on the Plan-Do-Check-Act (PDCA) model (see section 2.6), is established and capable of receiving inputs for improvements from any planning perspective.

Guidance on Service Measurement, demonstrating value with metrics, developing baselines and maturity assessments are among the key topics.

2.6 LIFECYCLE QUALITY CONTROL

Consistent with the structures adopted by high-performing businesses today and standards bodies around the world, the ITIL Service Lifecycle approach embraces and enhances the interpretation of the Deming Quality Cycle (Figure 2.1) of Plan-Do-Check-Act. You will see this quality cycle used in the structure of the practices in each of the core guides.

The ITIL framework incorporates the Deming Quality Cycle by applying it to the Service Lifecycle stages. This helps align the practices of ITIL to the structure of external practices such as COBIT and ISO/IEC 20000.

2.7 ITIL CONFORMANCE OR COMPLIANCE – PRACTICE ADAPTATION

An important aspect of ITIL is the 'open-source' nature of its practices. It is intended and strongly recommended that organizations adapt ITIL practices within their own context, and entrench their own best practices within an overall Service Management framework.

For example, within Service Transition, ITIL provides a selection of Change Management models for standard, normal and emergency Changes. In many cases, these models as described in Service Transition may be all you need and they cover the range of possible change types in

Figure 2.1 The Deming Quality Cycle

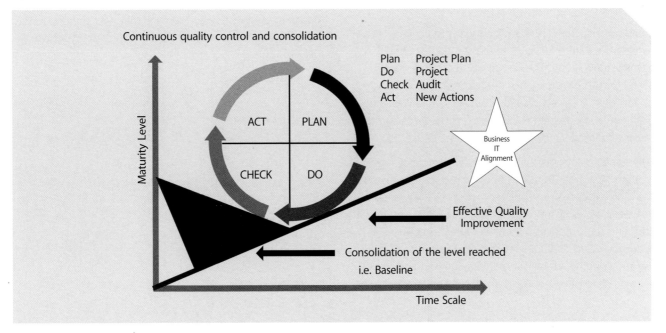

an organization. Within each model, a specific flow of process and procedure is provided. If in your organization, more steps for an emergency change make sense to meet your requirements and objectives, then you should adapt these into the generic ITIL Change process flow. Doing so does not mean you no longer conform to ITIL. As long as the main ITIL process steps, inputs and outputs are included and the objectives met, that is your best practice and is fit for purpose in your organizational context.

ITIL is a framework an organization conforms to, not complies with. There is a major difference between these two things and one that is often misunderstood.

Conformity allows flexibility in the adaptation of practices within an organizational context while maintaining the overall structure of the framework. **Compliance** is highly specific, often audited to a formal standard and the organization's practices must mimic externally defined practices. There is a need for both within certain contexts, but a key to agile service management practices is knowing which, in what blend and in what context conformance or compliance should apply.

Many organizations use ITIL as a means to achieve compliance with a formal, audited standard such as ISO/IEC 20000:2005. The design of ITIL is particularly useful for this purpose since the framework is architected to ensure that an organization's service capabilities are designed and operated using the practices that align to these standards.

This standard set outs the key areas of compliance and requires that organizations can demonstrate that they use the management systems and practices in these areas in order to be compliant to the standard. Experts agree that adopting ITIL produces a framework best suited to achieving ISO/IEC 20000 certification. Later in this book a list of common external frameworks, method and standards are provided that have a solid alignment to the

practices of ITIL and fit well into any organization's service practices.

2.8 GETTING STARTED – SERVICE LIFECYCLE PRINCIPLES

In the following chapters you will learn about the key concepts within the ITIL Service Lifecycle. You begin by working your way from the core of the lifecycle, Service Strategy, then around the revolving lifecycle practices of Service Design, Transition and Operation, finishing with Continual Service Improvement. Afterward, you should have a clear understanding of the basic concepts of the ITIL Service Lifecycle and how the core practice publications can be useful to you. This will help readers to further examine particular areas within any of the core guidance books that offer detailed practice information in areas that support your day-to-day service management role.

The following table gives a general view of some of the more common roles in organizations and the ITIL service management practice core guides that host the day-to-day practices, processes and activities most related to those roles.

Table 2.1 Roles and core guides

Role	Core guide
Service Desk Manager/staff	Service Operation
Incident Manager/Technical Support staff	Service Transition and Service Operation
Operations Management	Service Transition and Service Operation
Change Manager/Change Requestor	Service Transition
Solution Development	Service Design
Testing/Production Assurance	Service Transition and Service Operation
Service Level Manager	All core publications
Application/Infrastructure Architect	All core publications
Supplier Relationship Management	Service Design
IT Steering/Governance	Service Strategy, Service Design
CIO/IT Director	All core publications
IT Service Manager	All core publications
Portfolio Manager	All core publications

NOTE: It is extremely important to reiterate that no one core book exists in isolation, just as no one part of service management practice does. Organizations interested in adopting ITIL or further maturing their current ITIL practice must consider the lifecycle in its entirety and the benefit all five of the core books provide. Just as this Introduction book is not a substitute for the core library, one core guide alone is not sufficient to adopt and use the practices to their full potential.

The ITIL Service Management Lifecycle – core of practice

3

3   The ITIL Service Management Lifecycle – core of practice

The Service Lifecycle contains five elements as shown in Figure 3.1, each of which rely on service principles, processes, roles and performance measures. The Service Lifecycle uses a hub and spoke design, with Service Strategy at the hub, Service Design, Transition and Operation as the revolving lifecycle stages, and anchored by Continual Service Improvement. Each part of the lifecycle exerts influence on the other and relies on the other for inputs and feedback. In this way, a constant set of checks and balances throughout the Service Lifecycle ensures that as business demand changes with business need, the services can adapt and respond effectively to them.

At the heart of the Service Lifecycle is the key principle – all services must provide measurable value to business objectives and outcomes. ITIL Service Management focuses on business value as its prime objective. Each practice revolves around ensuring that everything a service provider does to manage IT services for the business

Figure 3.1 The ITIL Service Lifecycle

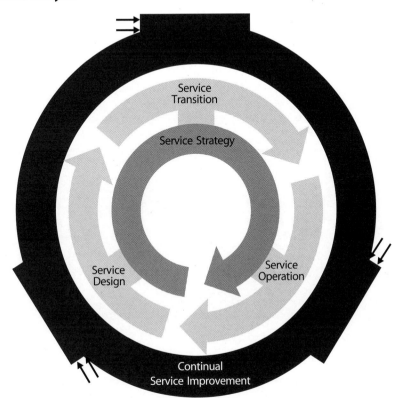

customer can be measured and quantified in terms of business value. This has become extremely important today as IT organizations must operate themselves as businesses in order to demonstrate a clear return on investment and equate service performance with business value to the customer.

3.1 FUNCTIONS AND PROCESSES ACROSS THE LIFECYCLE

3.1.1 Functions

Functions are units of organizations specialized to perform certain types of work and responsible for specific outcomes. They are self-contained with capabilities and resources necessary to their performance and outcomes. Capabilities include work methods internal to the functions. Functions have their own body of knowledge, which accumulates from experience. They provide structure and stability to organizations.

Functions typically define roles and the associated authority and responsibility for a specific performance and outcomes. Coordination between functions through shared processes is a common pattern in organization design. Functions tend to optimize their work methods locally to focus on assigned outcomes. Poor coordination between functions combined with an inward focus leads to functional silos that hinder alignment and feedback critical to the success of the organization as a whole. Process models help avoid this problem with functional hierarchies by improving cross-functional coordination and control. Well-defined processes can improve productivity within and across functions.

3.1.2 Processes

Processes are examples of closed-loop systems because they provide change and transformation towards a goal, and use feedback for self-reinforcing and self-corrective action (Figure 3.2). It is important to consider the entire process or how one process fits into another.

Figure 3.2 Process architecture

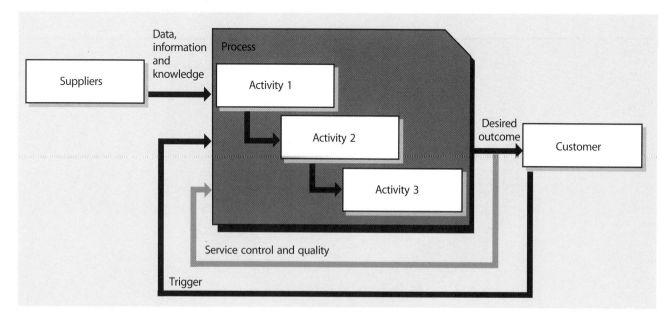

Process definitions describe actions, dependencies and sequence. Processes have the following characteristics:

- They are measurable and are performance driven. Managers want to measure cost, quality and other variables while practitioners are concerned with duration and productivity.
- They have specific results. The reason a process exists is to deliver a specific result. This result must be individually identifiable and countable.
- They deliver to customers. Every process delivers its primary results to a customer or stakeholder. They may be internal or external to the organization but the process must meet their expectations.
- They respond to a specific event. While a process may be ongoing or iterative, it should be traceable to a specific trigger.

3.1.3 Specialization and coordination across the lifecycle

Specialization and coordination are necessary in the lifecycle approach. Feedback and control between the functions and processes within and across the elements of the lifecycle make this possible. The dominant pattern in the lifecycle is the sequential progress starting from Service Strategy (SS) through Service Delivery (SD) – Service Transition (ST) – Service Operation (SO) and back to SS through Continual Service Improvement (CSI). That, however, is not the only pattern of action. Every element of the lifecycle provides points for feedback and control.

The combination of multiple perspectives allows greater flexibility and control across environments and situations. The lifecycle approach mimics the reality of most organizations where effective management requires the use of multiple control perspectives. Those responsible for the design, development and improvement of processes for service management can adopt a process-based control perspective. For those responsible for managing agreements, contracts and services may be better served by a lifecycle-based control perspective with distinct phases. Both these control perspectives benefit from systems thinking. Each control perspective can reveal patterns that may not be apparent from the other.

3.1.4 Feedback throughout the Service Lifecycle

The strength of the ITIL Service Lifecycle rests upon continual feedback throughout each stage of the lifecycle. This feedback ensures that service optimization is managed from a business perspective and is measured in terms of the value business derives from services at any point in time through the Service Lifecycle. The ITIL Service Lifecycle is non-linear in design. At every point in the Service Lifecycle, monitoring, assessment and feedback flows between each stage of the lifecycle which drive decisions about the need for minor course corrections or major service improvement initiatives. The following figure illustrates some examples of the continual feedback system built into the ITIL Service Lifecycle.

Figure 3.3 Continual feedback loop

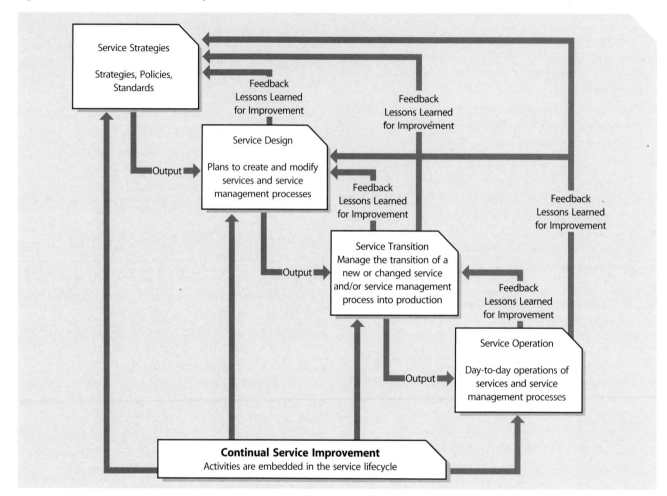

Service Strategy –
governance and
decision-making

4

4 Service Strategy – governance and decision-making

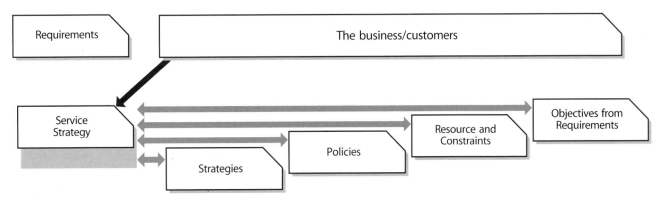

As the core of the ITIL Service Lifecycle, Service Strategy sets the stage for developing a service provider's core capabilities. This chapter will discuss a selection of the key concepts from the Service Strategy book to help aid the understanding of the role of Service Strategy in the ITIL Service Lifecycle.

Imagine you have been given responsibility for an IT organization. This organization could be internal or external, commercial or not-for-profit. How would you go about deciding on a strategy to serve customers? What if you have a variety of customers, all with specific needs and demands? How do you define your service strategy to meet all of them?

Service Strategy provides guidance to help answer that key question. It is comprised of the following key concepts.

- Value creation
- Service assets
- Service Provider types
- Service capabilities and resources
- Service structures

- Defining the service market
- Developing service offerings
- Financial Management
- Service Portfolios
- Demand Management
- Service assessment
- Return on investment.

4.1 STRATEGIC ASSESSMENT

In crafting a service strategy, a provider should first take a careful look at what it does already. It is likely there already exists a core of differentiation. An established service provider frequently lacks an understanding of its own unique differentiators. The following questions can help expose a service provider's distinctive capabilities:

Which of our services or service varieties are the most distinctive?

Are there services that the business or customer cannot easily substitute? The differentiation can come in the form of barriers to entry, such as the organization's know-how of the customer's business or the broadness of service offerings. Or it may be in the form of raised switching costs, due to lower cost structures generated through specialization or service sourcing. It may be a particular attribute not readily found elsewhere, such as product knowledge, regulatory compliance, provisioning speeds, technical capabilities or global support structures.

Which of our services or service varieties are the most profitable?

The form of value may be monetary, as in higher profits or lower expenses, or social, as in saving lives or collecting taxes. For non-profit organizations, are there services that allow the organization to perform its mission better? Substitute 'profit' with 'benefits realized'.

Which of our customers and stakeholders are the most satisfied?

Which customers, channels or purchase occasions are the most profitable?

Again, the form of value can be monetary, social or other.

Which of our activities in our value chain or value network are the most different and effective?

The answers to these questions will likely reveal patterns that lend insight to future strategic decisions. These decisions, and related objectives, form the basis of a strategic assessment.

Service Providers can be present in more than one market space. As part of strategic planning, Service Providers should analyse their presence across various market spaces. Strategic reviews include the analysis of strengths, weaknesses, opportunities and threats in each market space. Service Providers also analyse their business

Table 4.1 Factors in strategic assessment

Factor	Description
Strengths and weaknesses	The attributes of the organization. For example, resources and capabilities, service quality, operating leverage, experience, skills, cost structures, customer service, global reach, product knowledge, customer relationships and so on.
Distinctive competencies	As discussed throughout the chapter, 'What makes the service provider special to its business or customers?'
Business strategy	The perspective, position, plans and patterns received from a business strategy. For example, a Type I and II may be directed, as part of a new business model, to expose services to external partners or over the internet.
	This is also where the discussion on customer outcomes begins and is carried forward into objectives setting.
Critical success factors	How will the Service Provider know when it is successful? When must those factors be achieved?
Threats and opportunities	Includes competitive thinking. For example, 'Is the service provider vulnerable to substitution?'
	Or, 'Is there a means to outperform competing alternatives?'

potential based on un-served or underserved market spaces. This is an important aspect of leadership and direction provided by the senior management of Service Providers. The long-term vitality of the Service Provider rests on supporting customer needs as they change or grow as well exploiting new opportunities that emerge. This analysis identifies opportunities with current and prospective customers. It also prioritizes investments in service assets based on their potential to serve market spaces of interest. For example, if a Service Provider has strong capabilities and resources in service recovery, it explores all those market spaces where such assets can deliver value for customers.

4.2 DEVELOPING STRATEGIC CAPABILITIES

To operate and grow successfully in the long term, service providers must have the ability to think and act in a strategic manner. The purpose of Service Strategy is to help organizations develop such abilities. The achievement of strategic goals or objectives requires the use of strategic assets. The guidance shows how to transform service management into a strategic asset. Readers benefit from seeing the relationships between various services, systems or processes they manage and the business models, strategies or objectives they support. The guidance answers questions of the following kind:

- What services should we offer and to whom?
- How do we differentiate ourselves from competing alternatives?
- How do we truly create value for our customers?
- How can we make a case for strategic investments?
- How should we define service quality?
- How do we efficiently allocate resources across a portfolio of services?
- How do we resolve conflicting demands for shared resources?

A multi-disciplinary approach is required to answer such questions. Technical knowledge of IT is necessary but not sufficient. The guidance is pollinated with knowledge from the disciplines such as operations management, marketing, finance, information systems, organizational development, systems dynamics and industrial engineering. The result is a body of knowledge robust enough to be effective across a wide range of business environments. Some organizations are putting in place the foundational elements of service management. Others are further up the adoption curve, ready to tackle challenges and opportunities with higher levels of complexity and uncertainty.

4.3 SERVICE PROVIDER TYPES – MATCHING NEED TO CAPABILITY

The aim of service management is to make available capabilities and resources useful to the customer in the highly usable form of services at acceptable levels of quality, cost and risks. Service Providers help relax the constraints on customers of ownership and control of specific resources. In addition to the value from utilizing such resources now offered as services, customers are freed to focus on what they consider to be their core competence. The relationship between customers and Service Providers varies by specialization in ownership and control of resources and the coordination of dependencies between different pools of resources.

Service Strategy defines three broad types of Service Providers with whom a customer is likely to engage in accessing services.

- Type I – Internal Service Provider
  Type I providers are typically business functions embedded within the business units they serve. The business units themselves may be part of a larger enterprise or parent organization. Business functions such as finance, administration, logistics, human

resources and IT provide services required by various parts of the business. They are funded by overheads and are required to operate strictly within the mandates of the business. Type I providers have the benefit of tight coupling with their owner-customers, avoiding certain costs and risks associated with conducting business with external parties.

- Type II – Shared Service Provider
  Business functions such as finance, IT, human resources and logistics are not always at the core of an organization's competitive advantage. Hence, they need not be maintained at the corporate level where they demand the attention of the chief executive's team. Instead, the services of such shared functions are consolidated into an autonomous special unit called a shared services unit (SSU). This model allows a more devolved governing structure under which an SSU can focus on serving business units as direct customers. SSUs can create, grow and sustain an internal market for their services and model themselves along the lines of service providers in the open market. Like corporate business functions, they can leverage opportunities across the enterprise and spread their costs and risks across a wider base.

- Type III – External Service Provider
  Type III providers can offer competitive prices and drive down unit costs by consolidating demand. Certain business strategies are not adequately served by internal Service Providers such as Type I and Type II. Customers may pursue sourcing strategies requiring services from external providers. The motivation may be access to knowledge, experience, scale, scope, capabilities and resources that are either beyond the reach of the organization or outside the scope of a carefully considered investment portfolio. Business strategies often require reductions in the asset base, fixed costs, operational risks or the redeployment of financial assets. Competitive business environments often require customers to have flexible and lean structures. In such cases it is better to buy services rather than own and operate the assets necessary to execute certain business functions and processes. For such customers, Type III is the best choice for a given set of services.

Today, it is common to see all three types combining capabilities to manage services for a customer. The power of this approach lies in selecting the right blend and balance.

The Service Strategy publication provides detailed guidance on provider types and how to decide on the right blend.

4.4 SERVICES AS ASSETS – VALUE CREATION

A good business model describes the means of fulfilling an organization's objectives. However, without a strategy that in some way makes a Service Provider uniquely valuable to the customer, there is little to prevent alternatives from displacing the organization, degrading its mission or entering its market space. A service strategy therefore defines a unique approach for delivering better value. The need for having a service strategy is not limited to Service Providers who are commercial enterprises. Internal Service Providers need just as much to have a clear perspective, positioning and plans to ensure they remain relevant to the business strategies of their enterprises.

Service assets have two main characteristics:

- **Utility** is perceived by the customer from the attributes of the service that have a *positive effect* on the performance of tasks associated with desired business outcomes. This is fit for purpose.
- **Warranty** is derived from the *positive effect* being available when needed, in sufficient capacity or magnitude, and dependably in terms of continuity and security. This is fit for use.

Utility is what the customer gets, and warranty is how it is delivered.

Resources and capabilities are types of assets that, when combined in various ways, produce service utility and warranty. Organizations use them to create value in the form of goods and services. Resources are direct inputs for production. Management, organization, people and knowledge are used to transform resources. Capabilities represent an organization's ability to coordinate, control and deploy resources to produce value. They are typically experience-driven, knowledge-intensive, information-based and firmly embedded within an organization's people, systems, processes and technologies.

Customers perceive benefits in a continued relationship, and entrust the provider with the business of increasing value and also adding new customers and market spaces to the realm of possibilities. This justifies further investments in service management in terms of capabilities and resources, which have a tendency to reinforce each other.

Customers may initially trust the provider with low-value contracts or non-critical services. Service management

responds by delivering the performance expected of a strategic asset. The performance is rewarded with contract renewals, new services and customers, which together represent a larger value of business. To handle this increase in value, service management must invest further in assets such as process, knowledge, people, applications and infrastructure. Successful learning and growth enables commitments of higher service levels as service management gets conditioned to handle bigger challenges.

4.5 DEFINING THE MARKET SPACE

A market space is defined by a set of business outcomes, which can be facilitated by a service. The opportunity to facilitate those outcomes defines a market space. The following are examples of business outcomes that can be the bases of one or more market spaces:

- Sales teams are productive with sales management system on wireless computers
- E-commerce website is linked to the warehouse management system
- Key business applications are monitored and secure

Figure 4.1 Service Provider capabilities and resources

Capabilities		Resources	
A1	Management	Financial capital	A9
A2	Organization	Infrastructure	A8
A3	Processes	Applications	A7
A4	Knowledge	Information	A6
	People	A5 People	

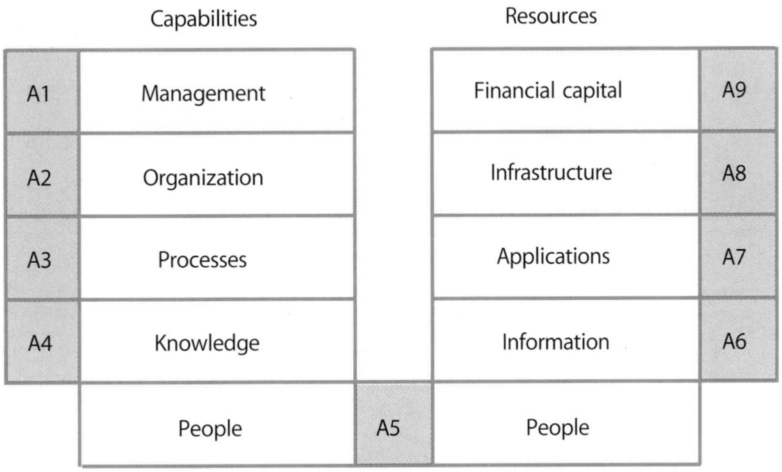

- Loan officers have faster access to information required on loan applicants
- Online bill payment service offers more options for shoppers to pay
- Business continuity is assured.

Each of the conditions is related to one or more categories of customer assets, such as people, infrastructure, information, accounts receivables and purchase orders, and can then be linked to the services that make them possible.

Customers will prefer the one that means lower costs and risks. Service Providers create these conditions through the services they deliver and thereby provide support for customers to achieve specific business outcomes.

A market space therefore represents a set of opportunities for Service Providers to deliver value to a customer's business through one or more services. This approach has definite value for Service Providers in building strong relationships with customers. Often it is not clear how services create value for customers. Services are often defined in terms of resources made available for use by customers. Service definitions lack clarity in the context in which such resources are useful, and the business outcomes that justify their cost from a customer's perspective. This problem leads to poor designs, ineffective operation and lacklustre performance in service contracts. Service improvements are difficult when it is not clear where improvements are truly required. Customers can understand and appreciate improvements only within the context of their own business assets, performances and outcomes. It is therefore important the Service Providers identify their market spaces by ensuring they define service by business outcomes such as those described above and in Figure 4.2.

4.6 SERVICE PORTFOLIOS

The Service Portfolio (Figure 4.3) represents the commitments and investments made by a Service Provider across all customers and market spaces. It represents

Figure 4.2 Actionable components of service definitions in terms of utility

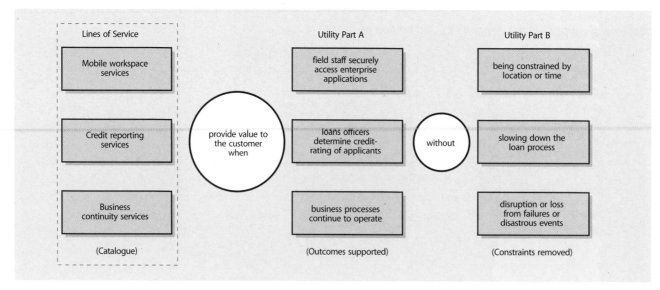

present contractual commitments, new service development, and ongoing service improvement programmes initiated by Continual Service Improvement. The portfolio also includes third-party services, which are an integral part of service offerings to customers. Some third-party services are visible to the customers while others are not.

The Service Portfolio represents all the resources presently engaged or being released in various phases of the Service Lifecycle. Each phase requires resources for completion of projects, initiatives and contracts. This is a very important governance aspect of Service Portfolio Management (SPM). Entry, progress and exit are approved only with approved funding and a financial plan for recovering costs or showing profit as necessary. The Portfolio should have the right mix of services in development for the market spaces and the Service Catalogue (Figure 4.4) to secure the financial viability of the Service Provider. The Service Catalogue is the only part of the Portfolio that recovers costs or earns profits.

Figure 4.3 Service Portfolio

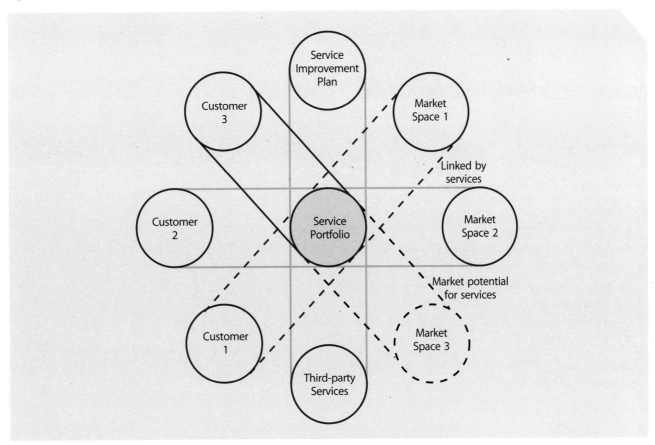

Figure 4.4 Elements of a Service Portfolio and Service Catalogue

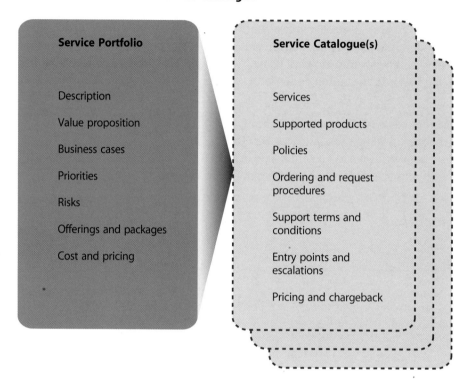

If we think of SPM as a dynamic and ongoing process set, it should include the following work methods:

- **Define**: inventory services, ensure business cases and validate portfolio data
- **Analyse**: minimize portfolio value, align and prioritize and balance supply and demand
- **Approve**: finalize proposed portfolio, authorize services and resources
- **Charter**: communicate decisions, allocate resources and charter services.

Figure 4.5 Service Portfolio management

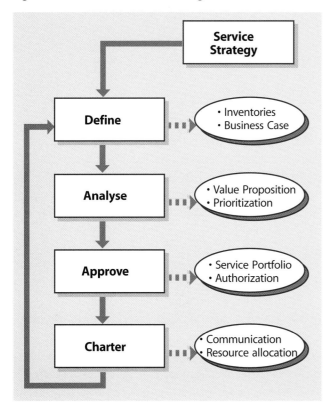

4.6.1 Service Pipeline

The Service Pipeline consists of services under development for a given market space or customer. These services are to be phased into operation by Service Transition after completion of design, development and testing. The Pipeline represents the Service Provider's growth and strategic outlook for the future. The general health of the provider is reflected in the Pipeline. It also reflects the extent to which new service concepts and ideas for improvement are being fed by Service Strategy, Service Design and Continual Service Improvement. Good financial management is necessary to ensure adequate funding for the Pipeline.

4.6.2 Service Catalogue

The Service Catalogue is the subset of the Service Portfolio visible to customers. It consists of services presently active in the Service Operation phase and those approved to be readily offered to current or prospective customers. Items can enter the Service Catalogue only after due diligence has been performed on related costs and risks. Resources are engaged to fully support active services.

The Service Catalogue is useful in developing suitable solutions for customers from one or more services. Items in the Service Catalogue can be configured and suitably priced to fulfil a particular need. The Service Catalogue is an important tool for Service Strategy because it is the virtual projection of the Service Provider's actual and present capabilities. Many customers are only interested in what the provider can commit now, rather than in future.

4.7 SERVICE OUTSOURCING – PRACTICAL DECISION-MAKING

A service strategy should enhance an organization's special strengths and core competencies. Each component should reinforce the other. Change any one and you have a different model. As organizations seek to improve their performance, they should consider which competencies are essential and know when to extend their capabilities by partnering in areas both inside and outside their enterprise.

Outsourcing is the moving of a value-creating activity that was performed inside the organization to outside the organization where it is performed by another company. What prompts an organization to outsource an activity is the same logic that determines whether an organization makes or buys inputs. Namely, does the extra value generated from performing an activity inside the organization outweigh the costs of managing it? This decision can change over time.

Table 4.2 Types of sourcing structures

Sourcing structure	Description
Internal (Type I)	The provision and delivery of services by internal staff. Does not typically include standardization of service delivery across business units.
	Provides the most control but also the most limited in terms of scale.
Shared services (Type II)	An internal business unit. Typically operates its profit and loss, and a chargeback mechanism. If cost recovery is not used, then it is internal not shared services.
	Lower costs than Internal with a similar degree of control. Improved standardization but limited in terms of scale.
Full service outsourcing	A single contract with a single Service Provider. Typically involves significant asset transfer.
	Provides improved scale but limited in terms of best-in-class capabilities. Delivery risks are higher than prime, consortium or selective outsourcing as switching to an alternative is difficult.
Prime	A single contract with a single Service Provider who manages service delivery but engages multiple providers to do so. The contract stipulates that the prime vendor will leverage the capabilities of other best-in-class Service Providers.
	Capabilities and risk are improved from single-vendor outsourcing but complexity is increased.
Consortium	A collection of Service Providers explicitly selected by the service recipient. All providers are required to come together and present a unified management interface.
	Fulfils a need that cannot be satisfied by any single-vendor outsourcer. Provides best-in-class capabilities with greater control than prime. Risk is introduced in the form of providers forced to collaborate with competitors.
Selective outsourcing	A collection of Service Providers explicitly selected and managed by the service recipient.
	This is the most difficult structure to manage. The service recipient is the service integrator, responsible for gaps or cross-provider disputes.
	The term 'co-sourcing' refers to a special case of selective outsourcing. In this variant, the service recipient maintains an internal or shared services structure and combines it with external providers. The service recipient is the service integrator.

Sourcing requires businesses to formally consider a sourcing strategy, the structure and role of the retained organization, and how decisions are made. When sourcing services, the enterprise retains the responsibility for the adequacy of services delivered. Therefore, the enterprise retains key overall responsibility for governance. The enterprise should adopt a formal governance approach in order to create a working model for managing its outsourced services as well as the assurance of value delivery. This includes planning for the organizational change precipitated by the sourcing strategy and a formal and verifiable description as to how decisions on services are made. Table 4.2 describes the generic forms of service sourcing structures.

Partnering with providers who are ISO/IEC 20000 compliant can be an important element in reducing the risk of service sourcing. Organizations who have achieved this certification are more likely to meet service levels on a sustained basis. This credential is particularly important in multi-sourced environments where a common framework promotes better integration. Multi-sourced environments require common language, integrated processes and a management structure between internal and external providers. ISO/IEC 20000 does not provide all of this but it provides a foundation on which it can be built.

4.7.1 Sourcing governance

There is a frequent misunderstanding of the definition of 'governance', particularly in a sourcing context. Companies have used the word interchangeably with 'vendor management', 'retained staff' and 'sourcing management organization'. Governance is none of these.

Management and governance are different disciplines. Management deals with making decisions and executing processes. Governance only deals with making sound decisions. It is the framework of decision rights that encourages desired behaviours in the sourcing and the sourced organization. When companies confuse

management and governance, they inevitably focus on execution at the expense of strategic decision-making. Both are vitally important. Further complicating matters is the requirement of sharing decision rights with the Service Providers. When a company places itself in a position to make operational decisions on behalf of an outsourcer, the outcomes are inevitably poor service levels and contentious relationship management.

Governance is invariably the weakest link in a service sourcing strategy. A few simple constructs have been shown to be effective at improving that weakness:

- **A governance body** – By forming a manageably sized governance body with a clear understanding of the service sourcing strategy, decisions can be made without escalating to the highest levels of senior management. By including representation from each Service Provider, stronger decisions can be made.
- **Governance domains** – Domains can cover decision-making for a specific area of the service sourcing strategy. Domains can cover, for example, service delivery, communication, sourcing strategy or contract management. Remember, a governance domain does not include the responsibility for its execution, only its strategic decision-making.
- **Creation of a decision-rights matrix** – This ties all three recommendations together. RACI or RASIC charts are common forms of a decision-rights matrix.

4.8 RETURN ON INVESTMENT (ROI)

Return on investment (ROI) is a concept for quantifying the value of an investment. Its use and meaning are not always precise. When dealing with financial officers, ROI most likely means ROIC (return on invested capital), a measure of business performance. In service management, ROI is used as a measure of the ability to use assets to generate additional value. In the simplest sense, it is the net profit of an investment divided by the net worth of the assets invested. The resulting percentage is applied to either additional top-line revenue or the elimination of bottom-line cost.

It is not unexpected that companies seek to apply ROI in deciding to adopt service management. ROI is appealing because it is self-evident. The measure either meets or does not meet a numerical criterion. The challenge is when ROI calculations focus on the short term. The application of service management has different degrees of ROI, depending on business impact (see Figure 4.6). Moreover, there are often difficulties in quantifying the complexities involved in implementations.

While a service can be directly linked and justified through specific business imperatives, few companies can readily identify the financial return for the specific aspects of service management. It is often an investment that companies must make in advance of any return.

4.9 FINANCIAL MANAGEMENT

Operational visibility, insight and superior decision-making are the core capabilities brought to the enterprise through the rigorous application of Financial Management. Just as business units accrue benefits through the analysis of

Figure 4.6 Business impact and ROI outcome

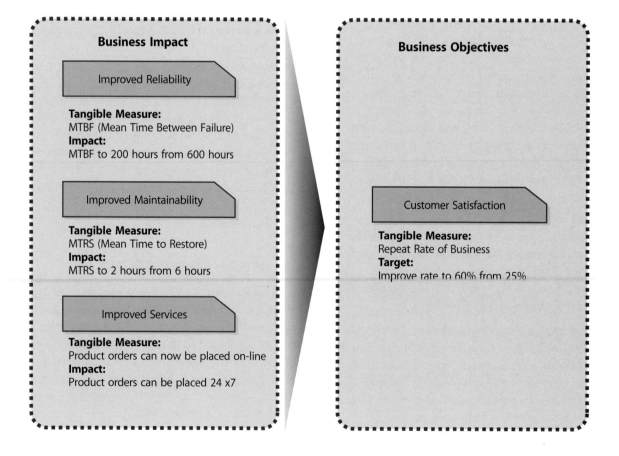

product mix and margin data, or customer profiles and product behaviour, a similar utility of financial data continues to increase the importance of Financial Management for IT and the business as well.

Financial Management as a strategic tool is equally applicable to all three Service Provider types. Internal service providers are increasingly asked to operate with the same levels of financial visibility and accountability as their business unit and external counterparts. Moreover, technology and innovation have become the core revenue-generating capabilities of many companies.

Financial Management provides the business and IT with the quantification, in financial terms, of the value of IT services, the value of the assets underlying the provisioning of those services, and the qualification of operational forecasting. Talking about IT in terms of services is the crux of changing the perception of IT and its value to the business. Therefore, a significant portion of Financial Management is working in tandem with IT and the business to help identify, document and agree on the value of the services being received, and the enablement of service demand modelling and management.

Much like their business counterparts, IT organizations are increasingly incorporating Financial Management in the pursuit of:

- Enhanced decision-making
- Speed of change
- Service Portfolio Management
- Financial compliance and control
- Operational control
- Value capture and creation.

One goal of Financial Management is to ensure proper funding for the delivery and consumption of services. Planning provides financial translation and qualification of expected future demand for IT services. Financial Management planning departs from historical IT planning

by focusing on demand and supply variances resulting from business strategy, capacity inputs and forecasting, rather than traditional individual line item expenditures or business cost accounts. As with planning for any other business organization, input should be collected from all areas of the IT organization and the business.

Planning can be categorized into three main areas, each representing financial results that are required for continued visibility and service valuation:

- Operating and capital planning processes are common and fairly standardized, and involve the translation of IT expenditures into corporate financial systems as part of the corporate planning cycle. Beyond this, the importance of this process is in communicating expected changes in the funding of IT services for consideration by other business domains. The impact of IT services on capital planning is largely underestimated, but is of interest to tax and fixed-asset departments if the status of an IT asset changes.
- Demand representing the need and use of IT services.
- Regulatory and environmental-related planning should get its triggers from within the business. However, Financial Management should apply the proper financial inputs to the related services value, whether cost-based or value-based.

4.9.1 Service valuation

Service valuation quantifies, in financial terms, the funding sought by the business and IT for services delivered, based on the agreed value of those services. Financial Management calculates and assigns a monetary value to a service or service component so that they may be disseminated across the enterprise once the business customer and IT identify what services are actually desired.

- Hardware and software licence costs
- Annual maintenance fees for hardware and software

- Personnel resources used in the support or maintenance of a service
- Utilities, data centre or other facilities charges
- Taxes, capital or interest charges
- Compliance costs.

Financial Management plays a translational role between corporate financial systems and service management. The result of a service-oriented accounting function is that far greater detail and understanding is achieved regarding service provisioning and consumption, and the generation of data that feeds directly into the planning process. The functions and accounting characteristics that come into play are discussed below:

- **Service recording** – The assignment of a cost entry to the appropriate service. Depending on how services are defined, and the granularity of the definitions, there may be additional sub-service components
- **Cost types** – These are higher-level expenses categories such as hardware, software, labour, administration etc. These attributes assist with reporting and analysing demand and usage of services and their components in commonly used financial terms
- **Cost classifications** – There are also classifications within services that designate the end purpose of the cost. These include classifications such as:
  - Capital/operational – this classification addresses different accounting methodologies that are required by the business and regulatory agencies
  - Direct/Indirect – this designation determines whether a cost will be assigned directly or indirectly to a consumer or service:
    - Direct costs are charged directly to a service since it is the only consumer of the expense
    - Indirect or shared costs are allocated across multiple services since each service may consume a portion of the expense

- Fixed/variable – this segregation of costs is based on contractual commitments of time or price. The strategic issue around this classification is that the business should seek to optimize fixed service costs and minimize the variable in order to minimize predictability and stability
- Cost units – a cost unit is the identified unit of consumption that is accounted for a particular service or service asset.

4.9.2 Variable cost dynamics

Variable cost dynamics (VCD) focuses on analysing and understanding the multitude of variables that impact service cost, how sensitive those elements are to variation, and the related incremental value changes that result.

Below is a very brief list of possible variable service cost components that could be included in such an analysis:

- Number and type of users
- Number of software licences
- Cost/operating foot of data centre
- Delivery mechanisms
- Number and type of resources
- Cost of adding one more storage device
- Cost of adding one more end-user license.

4.10 INCREASING SERVICE POTENTIAL

The capabilities and resources (service assets) of a Service Provider represent the service potential or the productive capacity available to customers through a set of services. Projects that develop or improve capabilities and resources increase the service potential. For example, implementation of a Configuration Management System leads to improved visibility and control over the productive capacity of service assets such as networks, storage and servers. It also helps quickly to restore such capacity in the event of failures or outages. There is

Table 4.3 Example of increased Service Potential

Service management initiative	Increasing service potential from capabilities	Increasing service potential from resources
Data centre rationalization	Better control over service operations Lower complexity in infrastructure Development of infrastructure and technology assets	Increases the capacity of assets Increases economies of scale and scope Capacity building in service assets
Training and certification	Knowledgeable staff in control of Service Lifecycle Improved analysis and decisions	Staffing of key competencies Extension of Service Desk hours
Implement Incident Management process	Better response to Service Incidents Prioritization of recovery activities	Reducing losses in resource utilization
Develop service design process	Systematic design of services Enrichment of design portfolio	Re-use of service components Fewer service failures through design
Thin-client computing	Increased flexibility in work locations Enhanced service continuity capabilities	Standardization and control of configurations Centralization of administration functions

greater efficiency in the utilization of those assets and therefore service potential because of capability improvements in Configuration Management. Similar examples are given in Table 4.3. One of the key objectives of service management is to improve the service potential of its capabilities and resources.

4.11 ORGANIZATIONAL DEVELOPMENT

When senior managers adopt a service management orientation, they are adopting a vision for the organization. Such a vision provides a model toward which staff can work. Organizational change, however, is not instantaneous. Senior managers often make the mistake of thinking that announcing the organizational change is the same as making it happen.

There is no one best way to organize. Elements of an organizational design, such as scale, scope and structure, are highly dependent on strategic objectives. Over time, an organization will likely outgrow its design. Certain organizational designs fit while others do not. The design challenge is to identify and select among often distinct choices. Thus the problem becomes much more solvable when there is an understanding of the factors that generate fit and the trade-offs involved, such as control and coordination.

It is common to think of organizational hierarchies in terms of functions. As the functional groups become larger, think of them in terms of departmentalization. A department can loosely be defined as an organizational activity involving over 20 people. When a functional group grows to departmental size, the organization can reorient the group to one of the following areas or a hybrid thereof:

- **Function** – preferred for specialization, the pooling of resources and reducing duplication
- **Product** – preferred for servicing businesses with strategies of diverse and new products, usually manufacturing businesses
- **Market space or customer** – preferred for organizing around market structures. Provides differentiation in the form of increased knowledge of and response to customer preferences
- **Geography** – the use of geography depends on the industry. By providing services in close geographical proximity, travel and distribution costs are minimized while local knowledge is leveraged
- **Process** – preferred for an end-to-end coverage of a process.

Certain basic structures are preferred for certain service strategies, as shown in Table 4.4.

Service strategies are executed by delivering and supporting the contract portfolio in a given market space. Contracts specify the terms and conditions under which value is delivered to customer through services. From an operational point of view this translates into specific levels of utility and warranty for every service. Since every service is mapped to one or more market spaces, it follows that the design of a service is related to categories of customer assets and the service models. These are the basic inputs for service design.

There is much more depth in Service Strategy than depicted in the preceding pages. As the core of the ITIL Service Lifecycle, Service Strategy is a prime component in a good service management practice. The key concepts have been outlined in this book to provide a basic understanding and illustrate the enormous benefits a

Table 4.4 Basic organizational structures for types of service strategies

Basic structure	Strategic considerations
Functional	Specialization
	Common standards
	Small size
Product	Product focus
	Strong product knowledge
Market space or customer	Service unique to segment
	Customer service
	Buyer strength
	Rapid customer service
Geography	Onsite services
	Proximity to customer for delivery and support
	Organization perceived as local
Process	Need to minimize process cycle times
	Process excellence

sound service strategy offers to every IT organization and their customers. You are encouraged to read the Service Strategy core guidance in its entirety as the best place to start in expanding your knowledge of service management practices.

Service Design – building structural service integrity

5

5 Service Design – building structural service integrity

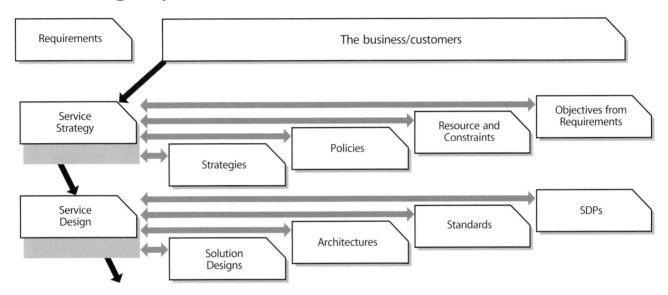

Following on from Service Strategy, Service Design is the next stage in the ITIL Service Lifecycle. While the lifecycle is not entirely linear, we will portray each stage from a logical progression. The key concepts of Service Design revolve around the five design aspects and the design of services, service processes and service capabilities to meet business demand. The primary topics that will be discussed here are not the entire spectrum of Service Design, but the main elements that illustrate the objectives of this stage in the Service Lifecycle:

- Aspects of Service Design
- Service Catalogue Management
- Service Requirements
- Service Design Models
- Capacity Management
- Availability Management
- Service Level Management.

The Service Design publication provides a greater level of detail on these and also on application and infrastructure design principles.

The main purpose of the Service Design stage of the lifecycle is the design of new or changed service for introduction into the live environment. It is important that a holistic approach to all aspects of design is adopted and that when changing or amending any of the individual elements of design all other aspects are considered. Thus when designing and developing a new application, this shouldn't be done in isolation, but should also consider the impact on the overall service, the management systems and tools (e.g. the Service Portfolio and Catalogue), the architectures, the technology, the Service Management processes and the necessary measurements and metrics. This will ensure that not only the functional elements are addressed by the design, but also that all of the management and operational requirements are addressed as a fundamental part of the design and are not added as an afterthought.

The main aim of Service Design is the design of new or changed services. The requirements for these new services are extracted from the Service Portfolio and each requirement is analysed, documented and agreed and a solution design is produced that is then compared with the strategies and constraints from Service Strategy to ensure that it conforms to corporate and IT policies.

5.1 BUSINESS VALUE

With good Service Design it will be possible to deliver quality, cost-effective services and to ensure that the business requirements are being met.

The following benefits are as a result of good Service Design practice:

- **Reduced total cost of ownership (TCO)**: cost of ownership can only be minimized if all aspects of services, processes and technology are designed properly and implemented against the design
- **Improved quality of service**: both service and operational quality will be enhanced
- **Improved consistency of service**: as services are designed within the corporate strategy, architectures and constraints
- **Easier implementation of new or changed services**: as there is integrated and full Service Design, and the production of comprehensives Service Design Packages
- **Improved service alignment**: involvement from the conception of the service ensuring that new or changed services match business needs, with services designed to meet Service Level Requirements
- **More effective service performance**: with incorporation and recognition of Capacity, Financial, Availability and IT Service Continuity plans

- **Improved IT governance**: assists with the implementation and communication of a set of controls for effective governance of IT
- **More effective service management and IT processes**: processes will be designed with optimal quality and cost-effectiveness
- **Improved information and decision-making**: more comprehensive and effective measurements and metrics will enable better decision-making and continual improvement of service management practices in the design stage of the Service Lifecycle.

5.2 FIVE ASPECTS OF SERVICE DESIGN

There are five aspects of design that need to be considered:

1 The design of the services, including all of the functional requirements, resources and capabilities needed and agreed

2 The design of service management systems and tools, especially the Service Portfolio, for the management and control of services through their lifecycle

3 The design of the technology architectures and management systems required to provide the services

4 The design of the processes needed to design, transition, operate and improve the services, the architectures and the processes themselves

5 The design of the measurement methods and metrics of the services, the architectures and their constituent components and the processes.

A results-driven approach should be adopted for each of the above five aspects. In each, the desired business outcomes and planned results should be defined so that what is delivered meets the expectation of the customers and users. Thus this structured approach should be adopted within each of the five aspects to deliver quality, repeatable consistency and continual improvement throughout the organization. There are no situations within IT service provision with either internal or external service providers where there are no processes in the Service Design area. All IT Service Provider organizations already have some elements of their approach to these five aspects in place, no matter how basic. Before starting on the implementation of the improvement of activities and processes a review should be conducted of what elements are in place and working successfully. Many Service Provider organizations already have mature processes in place for designing IT services and solutions.

5.3 IDENTIFYING SERVICE REQUIREMENTS

Service Design must consider all elements of the service by taking a holistic approach to the design of a new service. This approach should consider the service and its constituent components and their inter-relationships, ensuring that the services delivered meet the functionality and quality of service expected by the business in all areas:

- The scalability of the service to meet future requirements, in support of the long-term business objectives
- The business processes and business units supported by the service
- The IT service and the agreed business functionality and requirements
- The service itself and its Service Level Requirement (SLR) or Service Level Agreement (SLA)
- The technology components used to deploy and deliver the service, including the infrastructure, the environment, the data and the applications
- The internally supported services and components and their associated Operational Level Agreements (OLAs)

- The externally supported services and components and their associated Underpinning Contracts (UCs), which will often have their own related agreements and/or schedules
- The performance measurements and metrics required
- The legislated or required security levels.

The relationships and dependencies between these elements are illustrated in Figure 5.1.

The design needs to be holistic, and the main problem today is that organizations often only focus on the functional requirements. A design or architecture by very definition needs to consider all aspects. It is not a smaller organization that combines these aspects, it is a sensible one.

The design process activities are:

- Requirements collection, analysis and engineering to ensure that business requirements are clearly documented and agreed
- Design of appropriate services, technology, processes, information and process measurements to meet business requirements
- Review and revision of all processes and documents involved in Service Design, including designs, plans, architectures and policies
- Liaison with all other design and planning activities and roles, e.g. solution design
- Production and maintenance of IT policies and design documents, including designs, plans, architectures and policies
- Revision of all design documents and planning for the deployment and implementation of IT strategies using roadmaps, programmes and project plans
- Risk assessment and management of all design processes and deliverables
- Ensuring alignment with all corporate and IT strategies and policies.

Figure 5.1 Design dependencies

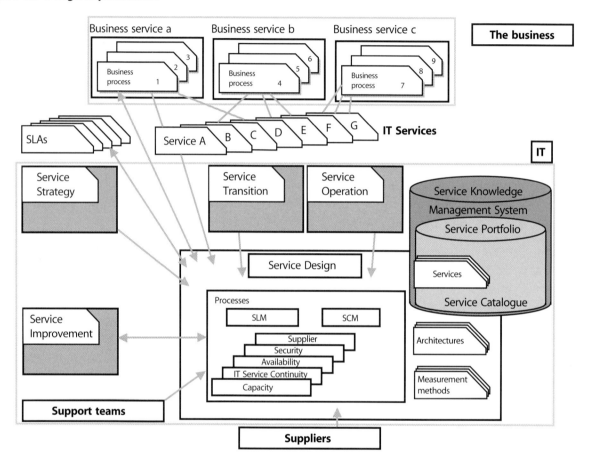

5.4 SERVICE DESIGN MODELS

Before adopting a design model for a major new service, a review of the current capability and provisions with respect to all aspects regarding the delivery of IT services should be conducted. This review should consider all aspects of the new service including:

- Business drivers and requirements
- Scope and capability of the existing service provider unit
- Demands, targets and requirements of the new service

- Scope and capability of external suppliers
- Maturity of the organizations currently involved and their processes
- Culture of the organizations involved
- IT infrastructure, applications, data, services and other components involved
- Degree of corporate and IT governance and the level of ownership and control required
- Budgets and resources available
- Staff levels and skills.

5.5 DELIVERY MODEL OPTIONS

Although the readiness assessment determines the gap between the current and desired capabilities, an IT organization should not necessarily try to bridge that gap by itself. There are many different delivery strategies that can be used. Each one has its own set of advantages and disadvantages, but all require some level of adaptation and customization for the situation at hand. Table 5.1 lists the main categories of sourcing strategies with a short abstract for each. Delivery practices tend to fall into one of these categories or some variant of them.

Table 5.1 Delivery model options

Delivery strategy	Description
Insourcing	This approach relies on utilizing internal organizational resources in the design, development, transition, maintenance, operation and/or support of a new, changed or revised services or data centre operations
Outsourcing	This approach utilizes the resources of an external organization or organizations in a formal arrangement to provide a well-defined portion of a service's design, development, maintenance, operations and/or support. This includes the consumption of services from Application Service Providers (ASPs) described below
Co-sourcing	Often a combination of insourcing and outsourcing, using a number of outsourcing organizations working together to co-source key elements within the lifecycle. This generally will involve using a number of external organizations working together to design, develop, transition, maintain, operate and/or support a portion of a service
Partnership or multi-sourcing	Formal arrangements between two or more organizations to work together to design, develop, transition, maintain, operate and/or support IT service(s). The focus here tends to be on strategic partnerships that leverage critical expertise or market opportunities
Business process outsourcing (BPO)	The increasing trend of relocating entire business functions using formal arrangements between organizations where one organization provides and manages the other organization's entire business process(es) or function(s) in a low-cost location. Common examples are accounting, payroll and call-centre operations
Application service provision (ASP)	Involves formal arrangements with an ASP organization that will provide shared computer-based services to customer organizations over a network. Applications offered in this way are also sometimes referred to as 'on-demand software/applications'. Through ASPs the complexities and costs of such shared software can be reduced and provided to organizations that could otherwise not justify the investment
Knowledge process outsourcing (KPO)	The newest form of outsourcing, KPO is a step ahead of BPO in one respect. KPO organizations provide domain-based processes and business expertise rather than just process expertise and require advanced analytical and specialized skills from the outsourcing organization

5.6 SERVICE CATALOGUE MANAGEMENT

Over the years, organizations' IT infrastructures have grown and developed, and there may not always be a clear picture of all the services currently being provided or the customers of each service. In order to establish an accurate picture, it is recommended that an IT Service Portfolio containing a Service Catalogue is produced and maintained to provide a central accurate set of information on all services and to develop a service-focused culture.

In the preceding chapter, we learned about the Service Portfolio and its constituent elements. Among them is the Service Catalogue.

The objective of Service Catalogue Management is to manage the information contained within the Service Catalogue and to ensure that it is accurate and reflects the current details, status, interfaces and dependencies of all services that are being run or being prepared to run in the live environment.

The Service Catalogue provides business value as a central source of information on the IT services delivered by the service provider organization. This ensures that all areas of the business can view an accurate, consistent picture of the IT services, their details and their status. It contains a customer-facing view of the IT services in use, how they are intended to be used, the business processes they enable, and the levels and quality of service the customer can expect of each service.

Service Catalogue Management activities should include:

- Definition of the service
- Production and maintenance of an accurate Service Catalogue
- Interfaces, dependencies and consistency between the Service Catalogue and Service Portfolio

- Interfaces and dependencies between all services and supporting services within the Service Catalogue and the CMS
- Interfaces and dependencies between all services, and supporting components and Configuration Items (CIs) within the Service Catalogue and the CMS.

When initially completed, the Service Catalogue may consist of a matrix, table or spreadsheet. Many organizations integrate and maintain their Portfolio and Catalogue as part of their CMS. By defining each service as a CI and, where appropriate, relating these to form a service hierarchy, the organization is able to relate events such as Incidents and RFCs to the services affected, thus providing the basis for service monitoring and reporting using an integrated tool (e.g. 'list or give the number of Incidents affecting this particular service'). It is therefore essential that changes within the Service Portfolio and Service Catalogue are subject to the Change Management process.

The Service Catalogue can also be used for other Service Management purposes (e.g. for performing a Business Impact Analysis (BIA) as part of IT Service Continuity Planning, or as a starting place for redistributing workloads, as part of Capacity Management). The cost and effort of producing and maintaining the catalogue, with its relationships to the underpinning technology components, is therefore easily justifiable. If done in conjunction with prioritization of the BIA, then it is possible to ensure that the most important services are covered first.

The Service Catalogue has two aspects:

- **Business Service Catalogue**: containing details of all of the IT services delivered to the customer, together with relationships to the business units and the business processes that rely on the IT services. This is the customer view of the Service Catalogue

- **Technical Service Catalogue**: containing details of all the IT services delivered to the customer, together with relationships to the supporting services, shared services, components and CIs necessary to support the provision of the service to the business. This should underpin the Business Service Catalogue and not form part of the customer view.

The key activities within the Service Catalogue Management process should include:

- Agreeing and documenting a service definition with all relevant parties
- Interfacing with Service Portfolio Management to agree the contents of the Service Portfolio and Service Catalogue
- Producing and maintaining a Service Catalogue and its contents, in conjunction with the Service Portfolio

- Interfacing with the business and IT Service Continuity Management on the dependencies of business units and their business processes with the supporting IT services, contained within the Business Service Catalogue
- Interfacing with support teams, Suppliers and Configuration Management on interfaces and dependencies between IT services and the supporting services, components and CIs contained within the Technical Service Catalogue
- Interfacing with Business Relationship Management and Service Level Management to ensure that the information is aligned to the business and business process.

The Service Catalogue forms an integral part of the overall Service Portfolio and is a key, customer-facing view of the services on offer. It establishes the expectations of value and potential that customers can expect from their IT

Figure 5.2 Service Catalogue elements

The Service Catalogue

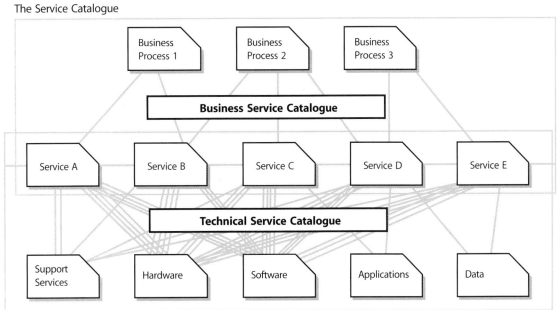

service provider(s). The Service Design core publication contains detailed guidance on the construction and management of a Service Catalogue.

5.7 SERVICE LEVEL MANAGEMENT

Service Level Management (SLM) negotiates, agrees and documents appropriate IT service targets with representatives of the business, and then monitors and produces reports on the Service Provider's ability to deliver the agreed level of service. SLM is a vital process for every IT Service Provider organization in that it is responsible for agreeing and documenting service level targets and responsibilities within Service Level Agreements (SLAs) and Service Level Requirements (SLRs), for every activity within IT. If these targets are appropriate and accurately reflect the requirements of the business, then the service delivered by the Service Providers will align with business requirements and meet the expectations of the customers and users in terms of service quality. If the targets are not aligned with business needs, then Service Provider activities and service levels will not be aligned with business expectations and problems will develop.

The SLA is effectively a level of assurance or warranty with regard to the level of service quality delivered by the Service Provider for each of the services delivered to the business. The success of SLM is very dependent on the quality of the Service Portfolio and the Service Catalogue and their contents, because they provide the necessary information on the services to be managed within the SLM process.

The objectives of SLM are to:

- Define, document, agree, monitor, measure, report and review the level of IT services provided
- Provide and improve the relationship and communication with the business and customers
- Ensure that specific and measurable targets are developed for all IT services

- Monitor and improve customer satisfaction with the quality of service delivered
- Ensure that IT and the customers have a clear and unambiguous expectation of the level of service to be delivered
- Ensure that proactive measures to improve the levels of service delivered are implemented wherever it is cost-justifiable to do so.

The key activities within the SLM process should include:

- Determine, negotiate, document and agree requirements for new or changed services in SLRs, and manage and review them through the Service Lifecycle into SLAs for operational services
- Monitor and measure service performance achievements of all operational services against targets within SLAs
- Collate, measure and improve customer satisfaction
- Produce service reports
- Conduct service review and instigate improvements within an overall Service Improvement Programme/Plan (SIP)
- Review and revise SLAs, service scope OLAs, contracts and any other underpinning agreements
- Develop and document contacts and relationships with the business, customers and stakeholders
- Develop, maintain and operate procedures for logging, actioning and resolving all complaints, and for logging and distributing compliments
- Log and manage all complaints and compliments
- Provide the appropriate management information to aid performance management and demonstrate service achievement
- Make available and maintain up-to-date SLM document templates and standards.

Figure 5.3 The Service Level Management process

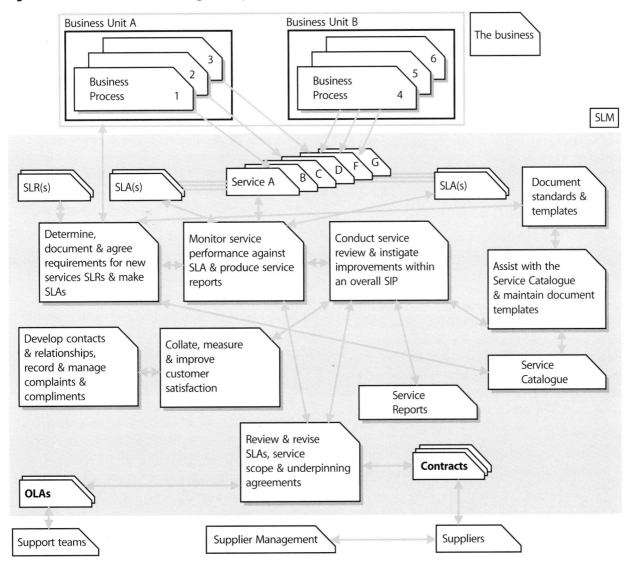

There are a number of potential options, including the following.

■ **Service-based SLA**

This is where an SLA covers one service for all the customers of that service – for example, an SLA may be established for an organization's e-mail service, covering all of the customers of that service. Where common levels of service are provided across all areas of the business, e.g. e-mail or telephony, the service-based SLA can be an efficient approach to use. Multiple classes of service, e.g. gold, silver and bronze, can also be used to increase the effectiveness of service-based SLAs.

■ **Customer-based SLA**

This is an agreement with an individual customer group covering all the services they use. For example, agreements may be reached with an organization's finance department covering, say, the finance system, the accounting system, the payroll system, the billing system, the procurement system, and any other IT systems that they use. Customers often prefer such an agreement, as all of their requirements are covered in a single document. Only one signatory is normally required, which simplifies this issue.

■ **Multi-level SLA**

Some organizations have chosen to adopt a multi-level SLA structure. For example, a three-layer structure as follows:

● Corporate level: covering all the generic SLM issues appropriate to every customer throughout the organization. These issues are likely to be less volatile, so updates are less frequently required

● Customer level: covering all SLM issues relevant to the particular customer group or business unit, regardless of the service being used

● Service level: covering all SLM issues relevant to the specific service, in relation to a specific customer group (one for each service covered by the SLA).

The wording of SLAs should be clear and concise and leave no room for ambiguity. There is normally no need for agreements to be couched in legal terminology, and plain language aids a common understanding. It is often helpful to have an independent person, who has not been involved with the drafting, to do a final read-through. This often throws up potential ambiguities and difficulties that can then be addressed and clarified. For this reason alone, it is recommended that all SLAs contain a glossary, defining any terms and providing clarity for any areas of ambiguity.

5.7.1 Service Level Requirements

This is one of the earliest activities within the Service Design stage of the Service Lifecycle. Once the Service Catalogue has been produced and the SLA structure has been agreed, a first SLR must be drafted. It is advisable to involve customers from the outset, but rather than going along with a blank sheet to start with, it may be better to produce a first outline draft of the performance targets and the management and operational requirements, as a starting point for more detailed and in-depth discussion. Be careful, though, not to go too far and appear to be presenting the customer with a fait accompli.

It cannot be overstressed how difficult this activity of determining the initial targets for inclusion with an SLR or SLA is. All of the other processes need to be consulted for their opinion on what are realistic targets that can be achieved, such as Incident Management on incident targets. The Capacity and Availability Management processes will be of particular value in determining appropriate service availability and performance targets.

5.7.2 Monitoring service level performance

Nothing should be included in an SLA unless it can be effectively monitored and measured at a commonly agreed point. The importance of this cannot be overstressed, as inclusion of items that cannot be effectively monitored almost always results in disputes and eventual loss of faith in the SLM process. A lot of organizations have discovered this the hard way and as a result have absorbed heavy costs, both in a financial sense as well as in terms of negative impacts on their credibility.

It is essential that monitoring matches the customer's true perception of the service. Unfortunately this is often very difficult to achieve. For example, monitoring of individual components, such as the network or server, does not guarantee that the service will be available so far as the customer is concerned. Where multiple services are delivered to a single workstation, it is probably more effective to record only downtime against the service the user was trying to access at the time (though this needs to be agreed with the customers).

There are a number of important *soft* issues that cannot be monitored by mechanistic or procedural means, such as customers' overall feelings (these need not necessarily match the *hard* monitoring). For example, even when there have been a number of reported service failures, customers may still feel positive about things, because they may feel satisfied that appropriate actions are being taken to improve things. Of course, the opposite may apply, and customers may feel dissatisfied with some issues (e.g. the manner of some staff on the Service Desk) when few or no SLA targets have been broken.

From the outset, it is wise to try to manage customers' expectations. This means setting proper expectations and appropriate targets in the first place, and putting a systematic process in place to manage expectations going forward, as satisfaction = perception – expectation (where a zero or positive score indicates a satisfied customer).

SLAs are just documents, and in themselves do not materially alter the quality of service being provided (though they may affect behaviour and help engender an appropriate service culture, which can have an immediate beneficial effect, and make longer-term improvements possible). A degree of patience is therefore needed and should be built into expectations.

5.7.3 Key performance indicators

Key performance indicators (KPIs) and metrics can be used to judge the efficiency and effectiveness of the SLM activities and the progress of the SIP. These metrics should be developed from the service, customer and business perspective and should cover both subjective and objective measurements such as the following.

- Objective:
  - Number or percentage of service targets being met
  - Number and severity of service breaches
  - Number of services with up-to-date SLAs
  - Number of services with timely reports and active service reviews
- Subjective:
  - Improvements in customer satisfaction.

Practising SLM can achieve a high trust factor between the business and the service provider. It establishes a pattern of quality and service management practices, demonstrated through reporting and interaction with the customer over time, that can instil a sense of trust and expectation from the business, which in turn engenders loyalty. No service provider should underestimate how important SLM is. The Service Design core publication offers detailed guidance in SLM.

5.8 CAPACITY MANAGEMENT

Capacity Management is a process that extends across the Service Lifecycle. A key success factor in managing capacity is ensuring it is considered during the Service

Design stage. It is for this reason that the Capacity Management Process is included in this book. Capacity Management is supported initially in Service Strategy where the decisions and analysis of business requirements and customer outcomes influencing the development of patterns of business activity (PBA), levels of service (LOS) and service level packages (SLPs) are identified. This provides the predictive and ongoing capacity indicators needed to align capacity to demand. An example of a component-based SLP is illustrated in Figure 5.4.

Capacity Management ensures that the capacity and performance of the IT services and systems match the evolving agreed demands of the business in the most cost-effective and timely manner. Capacity Management is essentially a balancing act:

■ Balancing costs against resources needed: the need to ensure that processing Capacity that is purchased is not only cost-justifiable in terms of business need, but also makes the most efficient use of those resources

■ Balancing supply against demand: the need to ensure that the available supply of IT processing power matches the demands made on it by the business, both now and in the future; it may also be necessary to manage or influence the demand for a particular resource.

Figure 5.4 Component-based Service Level Package

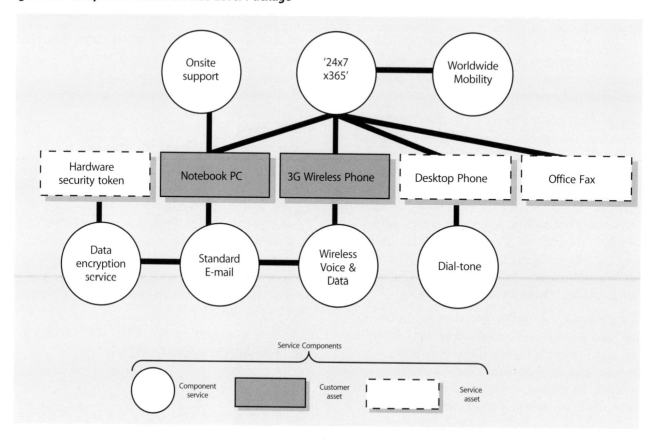

The objectives of Capacity Management are to:

- Produce and maintain an appropriate and up-to-date Capacity Plan, which reflects the current and future needs of the business
- Provide advice and guidance to all other areas of the business and IT on all capacity- and performance-related issues
- Ensure that service performance achievements meet or exceed all of their agreed performance targets, by managing the performance and capacity of both services and resources
- Assist with the diagnosis and resolution of performance- and capacity-related incidents and problems
- Assess the impact of all changes on the Capacity Plan, and the performance and capacity of all services and resources
- Ensure that proactive measures to improve the performance of services are implemented wherever it is cost-justifiable to do so.

The Capacity Management process should include:

- Monitoring patterns of business activity and service level plans through performance, utilization and throughput of IT services and the supporting infrastructure, environmental, data and applications components and the production of regular and ad hoc reports on service and component capacity and performance
- Undertaking tuning activities to make the most efficient use of existing IT resources
- Understanding the agreed current and future demands being made by the customer for IT resources and producing forecasts for future requirements
- Influencing demand management, perhaps in conjunction with Financial Management

- Producing a Capacity Plan that enables the Service Provider to continue to provide services of the quality defined in SLAs and that covers a sufficient planning timeframe to meet future service levels required as defined in the Service Portfolio and SLRs
- Assistance with the identification and resolution of any Incidents and Problems associated with service or component performance
- The proactive improvement of service or component performance wherever it is cost-justifiable and meets the needs of the business.

The elements of Capacity Management are illustrated in Figure 5.5.

5.8.1 Business Capacity Management

This sub-process translates business needs and plans into requirements for service and IT infrastructure, ensuring that the future business requirements for IT services are quantified, designed, planned and implemented in a timely fashion. This can be achieved by using the existing data on the current resource utilization by the various services and resources to trend, forecast, model or predict future requirements. These future requirements come from the Service Strategy and Service Portfolio detailing new processes and service requirements, changes, improvements and also the growth in the already existing services.

5.8.2 Service Capacity Management

The focus of this sub-process is the management, control and prediction of the end-to-end performance and capacity of the live, operational IT services usage and workloads. It ensures that the performance of all services, as detailed in service targets within SLAs and SLRs, is monitored and measured, and that the collected data is recorded, analysed and reported. Wherever necessary, proactive and reactive action should be instigated, to ensure that the performance of all services meets their agreed business targets. This is performed by staff with knowledge of all the areas of technology used in the delivery of end-to-end service, and often involves seeking advice from the specialists involved in Resource Capacity Management. Wherever possible, automated thresholds should be used to manage all operational services to ensure that situations where service targets are breached or threatened are rapidly identified and cost-effective actions to reduce or avoid their potential impact implemented.

5.8.3 Component Capacity Management

The focus in this sub-process is the management, control and prediction of the performance, utilization and capacity of individual IT technology components. It ensures that all components within the IT infrastructure that have finite resource are monitored and measured, and that the collected data is recorded, analysed and reported. Again, wherever possible, automated thresholds should be implemented to manage all components, to ensure that situations where service targets are breached or threatened by component usage or performance are rapidly identified, and cost-effective actions to reduce or avoid their potential impact are implemented.

There are many similar activities that are performed by each of the above sub-processes, but each sub-process has a very different focus. Business Capacity Management is focused on the current and future business requirements, while Service Capacity Management is focused on the delivery of the existing services that support the business, and Component Capacity Management is focused on the IT infrastructure that underpins service provision.

- The **Capacity Management Information System (CMIS)**: holds the information needed by all sub-processes within Capacity Management. For example, the data monitored and collected as part of Resource and Service Capacity Management is used in Business Capacity Management to determine what infrastructure components or upgrades to components are needed, and when

- The **Capacity Plan**: used by all areas of the business and IT management and is acted on by the IT Service Provider and senior management of the organization to plan the capacity of the IT infrastructure, it also provides planning input to many other areas of IT and the business. It contains information on the current usage of service and components and plans for the development of IT capacity to meet the needs in the growth of both existing service and any agreed new services. The Capacity Plan should be actively used as a basis of decision-making. Too often Capacity Plans are created and never referred to or used

- **Service performance information and reports**: used by many other processes. For example, the Capacity Management process assists Service Level Management with the reporting and reviewing of service performance and the development of new SLRs or changes to existing SLAs. It also assists the Financial Management process by identifying when money needs to be budgeted for IT infrastructure upgrades, or the purchase of new components

- **Workload analysis and reports**: used by IT operations to assess and implement changes in conjunction with Capacity Management to schedule or re-schedule when services or workloads are run, to ensure that the most effective and efficient use is made of the available resources

- **Ad hoc capacity and performance reports**: used by all areas of Capacity Management, IT and the business to analyse and resolve service and performance issues

- **Forecasts and predictive reports**: used by all areas to analyse, predict and forecast particular business and IT scenarios and their potential solutions

- **Thresholds, alerts and events**.

Figure 5.5 Capacity Management elements

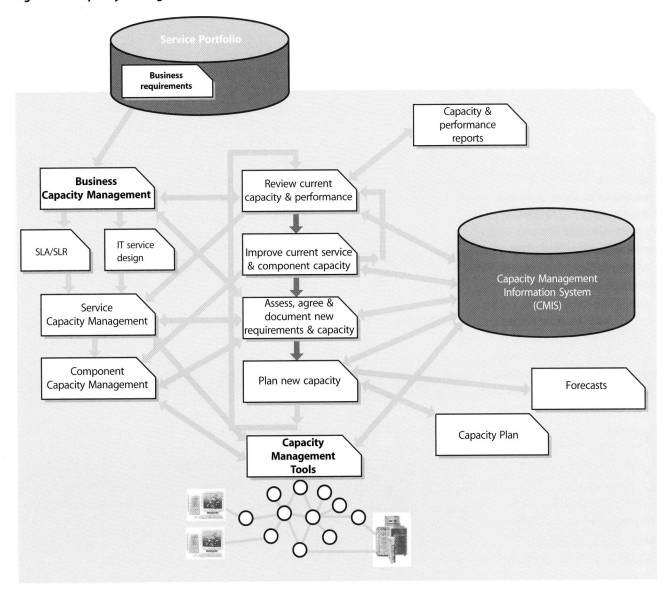

Additional detailed guidance can be found in the Service Design publication.

5.9 AVAILABILITY MANAGEMENT

Availability Management is the window of service quality to a business customer. A Service Provider who does not apply solid practices to AM and who cannot offer reliable, stable service availability will never have a customer's loyalty.

The objectives of Availability Management are to:

■ Produce and maintain an appropriate and up-to-date Availability Plan that reflects the current and future needs of the business

■ Provide advice and guidance to all other areas of the business and IT on all availability-related issues

■ Ensure that service availability achievements meet or exceed all of their agreed targets, by managing service- and resource-related availability performance

■ Assist with the diagnosis and resolution of availability-related Incidents and Problems

■ Assess the impact of all changes on the Availability Plan and the performance and capacity of all services and resources

■ Ensure that proactive measures to improve the availability of services are implemented wherever it is cost-justifiable to do so.

Availability Management should ensure the agreed level of availability is provided. The measurement and monitoring of IT availability is a key activity to ensure availability levels are being met consistently. Availability Management should look to continually optimize and proactively improve the availability of the IT infrastructure, the services and the supporting organization, in order to provide cost-effective availability improvements that can deliver business and customer benefits.

The Availability Management process should include:

■ Monitoring of all aspects of availability, reliability and maintainability of IT services and the supporting components, with appropriate events, alarms and escalation, with automated scripts for recovery

■ Maintenance of a set of methods, techniques and calculations for all availability measurements, metrics and reporting

■ Assistance with risk assessment and management activities

■ Collection of measurements, analysis and production of regular and ad hoc reports on service and component availability

■ Understanding the agreed current and future demands of the business for IT services and their availability

■ Influencing the design of services and components to align with business needs

■ Producing an Availability Plan that enables the Service Provider to continue to provide and improve services in line with availability targets defined in SLAs and to plan and forecast future availability levels required as defined in SLRs

■ Maintaining a schedule of tests for all resilient and failover components and mechanisms

■ Assistance with the identification and resolution of any Incidents and Problems associated with service or component unavailability

■ Proactive improvement of service or component availability wherever it is cost-justifiable and meets the needs of the business.

The Availability Management process (Figure 5.6) has two key elements:

- **Reactive activities**: the reactive aspect of Availability Management involves the monitoring, measuring, analysis and management of all events, Incidents and Problems involving unavailability. These activities are principally involved within operational roles
- **Proactive activities**: the proactive activities of Availability Management involve the proactive planning, design and improvement of availability. These activities are principally involved within design and planning roles.

Availability Management is completed at two interconnected levels:

- **Service availability**: involves all aspects of service availability and unavailability and the impact of component availability, or the potential impact of component unavailability on service availability
- **Component availability**: involves all aspects of component availability and unavailability.

A guiding principle of Availability Management is to recognize that it is still possible to gain customer satisfaction even when things go wrong. One approach to help achieve this requires Availability Management to ensure that the duration of any Incident is minimized to enable normal business operations to resume as quickly as is possible. An aim of Availability Management is to ensure the duration and impact from Incidents impacting IT services are minimized, to enable business operations to resume as quickly as is possible. The analysis of the 'expanded incident lifecycle' enables the total IT service downtime for any given Incident to be broken down and mapped against the major stages that all Incidents progress through (the lifecycle). Availability Management should work closely with Incident Management and Problem Management in the analysis of all Incidents causing unavailability.

5.9.1 Identifying vital business functions

The term 'vital business function' (VBF) is used to reflect the business-critical elements of the business process supported by an IT service. The service may also support less critical business functions and processes. It is important that the VBFs are recognized and documented to provide the appropriate business alignment and focus.

5.9.2 Designing for availability

The level of availability required by the business influences the overall cost of the IT service provided. In general, the higher the level of availability required by the business the higher the cost. These costs are not just the procurement of the base IT technology and services required to underpin the IT infrastructure. Additional costs are incurred in providing the appropriate service management processes, systems management tools and high availability solutions required to meet the more stringent availability requirements. The greatest level of availability should be included in the design of those services supporting the most critical of the VBFs.

When considering how the availability requirements of the business are to be met, it is important to ensure that the level of availability to be provided for an IT service is at the level actually required and is affordable and cost-justifiable to the business (Figure 5.7).

Figure 5.6 The Availability Management process

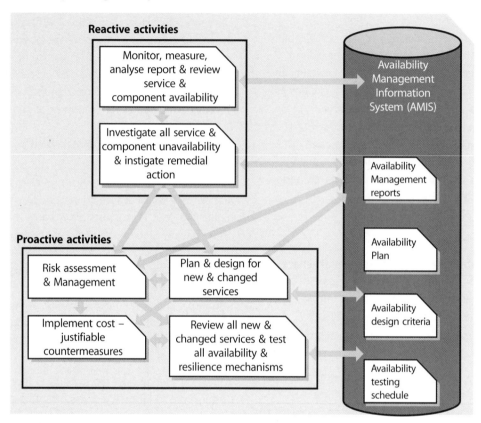

5.9.3 Service Failure Analysis

Service Failure Analysis (SFA) is a technique designed to provide a structured approach to identifying the underlying causes of service interruptions to the user. SFA utilizes a range of data sources to assess where and why shortfalls in availability are occurring. SFA enables a holistic view to be taken to drive not just technology improvements, but improvements to the IT support organization, processes, procedures and tools. SFA is run as an assignment or project and may utilize other Availability Management methods and techniques to formulate the recommendations for improvement. The detailed analysis of service interruptions can identify opportunities to enhance levels of availability. SFA is a structured technique to identify improvement opportunities in end-to-end service availability that can deliver benefits to the user. Many of the activities involved in SFA are closely aligned with those of Problem Management and in a number of organizations these activities are performed jointly by Problem and Availability Management.

The high-level objectives of SFA are:

■ To improve the overall availability of IT services by producing a set of improvements for implementation or input to the Availability Plan

Figure 5.7 Relationship between levels of availability and overall costs

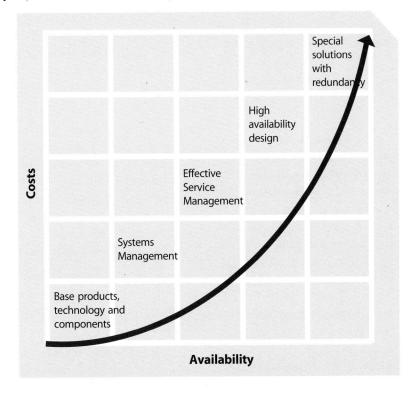

- To identify the underlying causes of service interruption to users
- To assess the effectiveness of the IT support organization and key processes
- To produce reports detailing the major findings and recommendations
- To ensure availability improvements derived from SFA-driven activities are measured.

SFA initiatives should use input from all areas and all processes including, most importantly, the business and users. Each SFA assignment should have a recognized sponsor(s) (ideally, joint sponsorship from the IT and business) and involve resources from many technical and process areas. The use of the SFA approach:

- Provides the ability to deliver enhanced levels of availability without major cost
- Provides the business with visible commitment from the IT support organization
- Develops in-house skills and competencies to avoid expensive consultancy assignments related to availability improvement
- Encourages cross-functional team working and breaks barriers between teams and is an enabler to lateral thinking, challenging traditional thoughts and providing innovative and often inexpensive solutions

- Provides a programme of improvement opportunities that can make a real difference to service quality and user perception
- Provides opportunities that are focused on delivering benefit to the user
- Provides an independent healthcheck of IT service management processes and is the stimulus for process improvements.

Designing for availability is a key activity, driven by Availability Management, which ensures that the stated availability requirements for an IT service can be met. However, Availability Management should also ensure that within this design activity there is focus on the design elements required to ensure that when IT services fail, the service can be reinstated to enable normal business operations to resume as quickly as is possible. 'Designing for Recovery' may at first sound negative. Clearly good availability design is about avoiding failures and delivering where possible a fault-tolerant IT infrastructure. However, with this focus, is too much reliance placed on technology and has as much emphasis been placed on the fault-tolerant aspects of the IT infrastructure? The reality is that failures will occur. The way the IT organization manages failure situations can have a positive effect on the perception of the business, customers and users of the IT services.

> **Key message**
> Every failure is an important moment of truth – an opportunity to make or break your reputation with the business.
>
> The process of Availability Management contains a number of methods, techniques and practices for assessing, preventing and analysing service failures. Details about these methods can be found in the Service Design publication.

5.10 IT SERVICE CONTINUITY MANAGEMENT

Service failures of extreme magnitude are not something any business or service provider wants to experience. Even the best-planned and managed services however, can be the victim of catastrophic failure through events that are not in the direct control of a service provider.

Most of us purchase insurance to protect us in the event something of great value, such as our home, becomes the victim of a catastrophic event. Insurance gives us peace of mind that if the unplanned happens, we have the means to recover from such disasters. The amount of insurance we purchase is gauged on the predicted replacement value of our possessions, the likelihood such a disaster could happen and how quickly we can restore our losses. This is a form of risk management.

IT Service Continuity Management is the part of ITIL practice that evaluates the level of *insurance* we need to protect service assets and a manuscript to recover from a disaster.

The goal of ITSCM is to support the overall Business Continuity Management process by ensuring that the required IT technical and service facilities (including computer systems, networks, applications, data repositories, telecommunications, environment, technical support and Service Desk) can be resumed within required, and agreed, business timescales.

The objectives of ITSCM are to:

- Maintain a set of IT Service Continuity Plans and IT recovery plans that support the overall Business Continuity Plans (BCPs) of the organization
- Complete regular Business Impact Analysis (BIA) exercises to ensure that all continuity plans are maintained in line with changing business impacts and requirements

- Conduct regular risk assessment and management exercises in conjunction particularly with the business and the Availability Management and Security Management processes that manages IT services within an agreed level of business risk
- Provide advice and guidance to all other areas of the business and IT on all continuity- and recovery-related issues
- Ensure that appropriate continuity and recovery mechanisms are put in place to meet or exceed the agreed business continuity targets
- Assess the impact of all changes on the IT Service Continuity Plans and IT recovery plans
- Ensure that proactive measures to improve the availability of services are implemented wherever it is cost-justifiable to do so
- Negotiate and agree the necessary contracts with suppliers for the provision of the necessary recovery capability to support all continuity plans in conjunction with the Supplier Management process.

The ITSCM process includes:

- The agreement of the scope of the ITSCM process and the policies adopted
- Business Impact Analysis (BIA) to quantify the impact that loss of IT service would have on the business
- Risk analysis – the risk identification and risk assessment to identify potential threats to continuity and the likelihood of the threats becoming reality. This also includes taking measures to manage the identified threats where this can be cost-justified
- Production of an overall ITSCM strategy that must be integrated into the BCM strategy. This can be produced following the two steps identified above and is likely to include elements of risk reduction as well as selection of appropriate and comprehensive recovery options

- Production of ITSCM plans, which again must be integrated with the overall BCM plans
- Testing of the plans
- The ongoing operation and maintenance of the plans.

Service continuity is implemented and managed in four stages (Figure 5.8):

1 **Initiation** – Policy setting, defining scope and terms of reference, project planning and resource allocation

2 **Requirements and strategy** – Business impact analysis, risk assessment

3 **Implementation** – Executing risk reduction measures, recovery option arrangements, testing the plans

4 **Ongoing operation** – Education and awareness, change control of ITSCM plans, ongoing testing.

A good place to start is by assessing the threats and risks to VBFs (as described in the preceding section on Availability Management). This will help reveal vulnerabilities to vital business operations and ensure that preventative and recovery plans and mechanisms are in place. Consistent with the ITSCM process, this should be continually evaluated to ensure that changes to services or business requirements have not affected the ability of the ITSCM process to be effective when needed.

The Service Design core publication offers detailed guidance on how to establish and maintain ITSCM.

Figure 5.8 Service Continuity lifecycle

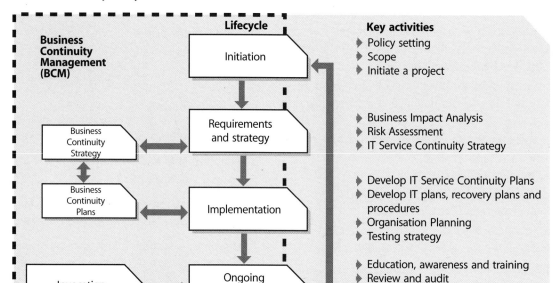

5.11 INFORMATION SECURITY MANAGEMENT

Across the world, organizations create value through the intellectual property they own and use to deliver products and services. Protecting intellectual capital is a primary need for business and is increasingly legislated by law. The technology today offers us unlimited potential to create, gather and amass vast quantities of information. A service provider is responsible to ensure that they can guarantee the business information is protected from intrusion, theft, loss and unauthorized access.

Information security is a management activity within the corporate governance framework, which provides the strategic direction for security activities and ensures objectives are achieved. It further ensures that that the information security risks are appropriately managed and enterprise information resources are used responsibly. The

purpose of ISM is to provide a focus for all aspects of IT security and manage all IT security activities.

The term 'information' is used as a general term and includes data stores, databases and metadata. The objective of information security is to protect the interests of those relying on information, and the systems and communications that deliver the information, from harm resulting from failures of availability, confidentiality and integrity.

For most organizations, the security objective is met when:

- Information is available and usable when required, and the systems that provide it can appropriately resist attacks and recover from or prevent failures (availability)
- Information is observed by or disclosed to only those who have a right to know (confidentiality)

- Information is complete, accurate and protected against unauthorized modification (integrity)
- Business transactions as well as information exchanges between enterprises, or with partners, can be trusted (authenticity and non-repudiation).

Prioritization of confidentiality, integrity and availability must be considered in the context of business and business processes. The primary guide to defining what must be protected and the level of protection has to come from the business. To be effective, security must address entire business processes from end to end and cover the physical and technical aspects. Only within the context of business needs and risks can management define security.

ISM activities should be focused on and driven by an overall Information Security Policy and a set of underpinning specific security policies. The policy should have the full support of top executive IT management and ideally the support and commitment of top executive business management. The policy should cover all areas of security, be appropriate, meet the needs of the business and should include:

- An overall Information Security Policy
- Use and misuse of IT assets policy
- An access control policy
- A password control policy
- An e-mail policy
- An internet policy
- An anti-virus policy
- An information classification policy
- A document classification policy
- A remote access policy
- A policy with regard to supplier access of IT services, information and components
- An asset disposal policy.

These policies should be widely available to all customers and users and their compliance should be referred to in all SLRs, SLAs, contracts and agreements. The policies should be authorized by top executive management within the business and IT, and compliance to them should be endorsed on a regular basis. All security policies should be reviewed and where necessary revised on at least an annual basis.

The five elements within an Information Security Management System (ISMS) framework are:

- **Control**

  The objectives of the control element of the ISMS are to:
  - Establish a management framework to initiate and manage information security in the organization
  - Establish an organization structure to prepare, approve and implement the information security policy
  - Allocate responsibilities
  - Establish and control documentation

- **Plan**

  The objective of the plan element of the ISMS is to devise and recommend the appropriate security measures, based on an understanding of the requirements of the organization.

  The requirements will be gathered from such sources as business and service risk, plans and strategies, SLAs and OLAs and the legal, moral and ethical responsibilities for information security. Other factors, such as the amount of funding available and the prevailing organization culture and attitudes to security, must be considered.

  The Information Security Policy defines the organization's attitude and stance on security matters. This should be an organization-wide document, not just applicable to the IT Service Provider. Responsibility for the upkeep of the document rests with the Information Security Manager

- **Implement**

  The objective of the implementation element of the ISMS is to ensure that appropriate procedures, tools and controls are in place to underpin the Information Security Policy.

  Amongst the measures are:

  - Accountability for assets – Configuration Management and the CMS are invaluable here
  - Information classification – information and repositories should be classified according to the sensitivity and the impact of disclosure

  The successful implementation of the security controls and measures is dependent on a number of factors:

  - The determination of a clear and agreed policy integrated with the needs of the business
  - Security procedures that are justified, appropriate and supported by senior management
  - Effective marketing and education in security requirements
  - A mechanism for improvement

- **Evaluation**

  The objectives of the evaluation element of the ISMS are to:

  - Supervise and check compliance with the security policy and security requirements in SLAs and OLAs
  - Carry out regular audits of the technical security of IT systems
  - Provide information to external auditors and regulators, if required

- **Maintain**

  The objectives of this maintain element of the ISMS are to:

  - Improve on security agreements as specified in, for example, SLAs and OLAs
  - Improve the implementation of security measures and controls

- This should be achieved using a PDCA (Plan-Do-Check-Act) cycle, which is a formal approach suggested by ISO 27001 for the establishment of the ISMS or Framework. This cycle is described in more detail in the Continual Service Improvement publication.

Security measures can be used at a specific stage in the prevention and handling of security incidents, as illustrated in Figure 5.9. Security incidents are not solely caused by technical threats – statistics show that, for example, the large majority stem from human errors (intended or not) or procedural errors, and often have implications in other fields such as safety, legal or health.

The following stages can be identified. At the start there is a risk that a threat will materialize. A threat can be anything that disrupts the business process or has negative impact on the business. When a threat materializes, we speak of a security incident. This security incident may result in damage (to information or to assets) that has to be repaired or otherwise corrected. Suitable measures can be selected for each of these stages. The choice of measures will depend on the importance attached to the information:

- **Preventive**: security measures are used to prevent a security incident from occurring. The best-known example of preventive measures is the allocation of access rights to a limited group of authorized people. The further requirements associated with this measure include the control of access rights (granting, maintenance and withdrawal of rights), authorization (identifying who is allowed access to which information and using which tools), identification and authentication (confirming who is seeking access) and access control (ensuring that only authorized personnel can gain access)

Figure 5.9 IT Security Management process

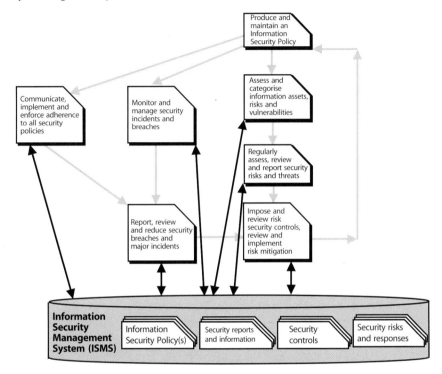

- **Reductive**: further measures can be taken in advance to minimize any possible damage that may occur. Familiar examples of reductive measures are making regular backups and the development, testing and maintenance of contingency plans
- **Detective**: if a security incident occurs, it is important to discover it as soon as possible – detection. A familiar example of this is monitoring, linked to an alert procedure. Another example is virus-checking software
- **Repressive**: measures are then used to counteract any continuation or repetition of the security incident. For example, an account or network address is temporarily blocked after numerous failed attempts to log on or the retention of a card when multiple attempts are made with a wrong PIN number

- **Corrective**: damage is repaired as far as possible using corrective measures. For example, corrective measures include restoring the backup, or returning to a previous stable situation (roll-back, back-out). Fallback can also been seen as a corrective measure.

The documentation of all controls should be maintained to reflect accurately their operation, maintenance and their method of operation.

ISM faces many challenges in establishing an appropriate Information Security Policy with an effective supporting process and controls. One of the biggest challenges is to ensure that there is adequate support from the business, business security and senior management. If these are not available, it will be impossible to establish an effective ISM process. If there is senior IT management support, but there is no support from the business, IT security controls and risk assessment will be severely limited in what they can achieve because of this lack of support from the business. It is pointless implementing security policies, procedures and controls in IT if these cannot be enforced throughout the business. The major use of IT services and assets is outside of IT, and so are the majority of security threats and risks.

In some organizations the business perception is that security is an IT responsibility, and therefore the business assumes that IT will be responsible for all aspects of IT security and that IT services will be adequately protected. However, without the commitment and support of the business and business personnel, money invested in expensive security controls and procedures will be largely wasted and they will mostly be ineffective.

Refer to the Service Design core publication for further guidance and detailed practices on Information Security Management.

5.12 SUPPLIER MANAGEMENT

The Supplier Management process ensures that suppliers and the services they provide are managed to support IT service targets and business expectations. The aim of this section is to raise awareness of the business context of working with partners and suppliers, and how this work can best be directed toward realizing business benefit for the organization.

It is essential that Supplier Management processes and planning are involved in all stages of the Service Lifecycle, from strategy and design, through transition and operation, to improvement. The complex business demands require the complete breadth of skills and capability to support provision of a comprehensive set of IT services to a business, therefore the use of value networks and the suppliers and the services they provide are an integral part of any end-to-end solution. Suppliers and the management

of suppliers and partners are essential to the provision of quality IT services (see Figure 5.10).

The main objectives of the Supplier Management process are to:

- Obtain value for money from supplier and contracts
- Ensure that underpinning contracts and agreements with suppliers are aligned to business needs, and support and align with agreed targets in SLRs and SLAs, in conjunction with SLM
- Manage relationships with suppliers
- Manage supplier performance
- Negotiate and agree contracts with suppliers and manage them through their lifecycle
- Maintain a supplier policy and a supporting supplier and contract database (SCD).

The Supplier Management process should include:

- Implementation and enforcement of the supplier policy
- Maintenance of an SCD
- Supplier and contract categorization and risk assessment
- Supplier and contract evaluation and selection
- Development, negotiation and agreement of contracts
- Contract review, renewal and termination
- Management of suppliers and supplier performance
- Agreement and implementation of service and supplier improvement plans
- Maintenance of standard contracts, terms and conditions
- Management of contractual dispute resolution
- Management of sub-contracted suppliers.

IT supplier management often has to comply with organizational or corporate standards, guidelines and requirements, particularly those of corporate legal, finance and purchasing.

Figure 5.10 Supplier Management – roles and interfaces

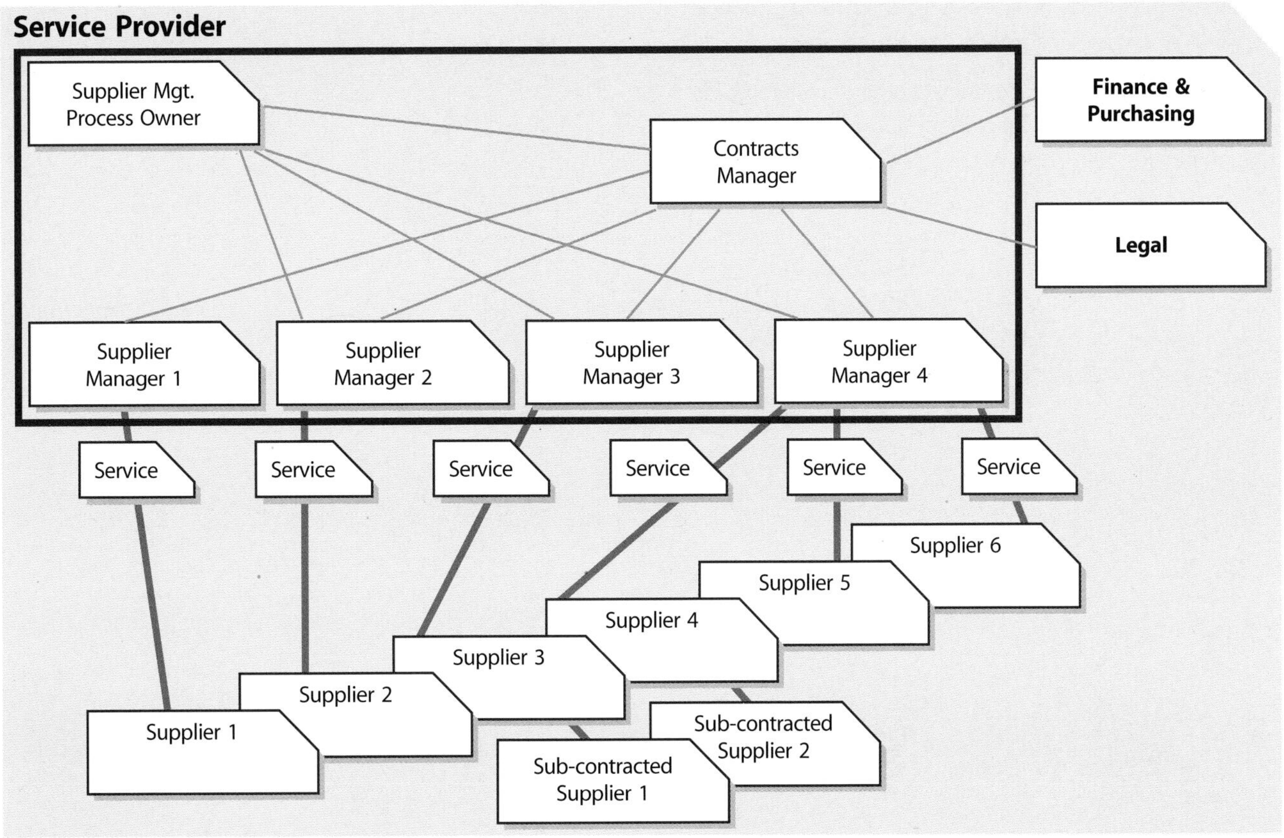

Satisfaction surveys also play an important role in revealing how well supplier service levels are aligned to business needs. A survey may reveal instances where there is dissatisfaction with the service, yet the supplier is apparently performing well against its targets (and vice versa). This may happen where service levels are inappropriately defined and should result in a review of the contracts, agreements and targets. Some service providers publish supplier league tables based on their survey results stimulating competition between suppliers.

For those significant supplier relationships in which the business has a direct interest, both the business (in conjunction with the procurement department) and IT will have established their objectives for the relationship, and defined the benefits they expect to realize. This forms a major part of the business case for entering into the relationship.

These benefits must be linked and complementary, and must be measured and managed. Where the business is seeking improvements in customer service, then IT supplier relationships contributing to those customer services must be able to demonstrate improved service in their own domain, and how much this has contributed to improved customer service.

Strong, trusted relationships with suppliers are an integral element of successful service management and enhance the value of any service provider to the business.

The Service Design book contains all the details to guide you through Supplier Management and achieve this level of relationships with suppliers.

Service Transition –
preparing for change

6

6   Service Transition – preparing for change

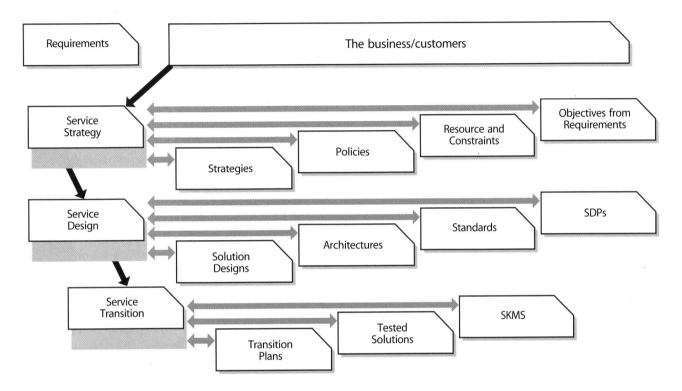

In the IT world, many business innovations are achieved through project initiatives that involve IT. In the end, whether these are minor operational improvements or major transformational events, they all produce change. In the preceding chapter we looked at creating and improving services through the design stage of the lifecycle. Now we must ensure that what is planned to be implemented will achieve the expected objectives. It is at this point the knowledge that has been generated and that will be needed to manage services once in the live environment, must be managed and shared across the organization. This is done through Service Transition.

In this chapter we will discuss a few of the key concepts within Service Transition:

- Transition Planning
- Asset and Configuration Management
- Release and Deployment Management
- Change Management
- Testing and Validation.

The purpose of Service Transition is to:

- Plan and manage the capacity and resources required to package, build, test and deploy a release into production and establish the service specified in the customer and stakeholder requirements

- Provide a consistent and rigorous framework for evaluating the service capability and risk profile before a new or changed service is released or deployed
- Establish and maintain the integrity of all identified service assets and configurations as they evolve through the Service Transition stage
- Provide good-quality knowledge and information so that Change and Release and Deployment Management can expedite effective decisions about promoting a release through the test environments and into production
- Provide efficient repeatable build and installation mechanisms that can be used to deploy releases to the test and production environments and be rebuilt if required to restore service
- Ensure that the service can be managed, operated and supported in accordance with the requirements and constraints specified within the Service Design.

Effective Service Transition can significantly improve a Service Provider's ability to handle high volumes of change and releases across its customer base. It enables the Service Provider to:

- Align the new or changed service with the customer's business requirements and business operations
- Ensure that customers and users can use the new or changed service in a way that minimizes value to the business operations.

Specifically, Service Transition adds value to the business by improving:

- The ability to adapt quickly to new requirements and market developments ('competitive edge')
- Transition management of mergers, de-mergers, acquisitions and transfer of services
- The success rate of changes and releases for the business

- The predictions of service levels and warranties for new and changed services
- Confidence in the degree of compliance with business and governance requirements during change
- The variation of actual against estimated and approved resource plans and budgets
- The productivity of business and customer staff because of better planning and use of new and changed services
- Timely cancellation or changes to maintenance contracts for hardware and software when components are disposed or decommissioned
- Understanding of the level of risk during and after change, e.g. service outage, disruption and re-work.

The processes covered in Service Transition (see Figure 6.1) are:

- Transition Planning and Support
- Change Management
- Service Asset and Configuration Management
- Release and Deployment Management
- Service Validation and Testing
- Evaluation
- Knowledge Management.

6.1 TRANSITION PLANNING AND SUPPORT

The goals of Transition Planning and Support are to:

- Plan and coordinate the resources to ensure that the requirements of Service Strategy encoded in Service Design are effectively realized in Service Operations
- Identify, manage and control the risks of failure and disruption across transition activities.

The objectives of Transition Planning and Support are to:

- Plan and coordinate the resources to establish successfully a new or changed service into production within the predicted cost, quality and time estimates

Figure 6.1 The Service Transition process

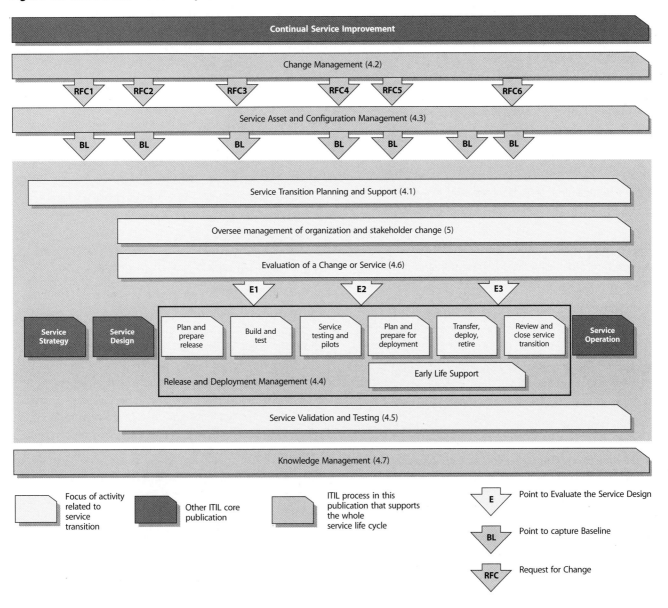

- Ensure that all parties adopt the common framework of standard re-usable processes and supporting systems in order to improve the effectiveness and efficiency of the integrated planning and coordination activities
- Provide clear and comprehensive plans that enable the customer and business change projects to align their activities with the Service Transition plans.

The organization should decide the most appropriate approach to Service Transition based on the size and nature of the core and supporting services, the number and frequency of releases required, and any special needs of the users – for example, if a phased rollout is usually required over an extended period of time.

The Service Transition strategy defines the overall approach to organizing Service Transition and allocating resources. The aspects to consider are:

- Purpose, goals and objectives of Service Transition
- Context, e.g. service customer, contract portfolios
- Scope – inclusions and exclusions
- Applicable standards, agreements, legal, regulatory and contractual requirements
- Organizations and stakeholders involved in transition
- Framework for Service Transition
- Criteria
- Identification of requirements and content of the new or changed service
- People
- Approach
- Deliverables from transition activities including mandatory and optional documentation for each stage
- Schedule of milestones
- Financial requirements – budgets and funding.

Service Design will – in collaboration with customers, external and internal suppliers and other relevant stakeholders – develop the Service Design and document it in a Service Design Package (SDP). The SDP includes the following information that is required by the Service Transition team:

- Applicable service packages (e.g. Core Service Package, Service Level Package)
- Service specifications
- Service models
- Architectural design required to deliver the new or changed Service including constraints
- Definition and design of each release package
- Detailed design of how the service components will be assembled and integrated into a release package
- Release and deployment plans
- Service Acceptance Criteria.

6.1.1 Planning an individual Service Transition

The release and deployment activities should be planned in stages as details of the deployment might not be known in detail initially. Each Service Transition plan should be developed from a proven Service Transition model wherever possible. Although Service Design provides the initial plan, the planner will allocate specific resources to the activities and modify the plan to fit in with any new circumstances, e.g. a test specialist may have left the organization.

A Service Transition plan describes the tasks and activities required to release and deploy a release into the test environments and into production, including:

- Work environment and infrastructure for the Service Transition
- Schedule of milestones, handover and delivery dates
- Activities and tasks to be performed
- Staffing, resource requirements, budgets and timescales at each stage
- Issues and risks to be managed

- Lead times and contingency.

Allocating resources to each activity and factoring in resource availability will enable the Service Transition planner to work out whether the transition can be deployed by the required date. If resources are not available, it may be necessary to review other transition commitments and consider changing priorities. Such changes need to be discussed with Change and Release Management as this may affect other changes that may be dependents or prerequisites of the release.

6.1.2 Integrated planning

Good planning and management are essential to deploy a release across distributed environments and locations into production successfully. An integrated set of transition plans should be maintained that are linked to lower-level plans such as release, build and test plans. These plans should be integrated with the change schedule, release and deployment plans. Establishing good-quality plans at the outset enables Service Transition to manage and coordinate the Service Transition resources, e.g. resource allocation, utilization, budgeting and accounting.

An overarching Service Transition plan should include the milestone activities to acquire the release components, package the release, build, test, deploy, evaluate and proactively improve the service through early life support. It will also include the activities to build and maintain the services and IT infrastructure, systems and environments and the measurement system to support the transition activities.

6.1.3 Adopting programme and project management best practices

It is best practice to manage several releases and deployments as a programme, with each significant deployment run as a project. The actual deployment may be carried out by dedicated staff, as part of broader responsibilities such as operations or through a team brought together for the purpose. Elements of the deployment may be delivered through external suppliers, and suppliers may deliver the bulk of the deployment effort, for example in the implementation of an off-the-shelf system such as an ITSM support tool.

Significant deployments will be complex projects in their own right. The steps to consider in planning include the range of elements comprising that service, e.g. people, application, hardware, software, documentation and knowledge. This means that the deployment will contain sub-deployments for each type of element comprising the service.

6.1.4 Reviewing the plans

The planning role should quality review all Service Transition, release and deployment plans. Wherever possible, lead times should include an element of contingency and be based on experience rather than merely supplier assertion. This applies even more for internal suppliers where there is no formal contract. Lead times will typically vary seasonally and they should be factored into planning, especially for long timeframe transitions, where the lead times may vary between stages of a transition, or between different user locations.

Before starting the release or deployment, the Service Transition planning role should verify the plans and ask appropriate questions such as:

- Are these Service Transition and release plans up to date?
- Have the plans been agreed and authorized by all relevant parties, e.g. customers, users, operations and support staff?
- Do the plans include the release dates and deliverables and refer to related Change Requests, Known Errors and Problems?

- Have the impacts on costs, organizational, technical and commercial aspects been considered?
- Have the risks to the overall services and operations capability been assessed?
- Has there been a compatibility check to ensure that the Configuration Items that are to be released are compatible with each other and with Configuration Items in the target environments?
- Have circumstances changed such that the approach needs amending?
- Were the rules and guidance on how to apply it relevant for current service and release packages?
- Do the people who need to use it understand and have the requisite skills to use it?
- Is the service release within the SDP and scope of what the transition model addresses?
- Has the Service Design altered significantly such that it is no longer appropriate?
- Have potential changes in business circumstances been identified?

Proper planning of service transition and support will reduce the need for corrective measures during and after release into live operation. Refer to the Service Transition core publication for full details on the Transition Planning and Support process.

6.2 CHANGE MANAGEMENT

The purpose of the Change Management process is to ensure that:

- Standardized methods and procedures are used for efficient and prompt handling of all changes
- All changes to Service Assets and Configuration Items are recorded in the configuration management system
- Overall business risk is optimized.

The goals of Change Management are to:

- Respond to the customer's changing business requirements while minimizing value and reducing incidents, disruption and re-work
- Respond to the business and IT requests for change that will align the services with the business needs.

Reliability and business continuity are essential for the success and survival of any organization. Service and infrastructure changes can have a negative impact on the business through service disruption and delay in identifying business requirements, but Change Management enables the service provider to add value to the business by:

- Prioritizing and responding to business and customer change proposals
- Implementing changes that meet the customers' agreed service requirements while optimizing costs
- Contributing to meet governance, legal, contractual and regulatory requirements
- Reducing failed changes and therefore service disruption, defects and re-work
- Delivering change promptly to meet business timescales
- Tracking changes through the Service Lifecycle and to the assets of its customers
- Contributing to better estimations of the quality, time and cost of change
- Assessing the risks associated with the transition of services (introduction or disposal)
- Aiding productivity of staff through minimizing disruptions due to high levels of unplanned or Emergency Change and hence minimizing service availability
- Reducing the mean time to restore service (MTRS), via quicker and more successful implementations of corrective changes

- Liaising with the business change process to identify opportunities for business improvement.

Policies that support Change Management include:

- Creating a culture of Change Management across the organization where there is zero tolerance for unauthorized change
- Aligning the service Change Management process with business, project and stakeholder change management processes
- Prioritization of change, e.g. innovation vs preventive vs detective vs corrective change
- Establishing accountability and responsibilities for changes through the Service Lifecycle
- Segregation of duty controls
- Establishing a single focal point for changes in order to minimize the probability of conflicting changes and potential disruption to the production environment
- Preventing people who are not authorized to make a change from having access to the production environment
- Integration with other service management processes to establish traceability of change, detect unauthorized change and identify change-related incidents
- Change windows – enforcement and authorization for exceptions
- Performance and risk evaluation of all changes that impact service capability
- Performance measures for the process, e.g. efficiency and effectiveness.

6.2.1 The seven Rs of Change Management

The following questions must be answered for all changes. Without this information, the impact assessment cannot be completed, and the balance of risk and benefit to the live service will not be understood. This could result in the change not delivering all the possible or expected business benefits or even having a detrimental, unexpected effect on the live service.

- Who RAISED the change?
- What is the REASON for the change?
- What is the RETURN required from the change?
- What are the RISKS involved in the change?
- What resources are REQUIRED to deliver the change?
- Who is RESPONSIBLE for the build, test and implementation of the change?
- What is the RELATIONSHIP between this change and other changes?

The Request for Change (RFC) is a key information source and the catalyst for the change activities of:

- Create and record
- Review
- Assess and evaluate
- Authorize
- Plan
- Coordinate
- Review
- Close.

Each RFC will follow a selected Change Model that is appropriate for the nature and type of change. Change Models are pre-established process flows with the necessary steps to satisfy the type of change and level of authorization needed to properly assess risk and impact.

Three basic Change Models are included in Service Transitions which can be adapted to suit individual organizational circumstances and need.

- **Standard Change Model** – Used for pre-authorized repetitive, low-risk, well-tested changes. Often these will be the model used for service operational maintenance changes

- **Normal Change Model** – The full model for changes that must go through assessment, authorization and Change Advisory Board (CAB) agreement before implementation

- **Emergency Change Model** – A model reserved only for highly critical changes needed to restore failed high availability or widespread service failure, or that will prevent such a failure from imminently occurring.

Figure 6.2 depicts the high-level flow of a Normal Change Model.

Figure 6.2 Normal Change Model

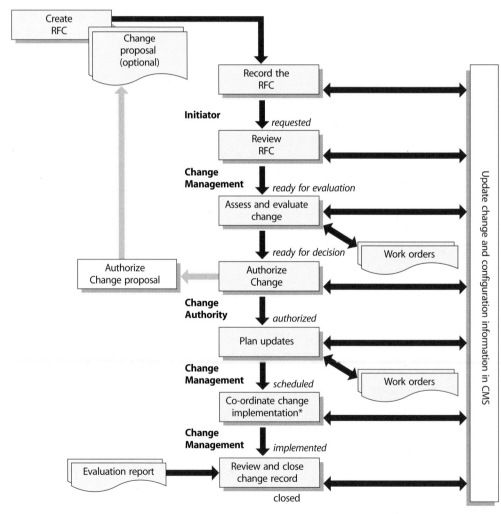

6.2.2 Change Advisory Board

The CAB is a body that exists to support the authorization of changes and to assist Change Management in the assessment and prioritization of changes. As and when a CAB is convened, members should be chosen who are capable of ensuring that all changes within the scope of the CAB are adequately assessed from both a business and a technical viewpoint.

The CAB may be asked to consider and recommend the adoption or rejection of changes appropriate for higher level authorization and then recommendations will be submitted to the appropriate change authority.

To achieve this, the CAB needs to include people with a clear understanding across the whole range of stakeholder needs. The Change Manager will normally chair the CAB and potential members include:

- Customer(s)
- User manager(s)
- User group representative(s)
- Applications developers/maintainers
- Specialists/technical consultants
- Services and operations staff, e.g. Service Desk, test management, ITSCM, security, capacity
- Facilities/office services staff (where changes may affect moves/accommodation and vice versa)
- Contractor's or third parties' representatives, e.g. in outsourcing situations.

The Service Transition core publication contains the full Change Management process.

6.3 ASSET AND CONFIGURATION MANAGEMENT

Within the human body lie a number of intricate systems. The respiratory, nervous and circulatory systems have distinct functions, but they also have a critical dependency on one another. If one system fails, the others will eventually succumb, unless provided additional life-supporting intervention. Services are systems with similar levels of interdependency. These are service assets which have configurations specific to the functions they perform and, ultimately, the service they collectively deliver.

No organization can be fully efficient or effective unless it manages its assets well, particularly those assets that are vital to the running of the customer's or organization's business. This process manages the service assets in order to support the other service management processes.

The goal of optimizing the performance of service assets and configurations improves the overall service performance and optimizes the costs and risks caused by poorly managed assets, e.g. service outages, fines, correct licence fees and failed audits.

Service Asset and Configuration Management (SACM) provides visibility of accurate representations of a service, release, or environment that enable:

- Better forecasting and planning of changes
- Changes and releases to be assessed, planned and delivered successfully
- Incidents and Problems to be resolved within the service level targets
- Service levels and warranties to be delivered
- Better adherence to standards, legal and regulatory obligations (fewer non-conformances)
- More business opportunities as able to demonstrate control of assets and services
- Changes to be traceable from requirements
- Creation of the ability to identify the costs for a service.

6.3.1 Configuration Items

A Configuration Item (CI) is an asset, service component or other item which is, or will be, under the control of Configuration Management. CIs may vary widely in complexity, size and type, ranging from an entire service or system including all hardware, software, documentation and support staff to a single software module or a minor hardware component. CIs may be grouped and managed together, e.g. a set of components may be grouped into a release. CIs should be selected using established selection criteria, grouped, classified and identified in such a way that they are manageable and traceable throughout the Service Lifecycle.

There will be a variety of CIs; the following categories may help to identify them.

- **Service Lifecycle CIs** such as the Business Case, service management plans, Service Lifecycle plans, Service Design Package, release and change plans, and test plans. They provide a picture of the Service Provider's services, how these services will be delivered, what benefits are expected, at what cost, and when they will be realized
- **Service CIs** such as:
  - Service capability assets: management, organization, processes, knowledge, people
  - Service resource assets: financial capital, systems, applications, information, data, infrastructure and facilities, people
  - Service model
  - Service package
  - Release package
  - Service acceptance criteria
- **Organization CIs** – some documentation will define the characteristics of a CI whereas other documentation will be a CI in its own right and need to be controlled, e.g. the organization's business strategy or other policies that are internal to the organization but independent of the Service Provider. Regulatory or statutory requirements also form external products that need to be tracked, as do products shared between more than one group

- **Internal CIs** comprising those delivered by individual projects, including tangible (data centre) and intangible assets such as software that are required to deliver and maintain the service and infrastructure
- **External CIs** such as external customer requirements and agreements, releases from suppliers or sub-contractors and external services
- **Interface CIs** that are required to deliver the end-to-end service across a Service Provider Interface (SPI).

6.3.2 Configuration Management System

To manage large and complex IT services and infrastructures, Service Asset and Configuration Management (SACM) requires the use of a supporting system known as the Configuration Management System (CMS).

The CMS holds all the information for CIs within the designated scope. Some of these items will have related specifications or files that contain the contents of the item, e.g. software, document or photograph. For example, a Service CI will include the details such as supplier, cost, purchase date and renewal date for licences and maintenance contracts and the related documentation such as SLAs and underpinning contracts.

The CMS is also used for a wide range of purposes; for example asset data held in the CMS may be made available to external financial asset management systems to perform specific asset management process reporting outside configuration management.

The CMS maintains the relationships between all service components and any related incidents, problems, known errors, change and release documentation and may also contain corporate data about employees, suppliers, locations and business units, customers and users.

Attributes for Configuration Items

Attributes describe the characteristics of a CI that are valuable to record and which will support SACM and the ITSM processes it supports.

The SACM plan references the configuration information and data architecture. This includes the attributes to be recorded for each type of asset or CI. Typical attributes include:

- Unique identifier
- CI type
- Name/description
- Version (e.g. file, build, baseline, release)
- Location
- Supply date
- Licence details, e.g. expiry date
- Owner/custodian
- Status
- Supplier/source
- Related document masters
- Related software masters
- Historical data, e.g. audit trail
- Relationship type
- Applicable SLA.

These attributes will define specific functional and physical characteristics of each type of asset and CI, e.g. size or capacity, together with any documentation or specifications.

The business value of SACM is often not recognized until the use of the CMS is used with other service management processes within the Service Lifecycle. The CMS is part of a larger Service Knowledge Management System (see the Service Transition core publication) that drives the effectiveness and value of service knowledge.

CI information is critical for responsive service provision and assists in areas such as:

- Service Desk – impact of service failure, SLA targets associated to the service that the CI(s) are supporting, owner and technical support information, recent changes to the CI to aid in Incident triage
- Event Management – trending of events logged against CI for possible service stability issues
- Incident Management – logging of faults against CIs and ability to see upstream and downstream impacts
- Financial Management – asset and replacement lifecycle information, contributing the service valuation activities
- Availability and Continuity – identification of point of failure vulnerability through CI relationship and redundancy information in the CMS
- Service Level Management – identifying dependencies and relationships of components that contribute to an end-to-end service
- Change Management – identification of impact of changes to services.

Figure 6.3 Service Asset and Configuration Management – interfaces to the lifecycle

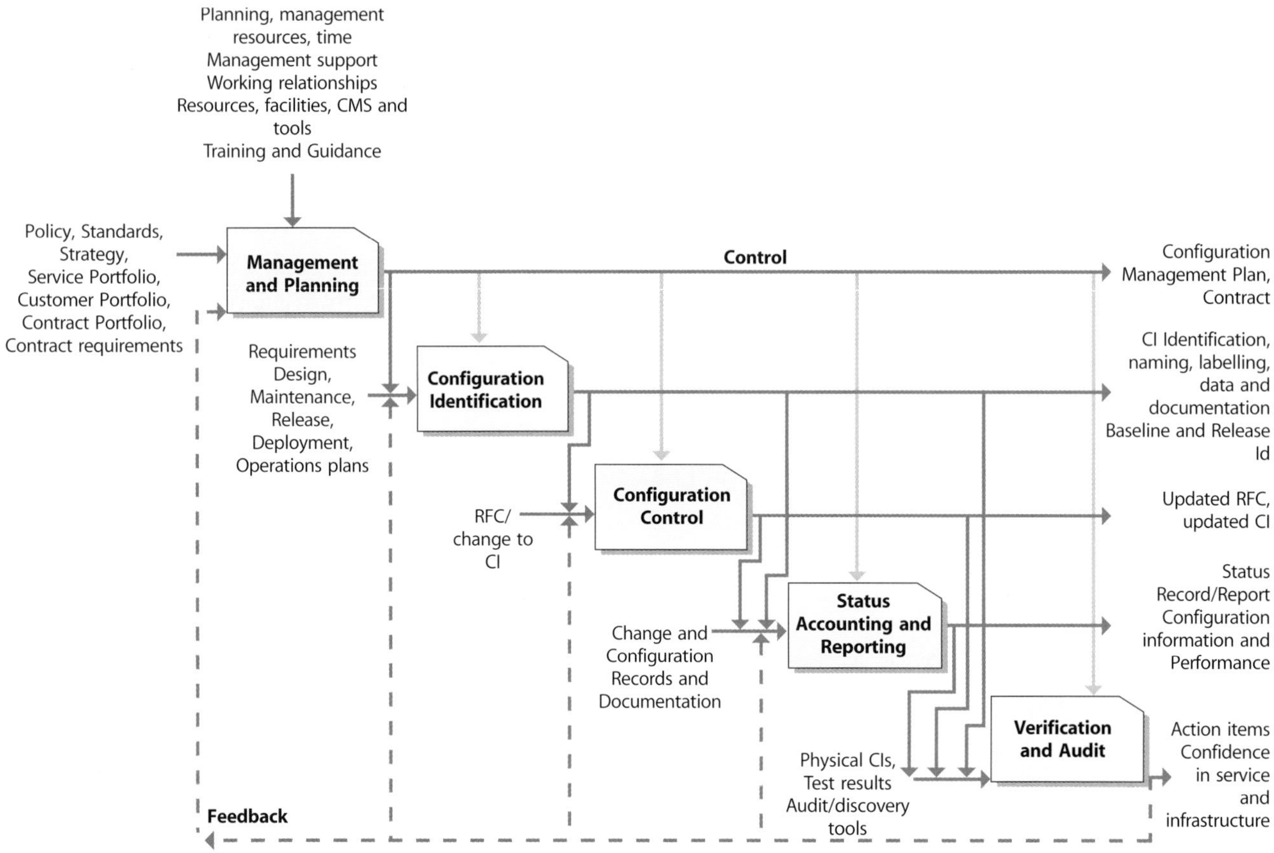

6.4 RELEASE AND DEPLOYMENT MANAGEMENT

Effective Release and Deployment Management practices enable the Service Provider to add value to the business by:

■ Delivering change, faster and at optimum cost and minimized risk

■ Assuring that customers and users can use the new or changed service in a way that supports the business goals

■ Improving consistency in implementation approach across the business change and service teams, suppliers and customers

■ Contributing to meeting auditable requirements for traceability through Service Transition.

Well-planned and implemented release and deployment will make a significant difference to an organization's service costs. A poorly designed release or deployment will, at best, force IT personnel to spend significant amounts of time troubleshooting problems and managing complexity. At worst, it can cripple the environment and degrade the live services.

The goal of Release and Deployment Management is to deploy releases into production and enable effective use of the service in order to deliver value to the customer.

The objective of Release and Deployment Management is to ensure that:

■ There are clear and comprehensive release and deployment plans that enable the customer and business change projects to align their activities with these plans

■ A release package can be built, installed, tested and deployed efficiently to a deployment group or target environment successfully and on schedule

■ A new or changed service and its enabling systems, technology and organization are capable of delivering the agreed service requirements, i.e. utilities, warranties and service levels

■ There is knowledge transfer to enable the customers and users to optimize their use of the service to support their business activities

■ Skills and knowledge are transferred to operations and support staff to enable them to effectively and efficiently deliver, support and maintain the service according to required warranties and service levels

■ There is minimal unpredicted impact on the production services, operations and support organization

■ Customers, users and service management staff are satisfied with the Service Transition practices and outputs, e.g. user documentation and training.

A key to Release and Deployment Management is defining the appropriate release package type for a given type of release. Figure 6.4 illustrates one example of a release package.

Figure 6.4 Example of a release package

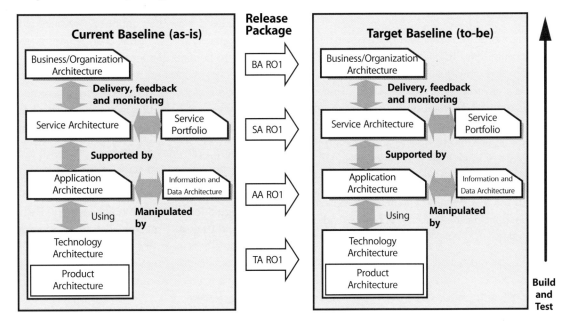

The general aim is to decide the most appropriate release-unit level for each service asset or component. An organization may, for example, decide that the release unit for business critical applications is the complete application in order to ensure that testing is comprehensive. The same organization may decide that a more appropriate release unit for a website is at the page level.

The following factors should be taken into account when deciding the appropriate level for release units:

■ The ease and amount of change necessary to release and deploy a release unit

■ The amount of resources and time needed to build, test, distribute and implement a release unit

■ The complexity of interfaces between the proposed unit and the rest of the services and IT infrastructure

■ The storage available in the build, test, distribution and live environments.

6.5 SERVICE VALIDATION AND TESTING RELEASES

Effective build and test environment management is essential to ensure that the builds and tests are executed in a repeatable and manageable manner. Inadequate control of these environments means that unplanned changes can compromise the testing activities and/or cause significant re-work. Dedicated build environments should be established for assembling and building the components for controlled test and deployment environments.

Preparation of the test environments includes building, changing or enhancing the test environments ready to receive the release.

An IT service is, on most occasions, built from a number of technology resources or management assets. In the build phase, these different blocks, often from different

suppliers, are installed and configured together to create the solution as designed. Standardization facilitates the integration of the different building blocks to provide a working solution and service.

Automating the installation of systems and application software onto servers and workstations reduces the dependencies on people and streamlines the procedures. Depending on the release and deployment plans, the installation may be performed in advance (for example, if equipment is being replaced) or it may have to occur *in situ* in the live environment.

The physical infrastructure elements, together with the environment in which they will operate, need to be tested appropriately. Part of the testing may be to test the replication of the infrastructure solution from one environment to another. This gives a better guarantee that the rollout to the production environment will be successful.

Test environments must be actively maintained and protected using service management best practices. For any significant change to a service, the question should be asked (as it is for the continued relevance of continuity and capacity plans): 'If this change goes ahead, will there need to be a consequential change to the test data?' During the build and test activities, operations and support teams need to be kept fully informed and involved as the solution is built to facilitate a structured transfer from the project to the operations team.

Figure 6.5 provides an example of service testing through the Service Transition stage of the lifecycle.

There is an invisible separation between Change, Configuration, Release and Deployment. Each works hand in hand to ensure minimal disruption and risk to the business during service transition. The Service Transition core publication contains full details of each of these important processes and guidance on how to implement and use them.

Figure 6.5 Service testing and validation

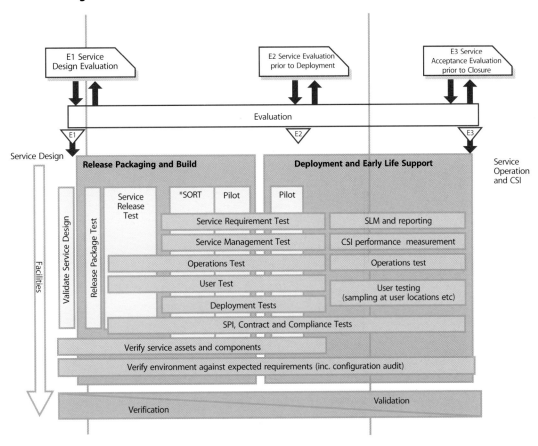

*Service Operational Readiness Test

Service Operation

7

7 Service Operation

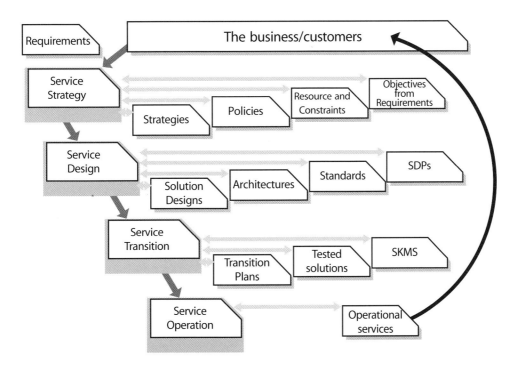

So far, we have learned some of the key concepts of ITIL Service Management – Strategy, Design and Transition. Each of these has demonstrated how they contribute to service quality, but it is in Service Operation that the business customer sees the quality of the strategy, the design and the transition come to life in everyday use of the services.

Service Operation is the phase in the ITIL Service Management Lifecycle that is responsible for business-as-usual activities.

Service Operation can be viewed as the 'factory' of IT. This implies a closer focus on the day-to-day activities and infrastructure that are used to deliver services. The overriding purpose of Service Operation is to deliver and

support services. Management of the infrastructure and the operational activities must always support this purpose.

Well-planned and implemented processes will be to no avail if the day-to-day operation of those processes is not properly conducted, controlled and managed. Nor will service improvements be possible if day-to-day activities to monitor performance, assess metrics and gather data are not systematically conducted during Service Operation.

The purpose of Service Operation is to coordinate and carry out the activities and processes required to deliver and manage services at agreed levels to business users and customers. Service Operation is also responsible for the ongoing management of the technology that is used to deliver and support services.

7.1 BUSINESS VALUE

Each stage in the ITIL Service Management Lifecycle provides value to business. For example, service value is modelled in Service Strategy; the cost of the service is designed, predicted and validated in Service Design and Service Transition; and measures for optimization identified in Continual Service Improvement. The operation of service is where these plans, designs and optimizations are executed and measured. From a customer viewpoint, Service Operation is where actual value is seen.

In all stages of the ITIL Service Management Lifecycle, there are distinct processes, functions and activities which work together to deliver the objectives of Service Operation. The following sections in this chapter touch on:

The processes of:

- Event Management
- Request Fulfilment
- Incident Management
- Problem Management
- Access Management

The functions of:

- Service Desk
- Technical Management
- IT Operations Management
- Application Management
- Monitoring and Control.

7.2 EVENT MANAGEMENT

An event can be defined as any detectable or discernible occurrence that has significance for the management of the IT infrastructure or the delivery of IT service and evaluation of the impact a deviation might cause to the services. Events are typically notifications created by an IT service, Configuration Item (CI) or monitoring tool (see Figure 7.1).

Effective Service Operation is dependent on knowing the status of the infrastructure and detecting any deviation from normal or expected operation. This is provided by good monitoring and control systems, which are based on two types of tools:

- Active monitoring tools that poll key CIs to determine their status and availability. Any exceptions will generate an alert that needs to be communicated to the appropriate tool or team for action
- Passive monitoring tools that detect and correlate operational alerts or communications generated by CIs.

Event Management can be applied to any aspect of service management that needs to be controlled and which can be automated. These include:

- Configuration Items:
  - Some CIs will be included because they need to stay in a constant state (e.g. a switch on a network needs to stay on and Event Management tools confirm this by monitoring responses to 'pings')
  - Some CIs will be included because their status needs to change frequently and Event Management can be used to automate this and update the CMS (e.g. the updating of a file server)
- Environmental conditions (e.g. fire and smoke detection)
- Software licence monitoring for usage to ensure optimum/legal licence utilization and allocation
- Security (e.g. intrusion detection)
- Normal activity (e.g. tracking the use of an application or the performance of a server).

Figure 7.1 The Event Management process

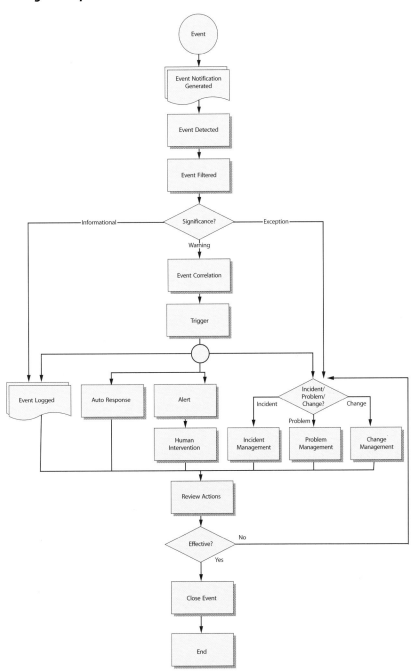

7.2.1 Value to business

Event Management's value to the business is generally indirect; however it is possible to determine the basis for its value as follows:

- Event Management provides mechanisms for early detection of incidents. In many cases it is possible for the incident to be detected and assigned to the appropriate group for action before any actual service outage occurs
- Event Management makes it possible for some types of automated activity to be monitored by exception – thus removing the need for expensive and resource-intensive real-time monitoring, while reducing downtime
- When integrated into other service management processes (such as, for example, Availability or Capacity Management), Event Management can signal status changes or exceptions that allow the appropriate person or team to perform early response, thus improving the performance of the process. This, in turn, will allow the business to benefit from more effective and more efficient Service Management overall
- Event Management provides a basis for automated operations, thus increasing efficiencies and allowing expensive human resources to be used for more innovative work, such as designing new or improved functionality or defining new ways in which the business can exploit technology for increased competitive advantage.

7.3 INCIDENT MANAGEMENT

Incident Management includes any event which disrupts, or which could disrupt, a service. This includes events which are communicated directly by users, either through the Service Desk or through an interface from Event Management to Incident Management tools.

Incidents can also be reported and/or logged by technical staff (if, for example, they notice something untoward with a hardware or network component they may report or log an incident and refer it to the Service Desk).

7.3.1 Value to business

Incident Management is highly visible to the business, and it is therefore easier to demonstrate its value than most areas in Service Operation. For this reason, Incident Management is often one of the first processes to be implemented in service management projects. The added benefit of doing this is that Incident Management can be used to highlight other areas that need attention – thereby providing a justification for expenditure on implementing other processes. Incident Management's value to the business includes:

- The ability to detect and resolve Incidents which results in lower downtime to the business, which in turn means higher availability of the service. This means that the business is able to exploit the functionality of the service as designed
- The ability to align IT activity to real-time business priorities. This is because Incident Management includes the capability to identify business priorities and dynamically allocate resources as necessary
- The ability to identify potential improvements to services. This happens as a result of understanding what constitutes an Incident and also from being in contact with the activities of business operational staff
- The Service Desk can, during its handling of Incidents, identify additional service or training requirements found in IT or the business.

7.3.2 Incident models

Many incidents are not new – they involve dealing with something that has happened before and may well happen again. For this reason, many organizations will find it helpful to pre-define standard Incident models – and apply them to appropriate Incidents when they occur.

An Incident model is a way of pre-defining the steps that should be taken to handle a process (in this case a process for dealing with a particular type of incident) in an agreed way. Support tools can then be used to manage the required process. This will ensure that standard incidents are handled in a pre-defined path and within pre-defined timescales.

The Incident model should include:

- Steps that should be taken to handle the Incident
- Chronological order these steps should be taken in, with any dependences or co-processing defined
- Responsibilities; who should do what
- Timescales and thresholds for completion of the actions
- Escalation procedures; who should be contacted and when
- Any necessary evidence-preservation activities (particularly relevant for security- and capacity-related incidents).

The models should be input to the Incident-handling support tools in use and the tools should then automate the handling, management and escalation of the process.

The Incident Management process is shown in Figure 7.2.

Incident logging

All incidents must be fully logged and date/time stamped, regardless of whether they are raised through a Service Desk telephone call or whether automatically detected via an event alert.

Incident categorization

Part of the initial logging must be to allocate suitable Incident categorization coding so that the exact type of the call is recorded. This will be important later when looking at Incident types/frequencies to establish trends for use in Problem Management, Supplier Management and other ITSM activities.

Incident prioritization

Prioritization can normally be determined by taking into account both the urgency of the Incident (how quickly the business needs a resolution) and the level of impact it is causing. An indication of impact is often (but not always) the number of users being affected. In some cases, and very importantly, the loss of service to a single user can have a major business impact.

Initial diagnosis

If the incident has been routed via the Service Desk, the Service Desk Analyst must carry out initial diagnosis, typically while the user is still on the telephone – if the call is raised in this way – to try to discover the full symptoms of the Incident and to determine exactly what has gone wrong and how to correct it. It is at this stage that diagnostic scripts and known error information can be most valuable in allowing earlier and accurate diagnosis.

Incident escalation

Functional escalation – As soon as it becomes clear that the Service Desk is unable to resolve the incident itself (or when target times for first-point resolution have been exceeded – whichever comes first!) the incident must be immediately escalated for further support.

Hierarchic escalation – If incidents are of a serious nature (for example Priority 1 incidents) the appropriate IT managers must be notified, for informational purposes at least. Hierarchic escalation is also used if the 'Investigation and Diagnosis' and 'Resolution and Recovery' steps are taking too long or proving too difficult. Hierarchic escalation should continue up the management chain so that senior managers are aware and can be prepared and take any necessary action, such as allocating additional

Figure 7.2 The Incident Management process flow

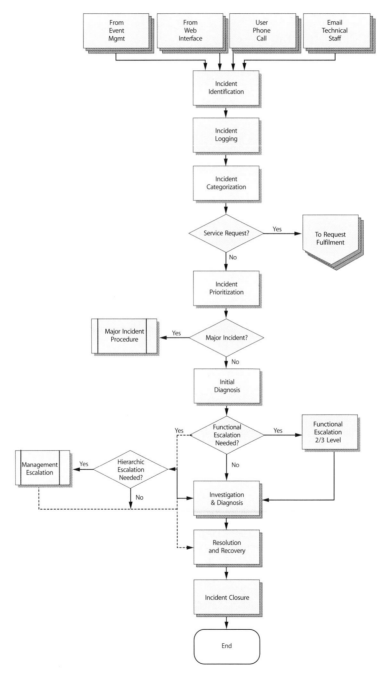

resources or involving suppliers/maintainers. Hierarchic escalation is also used when there is contention about to whom the incident is allocated.

Investigation and diagnosis

This will include a variety of activities depending on the type of incident but should include:

- Establishing exactly what has gone wrong or being sought by the user
- Understanding the chronological order of events
- Confirming the full impact of the incident, including the number and range of users affected
- Identifying any events that could have triggered the incident (e.g. a recent change, some user action?)
- Knowledge searches looking for previous occurrences by searching previous Incident/Problem Records and/or Known Error Databases or manufacturers'/suppliers' Error Logs or Knowledge Databases.

Resolution and recovery

When a potential resolution has been identified, this should be applied and tested. The specific actions to be undertaken and the people who will be involved in taking the recovery actions may vary, depending upon the nature of the fault – but could involve:

- Asking the user to undertake directed activities on their own desktop or remote equipment
- The Service Desk implementing the resolution either centrally (say, rebooting a server) or remotely using software to take control of the user's desktop to diagnose and implement a resolution
- Specialist support groups being asked to implement specific recovery actions (e.g. network support reconfiguring a router)
- A third-party supplier or maintainer being asked to resolve the fault.

Incident closure

The Service Desk should check that the incident is fully resolved and that the users are satisfied and willing to agree the Incident can be closed. The Service Desk should also check the following:

- **Closure categorization**. Check and confirm that the initial Incident categorization was correct or, where the categorization subsequently turned out to be incorrect, update the record so that a correct closure categorization is recorded for the Incident – seeking advice or guidance from the resolving group(s) as necessary
- **User satisfaction survey**. Carry out a user satisfaction call-back or e-mail survey for the agreed percentage of Incidents
- **Incident documentation**. Chase any outstanding details and ensure that the Incident Record is fully documented so that a full historic record at a sufficient level of detail is complete
- **Ongoing or recurring problem?** Determine (in conjunction with resolver groups) whether it is likely that the incident could recur and decide whether any preventive action is necessary to avoid this. In conjunction with Problem Management, raise a Problem Record in all such cases so that preventive action is initiated
- **Formal closure**. Formally close the Incident Record.

7.4 REQUEST FULFILMENT

The term 'Service Request' is used as a generic description for many varying types of demands that are placed upon the IT department by the users. Many of these are actually small changes – low risk, frequently occurring, low cost etc. (e.g. a request to change a password, a request to install an additional software application onto a particular workstation, a request to relocate some items of desktop equipment) or may be just a question requesting information – but their scale and frequent, low-risk nature means that they are better handled by a separate process, rather than being allowed to congest and obstruct the normal Incident and Change Management processes.

The process needed to fulfil a request will vary depending upon exactly what is being requested – but can usually be broken down into a set of activities that have to be performed. Some organizations will be comfortable to let the Service Requests be handled through their Incident Management processes (and tools) – with Service Requests being handled as a particular type of Incident (using a high-level categorization system to identify those Incidents that are in fact Service Requests).

Note, however, that there is a significant difference here – an Incident is usually an unplanned event whereas a Service Request is usually something that can and should be planned!

Therefore, in an organization where large numbers of Service Requests have to be handled, and where the actions to be taken to fulfil those requests are very varied or specialized, it may be appropriate to handle Service Requests as a completely separate work stream – and to record and manage them as a separate record type.

Many Service Requests will be frequently recurring, so a predefined process flow (a model) can be devised to include the stages needed to fulfil the request, the individuals or support groups involved, target timescales and escalation paths. Service Requests will usually be satisfied by implementing a Standard Change (see the Service Transition publication for further details on Standard Changes). The ownership of Service Requests resides with the Service Desk, which monitors, escalates, dispatches and often fulfils the user request.

7.4.1 Request models

Some Service Requests will occur frequently and will require handling in a consistent manner in order to meet agreed service levels. To assist this, many organizations will wish to create pre-defined Service Request models (which typically include some form of pre-approval by Change Management). This is similar in concept to the idea of Incident models, but applied to Service Requests.

Most requests will be triggered through either a user calling the Service Desk or a user completing some form of self-help web-based input screen to make their request. The latter will often involve a selection from a portfolio of available request types.

The primary interfaces with Request Fulfilment include:

- **Service Desk/Incident Management**: many Service Requests may come in via the Service Desk and may be initially handled through the Incident Management process. Some organizations may choose that all Requests are handled via this route – but others may choose to have a separate process, for reasons already discussed earlier in this chapter
- A strong link is also needed between **Request Fulfilment, Release, Asset and Configuration Management** as some requests will be for the deployment of new or upgraded components that can be automatically deployed. In such cases the release can be pre-defined, built and tested but only deployed upon request by those who want the release. Upon deployment, the CMS will have to be updated to reflect the change. Where appropriate, software licence checks/updates will also be necessary.

Where appropriate, it will be necessary to relate IT-related Service Requests to any Incidents or Problems that have initiated the need for the Request (as would be the case for any other type of change).

Request Fulfilment depends on the following critical success factors:

■ Agreement of what services will be standardized and who is authorized to request them. The cost of these services must also be agreed. This may be done as part of the SLM process. Any variances of the services must also be defined

■ Publication of the services to users as part of the Service Catalogue. It is important that this part of the Service Catalogue must be easily accessed, perhaps on the intranet, and should be recognized as the first source of information for users seeking access to a service

■ Definition of a standard fulfilment procedure for each of the services being requested. This includes all procurement policies and the ability to generate purchase orders and work orders

■ A single point of contact which can be used to request the service. This is often provided by the Service Desk or through an intranet request, but could be through an automated request directly into the Request Fulfilment or procurement system

■ Self-service tools needed to provide a front-end interface to the users. It is essential that these integrate with the back-end fulfilment tools, often managed through Incident or Change Management.

7.5 PROBLEM MANAGEMENT

ITIL defines a 'Problem' as the unknown cause of one or more Incidents.

Problem Management is the process responsible for managing the lifecycle of all problems. The primary objectives of Problem Management are to prevent Problems and resulting Incidents from happening, to eliminate recurring Incidents and to minimize the impact of Incidents that cannot be prevented.

7.5.1 Scope

Problem Management includes the activities required to diagnose the root cause of Incidents and to determine the resolution to those problems. It is also responsible for ensuring that the resolution is implemented through the appropriate control procedures, especially Change Management and Release Management.

Problem Management will also maintain information about Problems and the appropriate workarounds and resolutions, so that the organization is able to reduce the number and impact of Incidents over time. In this respect, Problem Management has a strong interface with Knowledge Management, and tools such as the Known Error Database will be used for both.

Although Incident and Problem Management are separate processes, they are closely related and will typically use the same tools, and may use similar categorization, impact and priority coding systems. This will ensure effective communication when dealing with related Incidents and Problems.

Problem Management consists of two major processes:

■ **Reactive** Problem Management, which is generally executed as part of Service Operation

■ **Proactive** Problem Management which is initiated in Service Operation, but generally driven as part of Continual Service Improvement.

7.5.2 Process

Problem detection

It is likely that multiple ways of detecting problems will exist in all organizations. These will include:

■ Suspicion or detection of an unknown cause of one or more Incidents by the Service Desk, resulting in a Problem Record being raised – the desk may have resolved the Incident but has not determined a

Figure 7.3 The Problem Management process flow

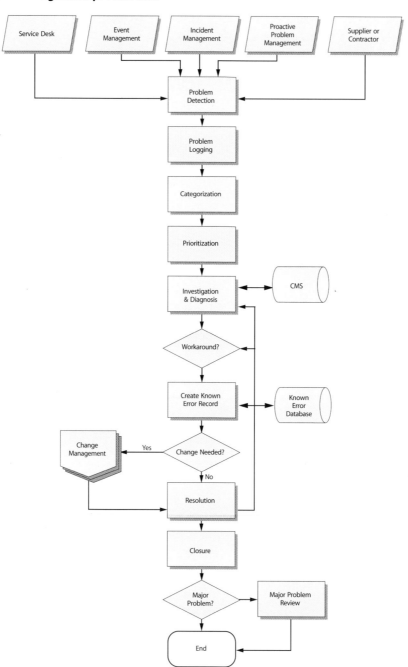

definitive cause and suspects that it is likely to recur, so will raise a Problem Record to allow the underlying cause to be resolved. Alternatively, it may be immediately obvious from the outset that an Incident, or Incidents, has been caused by a major problem, so a Problem Record will be raised without delay

■ Analysis of an incident by a technical support group which reveals that an underlying problem exists, or is likely to exist

■ Automated detection of an infrastructure or application fault, using event/alert tools automatically to raise an Incident which may reveal the need for a Problem Record

■ A notification from a supplier or contractor that a Problem exists that has to be resolved

■ Analysis of Incidents as part of proactive Problem Management – resulting in the need to raise a Problem Record so that the underlying fault can be investigated further.

Problem logging

A cross-reference must be made to the incident(s) which initiated the Problem Record – and all relevant details must be copied from the Incident Record(s) to the Problem Record. It is difficult to be exact, as cases may vary, but typically this will include details such as:

■ User details
■ Service details
■ Equipment details
■ Date/time initially logged
■ Priority and categorization details
■ Incident description
■ Details of all diagnostic or attempted recovery actions taken.

Problem categorization

Problems must be categorized in the same way as Incidents (and it is advisable to use the same coding system) so that the true nature of the Problem can be easily traced in the future and meaningful management information can be obtained.

Problem prioritization

Problems must be prioritized in the same way and for the same reasons as Incidents – but the frequency and impact of related Incidents must also be taken into account.

Problem prioritization should also take into account the severity of the Problem. Severity in this context refers to how serious the Problem is from an infrastructure perspective, for example:

■ Can the system be recovered, or does it need to be replaced?
■ How much will it cost?
■ How many people, with what skills, will be needed to fix the problem?
■ How long will it take to fix the problem?
■ How extensive is the problem (e.g. how many CIs are affected)?

Problem investigation and diagnosis

An investigation should be conducted to try to diagnose the root cause of the Problem – the speed and nature of this investigation will vary depending upon the impact, severity and urgency of the Problem – but the appropriate level of resources and expertise should be applied to finding a resolution commensurate with the priority code allocated and the service target in place for that priority level.

The CMS must be used to help determine the level of impact and to assist in pinpointing and diagnosing the exact point of failure. The Known Error Database (KEDB)

should also be accessed and Problem-matching techniques (such as keyword searches) should be used to see if the Problem has occurred before and, if so, to find the resolution.

It is often valuable to try to recreate the failure, so as to understand what has gone wrong, and then to try various ways of finding the most appropriate and cost-effective resolution to the Problem. To do this effectively without causing further disruption to the users, a test system will be necessary that mirrors the production environment.

There are many Problem analysis, diagnosis and solving techniques available and much research has been done in this area. The Service Operation publication details the types and how to use them.

Workarounds

In some cases it may be possible to find a workaround to the Incidents caused by the Problem – a temporary way of overcoming the difficulties. For example, a manual amendment may be made to an input file to allow a program to complete its run successfully and allow a billing process to complete satisfactorily, but it is important that work on a permanent resolution continues where this is justified – in this example the reason for the file becoming corrupted in the first place must be found and corrected to prevent this happening again.

In cases where a workaround is found, it is therefore important that the Problem Record remains open, and details of the workaround are always documented within the Problem Record.

Raising a Known Error Record

As soon as the diagnosis is complete, and particularly where a workaround has been found (even though it may not yet be a permanent resolution), a Known Error Record must be raised and placed in the Known Error Database –

so that if further Incidents or Problems arise, they can be identified and the service restored more quickly.

However, in some cases it may be advantageous to raise a Known Error Record even earlier in the overall process – just for information purposes, for example – even though the diagnosis may not be complete or a workaround found, so it is inadvisable to set a concrete procedural point exactly when a Known Error Record must be raised. It should be done as soon as it becomes useful to do so!

Problem resolution

Ideally, as soon as a solution has been found, it should be applied to resolve the Problem – but in reality safeguards may be needed to ensure that this does not cause further difficulties. If any change in functionality is required this will require an RFC to be raised and approved before the resolution can be applied. If the Problem is very serious and an urgent fix is needed for business reasons, then an Emergency RFC should be handled by the Emergency Change Advisory Board (ECAB) to facilitate this urgent action. Otherwise, the RFC should follow the established Change Management process for that type of Change – and the resolution should be applied only when the Change has been approved and scheduled for release. In the meantime, the KEDB should be used to help resolve quickly any further occurrences of the Incidents/Problems.

Problem closure

When any change has been completed (and successfully reviewed), and the resolution has been applied, the Problem Record should be formally closed – as should any related Incident Records that are still open. A check should be performed at this time to ensure that the record contains a full historical description of all events – and if not, the record should be updated.

The status of any related Known Error Records should be updated to show that the resolution has been applied.

Major Problem review

After every major Problem (as determined by the organization's priority system), while memories are still fresh a review should be conducted to learn any lessons for the future. Specifically, the review should examine:

- Those things that were done correctly
- Those things that were done wrong
- What could be done better in the future
- How to prevent recurrence
- Whether there has been any third-party responsibility and whether follow-up actions are needed.

Such reviews can be used as part of training and awareness activities for support staff – and any lessons learned should be documented in appropriate procedures, work instructions, diagnostic scripts or Known Error Records. The Problem Manager facilitates the session and documents any agreed actions.

Errors detected in the development environment

It is rare for any new applications, systems or software releases to be completely error-free. It is more likely that during testing of such new applications, systems or releases, a prioritization system will be used to eradicate the more serious faults, but it is possible that minor faults are not rectified – often because of the balance that has to be made between delivering new functionality to the business as quickly as possible and ensuring totally fault-free code or components.

Where a decision is made to release something into the production environment that includes known deficiencies, these should be logged as Known Errors in the KEDB, together with details of workarounds or resolution activities. There should be a formal step in the testing sign-off that ensures that this handover always takes place (see Service Transition publication).

7.6 ACCESS MANAGEMENT

Access Management is the process of granting authorized users the right to use a service, while preventing access to non-authorized users. It has also been referred to as 'rights management' or 'identity management' in different organizations.

Access Management is effectively the execution of both Availability and Information Security Management, in that it enables the organization to manage the confidentiality, availability and integrity of the organization's data and intellectual property.

Access Management ensures that users are given the right to use a service, but it does not ensure that this access is available at all agreed times – this is provided by Availability Management.

Access Management is a process that is executed by all Technical and Application Management functions and is usually not a separate function. However, there is likely to be a single control point of coordination, usually in IT Operations Management or on the Service Desk.

Access Management can be initiated by a Service Request through the Service Desk.

7.6.1 Value to business

- Controlled access to services ensures that the organization is able to maintain more effectively the confidentiality of its information
- Employees have the right level of access to execute their jobs effectively
- There is less likelihood of errors being made in data entry or in the use of a critical service by an unskilled user (e.g. production control systems)
- The ability to audit use of services and to trace the abuse of services
- The ability more easily to revoke access rights when needed – an important security consideration

- May be needed for regulatory compliance (e.g. SOX, HIPAA, COBIT).

7.6.2 Basic concepts

While each user has an individual identity, and each IT service can be seen as an entity in its own right, it is often helpful to group them together so that they can be managed more easily. Sometimes the terms 'user profile', 'user template' or 'user role' are used to describe this type of grouping.

Most organizations have a standard set of services for all individual users, regardless of their position or job (excluding customers – who do not have any visibility to internal services and processes). These will include services such as messaging, office automation, desktop support, telephony etc. New users are automatically provided with rights to use these services.

However, most users also have some specialized role that they perform. For example, in addition to the standard services, the user may also perform a marketing management role, which requires that they have access to some specialized marketing and financial modelling tools and data.

Some groups may have unique requirements – such as field or home workers who may have to dial in or use virtual private network (VPN) connections, with security implications that may have to be more tightly managed.

To make it easier for Access Management to provide the appropriate rights, it uses a catalogue of all the roles in the organization and which services support each role. This catalogue of roles should be compiled and maintained by Access Management in conjunction with HR and will often be automated in the directory services tools.

In addition to playing different roles, users may also belong to different groups. For example, all contractors may be required to log their timesheets in a dedicated time card system, which is not used by employees. Access Management will assess all the roles that a user plays as well as the groups that they belong to and ensure that they provide rights to use all associated services.

Note: All data held on users will be subject to data protection legislation (this exists in most geographic locations in some form or other) so should be handled and protected as part of the organization's security procedures.

7.6.3 Lifecycle activities

Within Access Management the following lifecycle flow is recommended:

- Requesting access
- Verification
- Providing rights
- Monitoring identity status
- Logging and tracking access
- Removing or restricting rights.

The Service Operation publication provides the detailed workflow for each of these activities.

7.7 SERVICE OPERATION FUNCTIONS

7.7.1 Monitoring and control

The measurement and control of services is based on a continual cycle of monitoring, reporting and subsequent action. This cycle is discussed in detail in this section because it is fundamental to the delivery, support and improvement of services.

It is also important to note that, although this cycle takes place during Service Operation, it provides a basis for setting strategy, designing and testing services and achieving meaningful improvement. It is also the basis for SLM measurement. Therefore, although monitoring is performed by Service Operation functions, it should not be seen as a purely operational matter. All phases of the

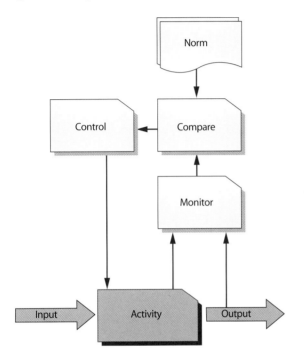

Service Lifecycle should ensure that measures and controls are clearly defined, executed and acted upon.

Figure 7.4 Single monitor control loop

Single monitor control loop

A single activity and its output are measured using a pre-defined norm, or standard, to determine whether it is within an acceptable range of performance or quality (Figure 7.4). If not, action is taken to rectify the situation or to restore normal performance.

Typically there are two types of monitor control loops:

■ **Open-loop systems** are designed to perform a specific activity regardless of environmental conditions. For example, a backup can be initiated at a given time and frequency – and will run regardless of other conditions

■ **Closed-loop systems** monitor an environment and respond to changes in that environment. For example, in network load balancing a monitor will evaluate the traffic on a circuit. If network traffic exceeds a certain range, the control system will begin to route traffic across a backup circuit. The monitor will continue to provide feedback to the control system which will continue to regulate the flow of network traffic between the two circuits.

To help clarify the difference, solving a Capacity Management problem through over-provisioning is open loop; a load-balancer that detects congestion/failure and redirects capacity is closed loop.

Complex monitor control loop

The monitor control loop in Figure 7.5 is a good basis for defining how Operations Management works, but within the context of ITSM the situation is far more complex. The figure illustrates a process consisting of three major activities. Each one has an input and an output, and the output becomes an input for the next activity.

In this diagram, each activity is controlled by its own Monitor Control Loop, using a set of norms for that specific activity. The process as a whole also has its own Monitor Control Loop, which spans all the activities and ensures that all norms are appropriate and are being followed.

One loop focuses purely on executing a defined standard, and the second evaluates the performance of the process and also the standards whereby the process is executed. An example of this would be if the first set of feedback loops at the bottom of the diagram represented individual stations on an assembly line and the higher-level loop represented quality assurance.

The complex monitor control loop is a good organizational learning tool (as defined by Chris Argyris (1976), *Increasing Leadership Effectiveness*, New York:

Figure 7.5 Complex monitor control loop

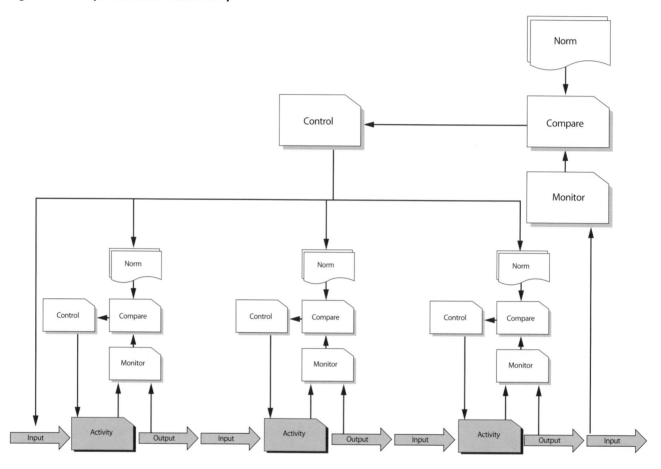

Wiley). The first level of feedback at individual activity level is concerned with monitoring and responding to data (single facts, codes or pieces of information). The second level is concerned with monitoring and responding to information (a collection of a number of facts about which a conclusion may be drawn). Refer to the Service Transition publication for a full discussion on data, information, knowledge and wisdom.

All of this is interesting theory, but does not explain how the monitor control loop concept can be used to operate

IT services. And especially – who defines the norm? Based on what has been described so far, monitor control loops can be used to manage:

■ **Performance of activities in a process or procedure**. Each activity and its related output can potentially be measured to ensure that problems with the process are identified before the process as a whole is completed. For example, in Incident Management, the Service Desk monitors whether a technical team has accepted an Incident in a specified time. If not, the Incident is escalated. This is done well before the target resolution time for that Incident because the aim of escalating that one activity is to ensure that the process as whole is completed in time

■ **Effectiveness of a process or procedure as a whole**. In this case the 'activity' box represents the entire process as a single entity. For example, Change Management will measure the success of the process by checking whether a change was implemented on time, to specification and within budget

■ **Performance of a device**. For example, the 'activity' box could represent the response time of a server under a given workload

■ **Performance of a series of devices**. For example, the end user response time of an application across the network.

ITSM monitor control loop

Each activity in a service management process (or each component used to provide a service) is monitored as part of the Service Operation processes. The operational team or department responsible for each activity or component will apply the monitor control loop as defined in the process, and using the norms that were defined during the Service Design processes. The role of operational monitoring and control is to ensure that the process or service functions exactly as specified, which is why they are primarily concerned with maintaining the status quo.

The norms and monitoring and control mechanisms are defined in Service Design, but they are based on the standards and architectures defined during Service Strategy. Any changes to the organization's Service Strategy, architecture, Service Portfolios or Service Level Requirements will precipitate changes to what is monitored and how it is controlled.

The monitor control loops are placed within the context of the organization. This implies that Service Strategy will primarily be executed by business and IT executives with

support from vendor account managers. Service Design acts as the bridge between Service Strategy and Service Operation and will typically involve representatives from all groups. The activities and controls will generally be executed by IT staff (sometimes involving users) and supported by IT managers and the vendors. Service Improvement spans all areas, but primarily represents the interests of the business and its users.

Notice that the second level of monitoring in this complex monitor control loop is performed by the CSI processes through Service Strategy and Service Design. These relationships are represented by the numbered arrows in Figure 7.6:

■ **Arrow 1**. In this case CSI has recognized that the service will be improved by making a change to the Service Strategy. This could be the result of the business needing a change to the Service Portfolio, or that the architecture does not deliver what was expected

■ **Arrow 2**. In this case the Service Level Requirements need to be adjusted. It could be that the service is too expensive; or that the configuration of the infrastructure needs to be changed to enhance performance; or because Operations Management is unable to maintain service quality in the current architecture

■ **Arrow 3**. In this case the norms specified in Service Design are not being adhered to. This could be because they are not appropriate or executable, or because of a lack of education or a lack of communication. The norms and the lack of compliance need to be investigated and action taken to rectify the situation.

There are many different types of monitoring tool and different situations in which each will be used. This section focuses on some of the different types of monitoring that can be performed and when they would be appropriate.

Figure 7.6 ITSM monitor control loop

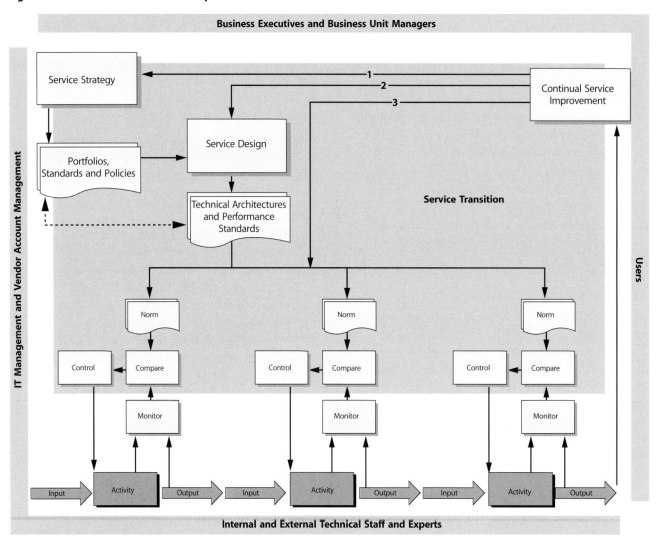

Active versus passive monitoring:

- **Active monitoring** refers to the ongoing interrogation of a device or system to determine its status. This type of monitoring can be resource intensive and is usually reserved to proactively monitor the availability of

critical devices or systems; or as a diagnostic step when attempting to resolve an Incident or diagnose a Problem

- **Passive monitoring** is more common and refers to generating and transmitting events to a listening device or monitoring agent. Passive monitoring depends on successful definition of events and instrumentation of the system being monitored (see section 4.1 of the Service Operation publication).

Reactive versus proactive monitoring:

- **Reactive monitoring** is designed to request or trigger action following a certain type of event or failure. For example, server performance degradation may trigger a reboot, or a system failure will generate an Incident. Reactive monitoring is not only used for exceptions. It can also be used as part of normal operations procedures, for example a batch job completes successfully, which prompts the scheduling system to submit the next batch job
- **Proactive monitoring** is used to detect patterns of events which indicate that a system or service may be about to fail. Proactive monitoring is generally used in more mature environments where these patterns have been detected previously, often several times. Proactive monitoring tools are therefore a means of automating the experience of seasoned IT staff and are often created through the Proactive Problem Management process (see Continual Service Improvement publication).

Operational monitoring and Continual Service Improvement

This section has focused on operational monitoring and reporting, but monitoring also forms the starting point for Continual Service Improvement (CSI). This is covered in the Continual Service Improvement publication, but key differences are outlined here.

Quality is the key objective of monitoring for CSI. Monitoring will therefore focus on the effectiveness of a service, process, tool, organization or CI. The emphasis is not on assuring real-time service performance; rather it is on identifying where improvements can be made to the existing level of service, or IT performance.

Monitoring for CSI will therefore tend to focus on detecting exceptions and resolutions. For example, CSI is not as interested in whether an Incident was resolved, but whether it was resolved within the agreed time and whether future Incidents can be prevented.

CSI is not only interested in exceptions, though. If an SLA is consistently met over time, CSI will also be interested in determining whether that level of performance can be sustained at a lower cost or whether it needs to be upgraded to an even better level of performance. CSI may therefore also need access to regular performance reports.

However, since CSI is unlikely to need, or be able to cope with, the vast quantities of data that are produced by all monitoring activity, they will most likely focus on a specific subset of monitoring at any given time. This could be determined by input from the business or improvements to technology.

This has two main implications:

- Monitoring for CSI will change over time. They may be interested in monitoring the e-mail service one quarter and then move on to look at HR systems in the next quarter
- This means that Service Operation and CSI need to build a process which will help them to agree on what areas need to be monitored and for what purpose.

7.7.2 Service Desk

A Service Desk is a functional unit made up of a dedicated number of staff responsible for dealing with a variety of service events, often made via telephone calls, web interface or automatically reported infrastructure events.

The Service Desk is a vitally important part of an organization's IT department and should be the single point of contact for IT users on a day-by-day basis – and will handle all Incidents and Service Requests, usually using specialist software tools to log and manage all such events.

The value of an effective Service Desk should not be underrated – a good Service Desk can often compensate for deficiencies elsewhere in the IT organization; but a poor Service Desk (or the lack of a Service Desk) can give a poor impression of an otherwise very effective IT organization!

It is therefore very important that the correct calibre of staff are used on the Service Desk and that IT managers do their best to make the Service Desk an attractive place to work in order to improve staff retention.

The primary aim of the Service Desk is to restore 'normal service' to the users as quickly as possible. In this context 'restoration of service' is meant in the widest possible sense. While this could involve fixing a technical fault, it could equally involve fulfilling a Service Request or answering a query – anything that is needed to allow the users to return to working satisfactorily.

Specific responsibilities will include:

- Logging all relevant Incident and Service Request details, allocating categorization and prioritization codes
- Providing first-line investigation and diagnosis
- Resolving those Incidents and Service Requests they are able to
- Escalating Incidents and Service Requests that they cannot resolve within agreed timescales
- Keeping users informed of progress
- Closing all resolved incidents, requests and other calls
- Conducting customer/user satisfaction call-backs/surveys as agreed
- Communication with users – keeping them informed of Incident progress, notifying them of impending changes or agreed outages etc.
- Updating the CMS under the direction and approval of Configuration Management if so agreed.

The following roles are needed for the Service Desk.

Service Desk manager

In larger organizations where the Service Desk is of a significant size, a Service Desk manager role may be justified with the Service Desk supervisor(s) reporting to them. In such cases this role may take responsibility for some of the activities listed above and may additionally perform the following activities:

- Manage the overall desk activities, including the supervisors
- Act as a further escalation point for the supervisor(s)
- Take on a wider customer-services role
- Report to senior managers on any issue that could significantly impact the business
- Attend Change Advisory Board meetings
- Take overall responsibility for Incident and Service Request handling on the Service Desk. This could also be expanded to any other activity taken on by the Service Desk – e.g. monitoring certain classes of event.

Note: In all cases, clearly defined job descriptions should be drafted and agreed so that specific responsibilities are known.

Service Desk supervisor

In very small Service Desks it is possible that the senior Service Desk analyst will also act as the supervisor – but in larger desks it is likely that a dedicated Service Desk supervisor role will be needed. Where shift hours dictate it, there may be two or more post-holders who fulfil the role, usually on an overlapping basis. The supervisor's role is likely to include:

- Ensuring that staffing and skill levels are maintained throughout operational hours by managing shift staffing schedules etc.
- Undertaking HR activities as needed

- Acting as an escalation point where difficult or controversial calls are received
- Production of statistics and management reports
- Representing the Service Desk at meetings
- Arranging staff training and awareness sessions
- Liaising with senior management
- Liaising with Change Management
- Performing briefings to Service Desk staff on changes or deployments that may affect volumes at the Service Desk
- Assisting analysts in providing first-line support when workloads are high, or where additional experience is required.

Service Desk analysts

The primary Service Desk analyst role is that of providing first-level support through taking calls and handling the resulting Incidents or Service Requests using the Incident Reporting and Request Fulfilment processes, in line with the objectives described earlier.

Super users

Super users are discussed in detail in the section on Service Desk staffing in paragraph 6.2.4 of the Service Operation publication. In summary, this role will consist of business users who act as liaison points with IT in general and the Service Desk in particular. The role of the Super User can be summarized as follows:

- To facilitate communication between IT and the business at an operational level
- To reinforce expectations of users regarding what Service Levels have been agreed
- Staff training for users in their area
- Providing support for minor incidents or simple request fulfilment
- Involvement with new releases and rollouts.

Metrics should be established so that performance of the Service Desk can be evaluated at regular intervals. This is important to assess the health, maturity, efficiency, effectiveness and any opportunities to improve Service Desk operations.

Metrics for Service Desk performance must be realistic and carefully chosen. It is common to select those metrics that are easily available and that may seem to be a possible indication of performance; however, this can be misleading. For example, the total number of calls received by the Service Desk is not in itself an indication of either good or bad performance and may in fact be caused by events completely outside the control of the Service Desk – for example a particularly busy period for the organization, or the release of a new version of a major corporate system.

An increase in the number of calls to the Service Desk can indicate less reliable services over that period of time – but may also indicate increased user confidence in a Service Desk that is maturing, resulting in a higher likelihood that users will seek assistance rather than try to cope alone. For this type of metric to be reliable for reaching either conclusion, further comparison of previous periods for any Service Desk improvements implemented since the last measurement baseline, or service reliability Changes, Problems etc. to isolate the true cause for the increase is needed.

Further analysis and more detailed metrics are therefore needed and must be examined over a period of time. These will include the call-handling statistics previously mentioned under telephony, and additionally:

- The first-line resolution rate: the percentage of calls resolved at first line, without the need for escalation to other support groups. This is the figure often quoted by organizations as the primary measure of the Service

Desk's performance – and used for comparison purposes with the performance of other Service Desks – but care is needed when making any comparisons

- Average time to resolve an Incident (when resolved at first line)
- Average time to escalate an Incident (where first-line resolution is not possible)
- Average Service Desk cost of handling an Incident
- Percentage of customer or user updates conducted within target times, as defined in SLA targets
- Average time to review and close a resolved call
- The number of calls broken down by time of day and day of week, combined with the average call-time metric, which is critical in determining the number of staff required.

7.7.3 Technical Management

Technical Management refers to the groups, departments or teams that provide technical expertise and overall management of the IT Infrastructure.

Technical Management plays a dual role:

- It is the custodian of technical knowledge and expertise related to managing the IT infrastructure. In this role, Technical Management ensures that the knowledge required to design, test, manage and improve IT services is identified, developed and refined
- It provides the actual resources to support the ITSM Lifecycle. In this role Technical Management ensures that resources are effectively trained and deployed to design, build, transition, operate and improve the technology required to deliver and support IT services.

By performing these two roles, Technical Management is able to ensure that the organization has access to the right type and level of human resources to manage technology and, thus, to meet business objectives. Defining the requirements for these roles starts in Service Strategy and is expanded in Service Design, validated in

Service Transition and refined in Continual Service Improvement (see other ITIL publications in this series).

Technical Management organization

Technical Management is not normally provided by a single department or group. One or more technical support teams or departments will be needed to provide Technical Management and support for the IT infrastructure. In all but the smallest organizations, where a single combined team or department may suffice, separate teams or departments will be needed for each type of infrastructure being used.

IT Operations Management consists of a number of technological areas. Each of these requires a specific set of skills to manage and operate it. Some skill sets are related and can be performed by generalists, whereas others are specific to a component, system or platform.

The primary criterion of the Technical Management organizational structure is that of specialization or division of labour. The principle is that people are grouped according to their technical skill sets, and that these skill sets are determined by the technology that needs to be managed.

This list provides some examples of typical Technical Management teams or departments:

- Mainframe team or department – if one or more mainframe types are still being used by the organization
- Server team or department – often split again by technology types (e.g. Unix server, Wintel server)
- Storage team or department, responsible for the management of all data storage devices and media
- Network support team or department, looking after the organization's internal WANs/LANs and managing any external network suppliers
- Desktop team or department, responsible for all installed desktop equipment

- Database team or department, responsible for the creation, maintenance and support of the organization's databases
- Middleware team or department, responsible for the integration, testing and maintenance of all middleware in use in the organization
- Directory services team or department, responsible for maintaining access and rights to service elements in the infrastructure
- Internet or web team or department, responsible for managing the availability and security of access to servers and content by external customers, users and partners
- Messaging team or department, responsible for e-mail services
- IP-based telephony team or department (e.g. VoIP).

7.7.4 Technical Management roles

The following roles are needed in the Technical Management areas.

Technical managers/team-leaders

A technical manager or team-leader (depending upon the size and/or importance of the team and the organization's structure and culture) may be needed for each of the technical teams or departments. The role will:

- Take overall responsibility for leadership, control and decision-making for the technical team or department
- Provide technical knowledge and leadership in the specific technical areas covered by the team or department
- Ensure necessary technical training, awareness and experience levels are maintained within the team or department
- Report to senior management on all technical issues relevant to their area of responsibility

- Perform line-management for all team or department members.

Technical analysts/architects

This term refers to any staff member in Technical Management who performs the activities listed in paragraph 7.7.3, excluding the daily operational actions, which are performed by operators in either Technical or IT Operations Management. Based on this list of generic activities, the role of technical analysts and architects includes:

- Working with users, sponsors, Application Management and all other stakeholders to determine their evolving needs
- Working with Application Management and other areas in Technical Management to determine the highest level of system requirements needed to meet the requirements within budget and technology constraints
- Defining and maintaining knowledge about how systems are related and ensuring that dependencies are understood and managed accordingly
- Performing cost-benefit analyses to determine the most appropriate means to meet the stated requirements
- Developing operational models that will ensure optimal use of resources and the appropriate level of performance
- Ensuring that the infrastructure is configured to be effectively managed given the organization's technology architecture, available skills and tools
- Ensuring the consistent and reliable performance of the infrastructure to deliver the required level of service to the business
- Defining all tasks required to manage the infrastructure and ensuring that these tasks are performed appropriately

- Input into the design of configuration data required to manage and track the application effectively.

7.8 IT OPERATIONS MANAGEMENT

In business, the term 'Operations Management' is used to mean the department, group or team of people responsible for performing the organization's day-to-day operational activities – such as running the production line in a manufacturing environment or managing the distribution centres and fleet movements within a logistics organization.

Operations Management generally has the following characteristics:

- There is activity to ensure that a device, system or process is actually running or working (as opposed to strategy or planning)
- This is where plans are turned into actions
- The focus is on daily or shorter-term activities, although it should be noted that these activities will generally be performed and repeated over a relatively long period (as opposed to one-off project type activities)
- These activities are executed by specialized technical staff, who often have to undergo technical training to learn how to perform each activity
- There is a focus on building repeatable, consistent actions that – if repeated frequently enough at the right level of quality – will ensure the success of the operation
- This is where the actual value of the organization is delivered and measured
- There is a dependency on investment in equipment or human resources or both

- The value generated must exceed the cost of the investment and all other organizational overheads (such as management and marketing costs) if the business is to succeed.

In a similar way, IT Operations Management can be defined as the function responsible for the ongoing management and maintenance of an organization's IT infrastructure to ensure delivery of the agreed level of IT services to the business.

IT Operations can be defined as the set of activities involved in the day-to-day running of the IT infrastructure for the purpose of delivering IT services at agreed levels to meet stated business objectives.

7.8.1 IT Operations Management role

The role of Operations Management is to execute the ongoing activities and procedures required to manage and maintain the IT infrastructure so as to deliver and support IT services at the agreed levels. These are summarized here for completeness:

- **Operations control**, which oversees the execution and monitoring of the operational activities and events in the IT infrastructure. This can be done with the assistance of an operations bridge or network operations centre. In addition to executing routine tasks from all technical areas, Operations Control also performs the following specific tasks:
  - **Console management**, which refers to defining central observation and monitoring capability and then using those consoles to exercise monitoring and control activities
  - **Job scheduling**, or the management of routine batch jobs or scripts
  - **Backup and restore** on behalf of all Technical and Application Management teams and departments and often on behalf of users

- **Print and output management** for the collation and distribution of all centralized printing or electronic output
- Performance of **maintenance activities** on behalf of Technical or Application Management teams or departments

■ **Facilities management**, which refers to the management of the physical IT environment, typically a data centre or computer rooms and recovery sites together with all the power and cooling equipment. Facilities Management also includes the coordination of large-scale consolidation projects, e.g. data centre consolidation or server consolidation projects. In some cases the management of a data centre is outsourced, in which case Facilities Management refers to the management of the outsourcing contract.

The objectives of IT Operations Management include:

■ Maintenance of the status quo to achieve stability of the organization's day-to-day processes and activities

■ Regular scrutiny and improvements to achieve improved service at reduced costs, while maintaining stability

■ Swift application of operational skills to diagnose and resolve any IT operations failures that occur.

7.9 APPLICATION MANAGEMENT

Application Management is responsible for managing applications throughout their lifecycle. The Application Management function is performed by any department, group or team involved in managing and supporting operational applications. Application Management also plays an important role in the design, testing and improvement of applications that form part of IT services. As such, it may be involved in development projects, but is not usually the same as the applications development teams.

Application Management high-level role

Application Management is to applications what Technical Management is to the IT infrastructure. Application Management plays a role in all applications, whether purchased or developed in-house. One of the key decisions that they contribute to is the decision of whether to buy an application or build it (this is discussed in detail in the Service Design publication). Once that decision is made, Application Management will play a dual role:

■ It is the custodian of technical knowledge and expertise related to managing applications. In this role Application Management, working together with Technical Management, ensures that the knowledge required to design, test, manage and improve IT services is identified, developed and refined

■ It provides the actual resources to support the ITSM Lifecycle. In this role, Application Management ensures that resources are effectively trained and deployed to design, build, transition, operate and improve the technology required to deliver and support IT services.

By performing these two roles, Application Management is able to ensure that the organization has access to the right type and level of human resources to manage applications and thus to meet business objectives. This starts in Service Strategy and is expanded in Service Design, tested in Service Transition and refined in Continual Service Improvement (see other ITIL publications in this series).

Part of this role is to ensure a balance between the skill level and the cost of these resources.

In additional to these two high-level roles, Application Management also performs the following two specific roles:

■ Providing guidance to IT Operations about how best to carry out the ongoing operational management of applications. This role is partly carried out during the

Service Design process, but it is also a part of everyday communication with IT Operations Management as they seek to achieve stability and optimum performance

■ The integration of the Application Management Lifecycle into the ITSM Lifecycle. This is discussed below.

The objectives, activities and structures that enable Application Management to play these roles effectively are discussed below.

Application Management objectives

The objectives of Application Management are to support the organization's business processes by helping to identify functional and manageability requirements for application software, and then to assist in the design and deployment of those applications and the ongoing support and improvement of those applications.

These objectives are achieved through:

■ Applications that are well designed, resilient and cost-effective

■ Ensuring that the required functionality is available to achieve the required business outcome

■ The organization of adequate technical skills to maintain operational applications in optimum condition

■ Swift use of technical skills to speedily diagnose and resolve any technical failures that do occur.

Application Management generic activities

While most Application Management teams or departments are dedicated to specific applications or sets of applications, there are a number of activities which they have in common (see Figure 7.7). These include:

■ Identifying the knowledge and expertise required to manage and operate applications in the delivery of IT services. This process starts during the Service Strategy phase, is expanded in detail in Service Design and is executed in Service Operation. Ongoing assessment and updating of these skills are done during Continual Service Improvement

■ Initiating training programmes to develop and refine the skills in the appropriate Application Management resources and maintaining training records for these resources

■ Recruiting or contracting resources with skills that cannot be developed internally, or where there are insufficient people to perform the required Application Management activities

■ Design and delivery of end-user training. Training may be developed and delivered by either the Application Development or Application Management groups, or by a third party, but Application Management is responsible for ensuring that training is conducted as appropriate

■ Insourcing for specific activities where the required skills are not available internally or in the open market, or where it is more cost-efficient to do so

■ Definition of standards used in the design of new architectures and participation in the definition of application architectures during the Service Strategy processes

■ Research and development of solutions that can help expand the Service Portfolio or which can be used to simplify or automate IT Operations, reduce costs or increase levels of IT service

■ Involvement in the design and building of new services. All Application Management teams or departments will contribute to the design of the technical architecture and performance standards for IT services. In addition they will also be responsible for specifying the operational activities required to manage applications on an ongoing basis

- Involvement in projects, not only during the Service Design process, but also for Continual Service Improvement or operational projects, such as operating system upgrades, server consolidation projects or physical moves
- Designing and performing tests for the functionality, performance and manageability of IT services (bearing in mind that testing should be controlled and performed by an independent tester – see Service Transition publication)
- Availability and Capacity Management are dependent on Application Management for contributing to the design of applications to meet the levels of service required by the business. This means that modelling and workload forecasting are often done together with Technical and Application Management resources
- Assistance in assessing risk, identifying critical service and system dependencies and defining and implementing countermeasures
- Managing vendors. Many Application Management departments or groups are the only ones who know exactly what is required of a vendor and how to measure and manage them. For this reason, many organizations rely on Application Management to manage contracts with vendors of specific applications. If this is the case it is important to ensure that these relationships are managed as part of the SLM process
- Involvement in definition of Event Management standards and especially in the instrumentation of applications for the generation of meaningful events
- Application Management as a function provides the resources that execute the Problem Management process. It is their technical expertise and knowledge that is used to diagnose and resolve Problems. It is also their relationship with the vendors that is used to escalate and follow up with vendor support teams or departments

- Application Management resources will be involved in defining coding systems that are used in Incident and Problem Management (e.g. Incident Categories)
- Application Management resources are used to support Problem Management in validating and maintaining the KEDB together with the Application Development teams
- Change Management relies on the technical knowledge and expertise to evaluate changes, and many changes will be built by Application Management teams
- Successful Release Management is dependent on involvement from Application Management staff. In fact they are frequently the drivers of the Release Management process for their applications
- Application Management will define, manage and maintain attributes and relationships of application CIs in the CMS
- Application Management is involved in the Continual Service Improvement processes, particularly in identifying opportunities for improvement and then in helping to evaluate alternative solutions
- Application Management ensures that all system and operating documentation is up to date and properly utilized. This includes ensuring that all design, management and user manuals are up to date and complete and that Application Management staff and users are familiar with their contents
- Collaboration with Technical Management on performing training needs analysis and maintaining skills inventories
- Assisting IT Financial Management to identify the cost of the ongoing management of applications
- Involvement in defining the operational activities performed as part of IT Operations Management. Many Application Management departments, groups or teams also perform the operational activities as part of an organization's IT Operations Management function

Figure 7.7 Role of Application Management in the application lifecycle

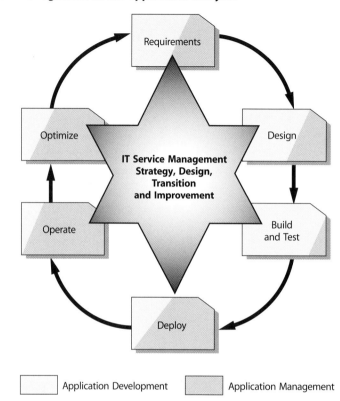

- Input into, and maintenance of, software configuration policies
- Together with software development teams, the definition and maintenance of documentation related to applications. These will include user manuals, administration and management manuals, as well as any standard operating procedures (SOPs) required to manage operational aspects of the application.

7.9.1 Application Management roles

Applications managers/team-leaders

An applications manager or team-leader should be considered for each of the applications teams or departments. The role will:

- Take overall responsibility for leadership, control and decision-making for the applications team or department
- Provide technical knowledge and leadership in the specific applications support activities covered by the team or department

- Ensure necessary technical training, awareness and experience levels are maintained within the team or department relevant to the applications being supported and processes being used
- Involve ongoing communication with users and customers regarding application performance and evolving requirements of the business
- Report to senior management on all issues relevant to the applications being supported
- Perform line-management for all team or department members.

Applications analyst/architect

Application analysts and architects are responsible for matching requirements to application specifications. Specific activities include:

- Working with users, sponsors and all other stakeholders to determine their evolving needs
- Working with Technical Management to determine the highest level of system requirements needed to meet the requirements within budget and technology constraints
- Performing cost-benefit analyses to determine the most appropriate means to meet the stated requirement
- Developing operational models that will ensure optimal use of resources and the appropriate level of performance
- Ensuring that applications are designed to be effectively managed given the organization's technology architecture, available skills and tools
- Developing and maintaining standards for application sizing, performance modelling etc.

- Generating a set of acceptance test requirements, together with the designers, test engineers and the user, which determine that all of the high-level requirements have been met, in both functionality and manageability
- Input into the design of configuration data required to manage and track the application effectively.

7.10 SERVICE OPERATION AND PROJECT MANAGEMENT

Because Service Operation is generally viewed as 'business as usual' and often focused on executing defined procedures in a standard way, there is a tendency not to use project management processes when they would in fact be appropriate. For example, major infrastructure upgrades, or the deployment of new or changed procedures, are significant tasks where formal project management can be used to improve control and manage costs/resources.

Using project management to manage these types of activity would have the following benefits:

- The project benefits are clearly stated and agreed
- There is more visibility of what is being done and how it is being managed, which makes it easier for other IT groups and the business to quantify the contributions made by operational teams
- This in turn makes it easier to obtain funding for projects that have traditionally been difficult to cost justify
- Greater consistency and improved quality
- Achievement of objectives results in higher credibility for operational groups.

7.11 ASSESSING AND MANAGING RISK IN SERVICE OPERATION

There will be a number of occasions where it is imperative that risk assessment to Service Operation is quickly undertaken and acted upon.

The most obvious area is in assessing the risk of potential changes or Known Errors (already covered elsewhere) but in addition Service Operation staff may need to be involved in assessing the risk and impact of:

■ Failures, or potential failures – either reported by Event Management or Incident/Problem Management, or warnings raised by manufacturers, suppliers or contractors

■ New projects that will ultimately result in delivery into the live environment

■ Environmental risk (encompassing IT Service Continuity-type risks to the physical environment and locale as well as political, commercial or industrial-relations related risks)

■ Suppliers, particularly where new suppliers are involved or where key service components are under the control of third parties

■ Security risks – both theoretical or actual arising from security related incidents or events

■ New customers/services to be supported.

7.12 OPERATIONAL STAFF IN SERVICE DESIGN AND TRANSITION

All IT groups will be involved during Service Design and Service transition to ensure that new components or services are designed, tested and implemented to provide the correct levels of functionality, usability, availability, capacity etc.

Additionally, Service Operation staff must be involved during the early stages of Service Design and Service Transition to ensure that when new services reach the live environment they are fit for purpose, from a Service Operation perspective, and are supportable in the future.

In this context, 'supportable' means:

■ Capable of being supported from a technical and operational viewpoint from within existing or pre-agreed additional resources and skills levels

■ Without adverse impact on other existing technical or operational working practices, processes or schedules

■ Without any unexpected operational costs or ongoing or escalating support expenditure

■ Without any unexpected contractual or legal complications

■ No complex support paths between multiple support departments of third-party organizations.

Continual Service Improvement 8

8 Continual Service Improvement

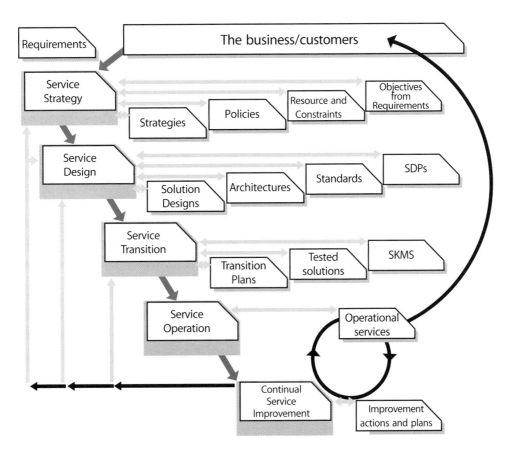

Continual Service Improvement (CSI) provides practical guidance in evaluating and improving the quality of services, overall maturity of the ITSM Service Lifecycle and its underlying processes, at three levels within the organization:

■ The overall health of ITSM as a discipline
■ The continual alignment of the portfolio of IT services with the current and future business needs

■ The maturity of the enabling IT processes required to support business processes in a continual Service Lifecycle model.

8.1 PURPOSE OF CSI

The primary purpose of CSI is to continually align and re-align IT services to the changing business needs by identifying and implementing improvements to IT services that support business processes. These improvement activities support the lifecycle approach through Service

Strategy, Service Design, Service Transition and Service Operation. In effect, CSI is about looking for ways to improve process effectiveness and efficiency as well as cost effectiveness.

8.2 CSI OBJECTIVES

- Review, analyse and make recommendations on improvement opportunities in each lifecycle phase: Service Strategy, Service Design, Service Transition and Service Operation
- Review and analyse Service Level achievement results
- Identify and implement individual activities to improve IT service quality and improve the efficiency and effectiveness of enabling ITSM processes
- Improve cost effectiveness of delivering IT services without sacrificing customer satisfaction
- Ensure applicable quality management methods are used to support continual improvement activities.

The following activities support a continual process improvement plan:

- Reviewing management information and trends to ensure that services are meeting agreed Service Levels
- Reviewing management information and trends to ensure that the output of the enabling ITSM processes are achieving the desired results
- Periodically conducting maturity assessments against the process activities and roles associated with the process activities to demonstrate areas of improvement or, conversely, areas of concern
- Periodically conducting internal audits verifying employee and process compliance
- Reviewing existing deliverables for relevance
- Making ad hoc recommendations for approval
- Conducting periodic customer satisfaction surveys
- Conducting external and internal service reviews to identify CSI opportunities.

These activities do not happen automatically. They must be owned within the IT organization which is capable of handling the responsibility and possesses the appropriate authority to make things happen. They must also be planned and scheduled on an ongoing basis. By default, 'improvement' becomes a process within IT with defined activities, inputs, outputs, roles and reporting. CSI must ensure that ITSM processes are developed and deployed in support of an end-to-end service management approach to business customers. It is essential to develop an ongoing continual improvement strategy for each of the processes as well as the services.

As Figure 8.1 shows, there are many opportunities for CSI. The figure also illustrates a constant cycle of improvement. The improvement process can be summarized in six steps:

- Embrace the vision by understanding the high-level business objectives. The vision should align the business and IT strategies
- Assess the current situation to obtain an accurate, unbiased snapshot of where the organization is right now. This baseline assessment is an analysis of the current position in terms of the business, organization, people, process and technology
- Understand and agree on the priorities for improvement based on a deeper development of the principles defined in the vision. The full vision may be years away but this step provides specific goals and a manageable timeframe
- Detail the CSI plan to achieve higher quality service provision by implementing ITSM processes
- Verify that measurements and metrics are in place to ensure that milestones were achieved, process compliance is high, and business objectives and priorities were met by the level of service
- Finally, the process should ensure that the momentum for quality improvement is maintained by assuring that changes become embedded in the organization.

Figure 8.1 Continual Service Improvement model

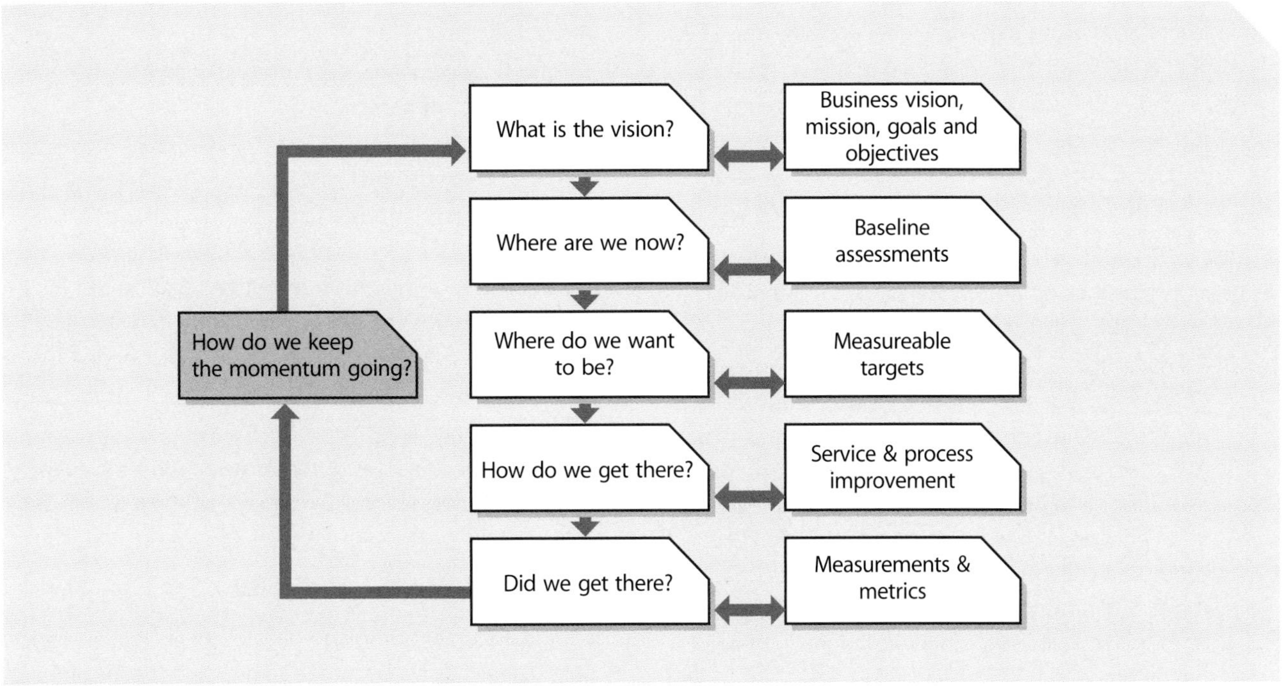

8.2.1 Perspectives on benefits

There are four commonly used terms when discussing service improvement outcomes:

- Improvements
- Benefits
- ROI (return on investment)
- VOI (value on investment).

Much of the angst and confusion surrounding IT process improvement initiatives can be traced to the misuse of these terms. Below is the proper use:

- **Improvements** – Outcomes that when compared to the 'before' state, show a measurable increase in a desirable metric or decrease in an undesirable metric
  - Example: ABC Corp achieved a 15% reduction in failed changes through implementation of a formal Change Management process

- **Benefits** – The gains achieved through realization of improvements, usually but not always expressed in monetary terms.
  - Example: ABC Corp's 15% reduction in failed changes has saved the company £395,000 in productivity and re-works costs in the first year

- **ROI** – The difference between the benefit (saving) achieved and the amount expended to achieve that benefit, expressed as a percentage. Logically, one would like to spend a little to save a lot
  - Example: ABC Corp spent £200,000 to establish the formal Change Management process that saved £395,000. The ROI at the end of the first year of operation was therefore £195,000 or 97.5%

- **VOI** – The extra value created by establishment of benefits that include non-monetary or long-term outcomes. ROI is a subcomponent of VOI
  - Example: ABC Corp's establishment of a formal Change Management process (which reduced the number of failed changes) improved the ability of ABC Corp to respond quickly to changing market conditions and unexpected opportunities resulting in an enhanced market position. In addition, it promoted collaboration between business units and the IT organization and freed up resources to work on other projects that otherwise might not have been completed.

8.3 BUSINESS DRIVERS

Businesses are becoming increasingly aware of the importance of IT as a service provider to not only support but also enable business operations. As a result the business leaders of today ask much more pointed and direct questions regarding the quality of IT services and the competency and efficiency of their provider. This higher level of scrutiny buttresses the expanding need for CSI, meaning that:

- IT does more than enable existing business operations; IT enables business change and is, therefore, an integral component of the business change programme

- There is additional focus on the quality of IT in terms of reliability, availability, stability, capacity, security and, especially, risk
- IT and IT governance is an integral component in corporate governance
- IT performance becomes even more visible – technical outages and customer dissatisfaction increasingly become boardroom issues
- IT organizations increasingly find themselves in a position where they have to not only realize but manage business-enabling technology and services that deliver the capability and quality demanded by the business
- IT must demonstrate value for money
- IT within e-business is not only supporting the primary business processes, but is the core of those processes.

8.4 TECHNOLOGY DRIVERS

The rapid pace of technology developments, within which IT provides solutions, becomes a core component of almost every area of business operations. As a result, IT services must:

- Understand business operations and advise about the short- and long-term opportunities (and limitations) of IT
- Be designed for agility and nimbleness to allow for unpredictability in business needs
- Accommodate more technological change, with a reduced cycle time, for realizing change to match a reduced window in the business cycle
- Maintain or improve existing quality of services while adding or removing technology components
- Ensure that quality of delivery and support matches the business use of new technology
- Bring escalating costs under control.

8.5 SERVICE MEASUREMENT

Critical elements of a service measurement framework:

- Integrated into business planning
- Focused on business and IT goals and objectives
- Cost-effective
- Balanced in its approach on what is measured
- Able to withstand change.

Performance measures that:

- Are accurate and reliable
- Are well defined, specific and clear
- Are relevant to meeting the objectives
- Do not create a negative behaviour
- Lead to improvement opportunities.

Performance targets that:

- Are SMART.

Defined roles and responsibilities

- Who defines the measures and targets?
- Who monitors and measures?
- Who gathers the data?
- Who processes and analyses the data?
- Who prepares the reports?
- Who presents the reports?

8.5.1 Baselines

An important beginning point for highlighting improvement is to establish baselines as markers or starting points for later comparison. Baselines are also used to establish an initial data point to determine if a service or process needs to be improved. As a result, it is important that baselines are documented, recognized and accepted throughout the organization. Baselines must be established at each level: strategic goals and objectives, tactical process maturity, and operational metrics and KPIs.

If a baseline is not initially established the first measurement efforts will become the baseline. That is why it is essential to collect data at the outset, even if the integrity of the data is in question. It is better to have data to question than to have no data at all.

8.5.2 Why do we measure?

- **To validate** – monitoring and measuring to validate previous decisions
- **To direct** – monitoring and measuring to set direction for activities in order to meet set targets. It is the most prevalent reason for monitoring and measuring
- **To justify** – monitoring and measuring to justify, with factual evidence or proof, that a course of action is required
- **To intervene** – monitoring and measuring to identify a point of intervention including subsequent changes and corrective actions.

The four basic reasons to monitor and measure lead to three key questions: 'Why are we monitoring and measuring?', 'When do we stop?' and 'Is anyone using the data?' To answer these questions, it is important to identify which of the above reasons is driving the measurement effort. Too often, we continue to measure long after the need has passed. Every time you produce a report you should ask: 'Do we still need this?'

8.6 CONTINUAL SERVICE IMPROVEMENT PROCESSES

The Seven-step Improvement Process is illustrated in Figure 8.2.

8.6.1 Step 1 – Define what you should measure

Compile a list of what you should measure. This will often be driven by business requirements. Don't try to cover every single eventuality or possible metric in the world.

Figure 8.2 Seven-step Improvement Process

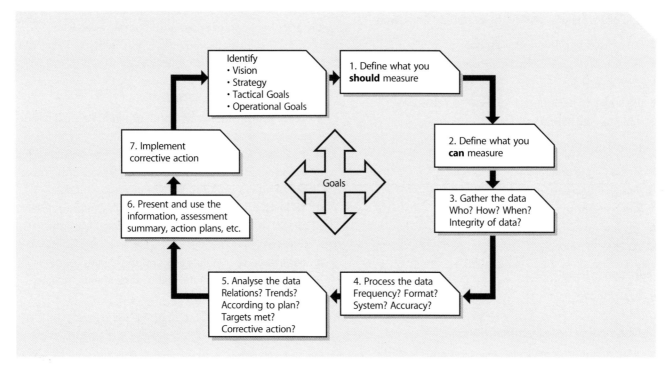

Make it simple. The number of things you should measure can grow quite rapidly. So too can the number of metrics and measurements.

Identify and link the following items:

- Corporate vision, mission, goals and objectives
- IT vision, mission, goals and objectives
- Critical success factors
- Service level targets
- Job description for IT staff.

Inputs:

- Service Level Requirements and targets
- Service Catalogue
- Vision and mission statements

- Corporate, divisional and departmental goals and objectives
- Legislative requirements
- Governance requirements
- Budget cycle
- Balanced Scorecard.

8.6.2 Step 2 – Define what you can measure

Every organization may find that they have limitations on what can actually be measured. If you cannot measure something then it should not appear in an SLA.

Compile a list of what each tool can currently measure without any configuration or customization. Stay away from customizing the tools as much as possible; configuring them is acceptable.

Perform a gap analysis between the two lists. Report this information back to the business, the customers and IT management. It is possible that new tools are required or that configuration or customization is required to be able to measure what is required.

Inputs:

- List of what you should measure
- Process flows
- Procedures
- Work instructions
- Technical and user manuals from existing tools
- Existing reports.

8.6.3 Step 3 – Gathering the data

Gathering data requires having some form of monitoring in place. Monitoring could be executed using technology such as application, system and component monitoring tools or could even be a manual process for certain tasks.

Quality is the key objective of monitoring for Continual Service Improvement. Monitoring will therefore focus on the effectiveness of a service, process, tool, organization or Configuration Item (CI). The emphasis is not on assuring real-time service performance, rather it is on identifying where improvements can be made to the existing level of service, or IT performance. Monitoring for CSI will therefore tend to focus on detecting exceptions and resolutions. For example, CSI is not as interested in whether an Incident was resolved, but whether it was resolved within the agreed time, and whether future Incidents can be prevented.

CSI is not only interested in exceptions, though. If a Service Level Agreement is consistently met over time, CSI will also be interested in determining whether that level of performance can be sustained at a lower cost or whether it needs to be upgraded to an even better level of performance. CSI may therefore also need access to regular performance reports.

However since CSI is unlikely to need, or be able to cope with, the vast quantities of data that are produced by all monitoring activity, they will most likely focus on a specific subset of monitoring at any given time. This could be determined by input from the business or improvements to technology.

When a new service is being designed or an existing one changed, this is a perfect opportunity to ensure that what CSI needs to monitor is designed into the service requirements (see Service Design publication).

This has two main implications:

- Monitoring for CSI will change over time. They may be interested in monitoring the e-mail service one quarter, and then move on to look at HR systems in the next quarter
- This means that Service Operation and CSI need to build a process which will help them to agree on what areas need to be monitored and for what purpose.

It is important to remember that there are three types of metrics that an organization will need to collect to support CSI activities as well as other process activities. The types of metrics are:

- Technology metrics – these metrics are often associated with component and application-based metrics such as performance, availability etc.
- Process metrics – these metrics are captured in the form of CSFs, KPIs and activity metrics for the service management processes. These metrics can help determine the overall health of a process. Four key questions that KPIs can help answer are around quality, performance, value and compliance in following the process. CSI would use these metrics as input in identifying improvement opportunities for each process

■ Service metrics – these metrics are the results of the end-to-end service. Component/technology metrics are used to compute the service metrics.

As much as possible, you need to standardize the data structure through policies and published standards. For example, how do you enter names in your tools – John Smith; Smith, John; or J. Smith? These can be the same or different individuals. Having three different ways of entering the same name would slow down trend analysis and will severely impede any CSI initiative.

Gathering data is defined as the act of monitoring and data collection. This activity needs to clearly define the following:

■ Who is responsible for monitoring and gathering the data?
■ How the data will be gathered?
■ When and how often is the data gathered?
■ Criteria to evaluate the integrity of the data

The answers will be different for every organization.

Service monitoring allows weak areas to be identified, so that remedial action can be taken (if there is a justifiable business case), thus improving future service quality. Service monitoring also can show where customer actions are causing the fault and thus lead to identifying where working efficiency and/or training can be improved.

Service monitoring should also address both internal and external suppliers since their performance must be evaluated and managed as well.

Service management monitoring helps determine the health and welfare of service management processes in the following manner:

■ Process compliance – Are the processes being followed? Process compliance seeks to monitor the compliance of the IT organization to the new or modified service management processes and also the use of the authorized service management tool that was implemented

■ Quality – How well are the processes working? Monitor the individual or key activities as they relate to the objectives of the end-to-end process
■ Performance – How fast or slow? Monitor the process efficiency such as throughput or cycle times
■ Value – Is this making a difference? Monitor the effectiveness and perceived value of the process to the stakeholders and the IT staff executing the process activities.

Monitoring is often associated with automated monitoring of infrastructure components for performance such as availability or capacity, but monitoring should also be used for monitoring staff behaviour such as adherence to process activities, use of authorized tools as well as project schedules and budgets.

Exceptions and alerts need to be considered during the monitoring activity as they can serve as early warning indicators that services are breaking down. Sometimes the exceptions and alerts will come from tools, but they will often come from those who are using the service or service management processes. We don't want to ignore these alerts.

Inputs to the gather-the-data activity:

■ New business requirements
■ Existing SLAs
■ Existing monitoring and data capture capability
■ Availability and Capacity Plans
■ Service Improvement Plans
■ Previous trend analysis reports
■ List of what you should measure
■ List of what you can measure
■ Gap analysis report
■ List of what to measure
■ Customer satisfaction surveys.

8.6.4 Step 4 – Processing the data

Once data is gathered, the next step is to process the data into the required format. Report-generating technologies are typically used at this stage as various amounts of data are condensed into information for use in the analysis activity. The data is also typically put into a format that provides an end-to-end perspective on the overall performance of a service. This activity begins the transformation of raw data into packaged information. Use the information to develop insight into the performance of the service and/or processes. Process the data into information (i.e. create logical groupings) which provides a better means to analyse the data – the next activity step in CSI.

The output of logical groupings could be in spreadsheets, reports generated directly from the service management tool suite, system monitoring and reporting tools, or telephony tools such as an automatic call distribution tool.

Processing the data is an important CSI activity that is often overlooked. While monitoring and collecting data on a single infrastructure component is important, it is also important to understand that components impact on the larger infrastructure and IT service. Knowing that a server was up 99.99% of the time is one thing, knowing that no one could access the server is another. An example of processing the data is taking the data from monitoring of the individual components such as the mainframe, applications, WAN, LAN, servers etc., and processing this into a structure of an end-to-end service from the customer's perspective.

Key questions that need to be addressed in the processing activity are:

- What is the frequency of processing the data? This could be hourly, daily, weekly or monthly. When introducing a new service or service management process it is a good idea to monitor and process in shorter intervals than longer intervals. How often analysis and trend investigation activities take place will drive how often the data is processed

- What format is required for the output? This is also driven by how analysis is done and ultimately how the information is used
- What tools and systems can be used for processing the data?
- How do we evaluate the accuracy of the processed data?

There are two aspects to data gathering. One is automated and the other is manual. While both are important and contribute greatly to the measuring process, accuracy is a major differentiator between the two types. The accuracy of the automated data gathering and processing is not the issue here. The vast majority of CSI-related data will be gathered by automated means. Human data gathering and processing is the issue. It is important for staff to properly document their compliance activities, to update logs and records. Common excuses are that people are too busy, that this is not important or that it is not their job. On-going communication about the benefits of performing administrative tasks is of utmost importance. Tying these administrative tasks to job performance is one way to alleviate this issue.

Inputs to the processing-the-data activity:

- Data collected through monitoring
- Reporting requirements
- SLAs
- OLAs
- Service Catalogue
- List of metrics, KPI, CSF, objectives and goals
- Report frequency
- Report template.

8.6.5 Step 5 – Analysing the data

Your organization's Service Desk has a trend of reduced call volumes consistently over the last four months. Even though this is a trend, you need to ask yourself the question: 'Is this a good trend or a bad trend?' You don't know if the call reduction is because you have reduced the number of recurring errors in the infrastructure by good Problem Management activities or if the customers feel that the Service Desk doesn't provide any value and they have started bypassing the Service Desk and going directly to second-level support groups.

Data analysis transforms the information into knowledge of the events that are affecting the organization. More skill and experience is required to perform data analysis than data gathering and processing. Verification against goals and objectives is expected during this activity. This verification validates that objectives are being supported and value is being added. It is not sufficient to simply produce graphs of various types but to document the observations and conclusions looking to answer the following questions:

- Are there any clear trends?
- Are they positive or negative trends?
- Are changes required?
- Are we operating according to plan?
- Are we meeting targets?
- Are corrective actions required?
- Are there underlying structural problems?
- What is the cost of the service gap?

It is interesting to note the number of job titles for IT professionals that contain the word 'analyst' and even more surprising to discover that few of them actually analyse anything. This step takes time. It requires concentration, knowledge, skills, experience etc. One of the major assumptions is that the automated processing, reporting, monitoring tool has actually done the analysis. Too often people simply point at a trend and say 'Look, numbers have gone up over the last quarter.' However, key questions need to be asked, such as:

- Is this good?

- Is this bad?
- Is this expected?
- Is this in line with targets?

Combining multiple data points on a graph may look nice but the real question is, what does it actually mean. 'A picture is worth a thousand words' goes the saying. In analysing the data an accurate question would be, 'Which thousand words?' To transform this data into knowledge, compare the information from Step 3 against both the requirements from Step 1 and what could realistically be measured from Step 2.

Be sure to also compare the clearly defined objectives against the measurable targets that were set in the Service Design, Transition and Operations lifecycle stages. Confirmation needs to be sought that these objectives and the milestones were reached. If not, have improvement initiatives been implemented? If so, then the CSI activities start again from the gathering data, processing data and analysing data steps to identify if the desired improvement in service quality has been achieved. At the completion of each significant stage or milestone, a review should be conducted to ensure the objectives have been met. It is possible here to use the Post-Implementation Review (PIR) from the Change Management process. The PIR will include a review of supporting documentation and the general awareness amongst staff of the refined processes or service. A comparison is required of what has been achieved against the original goals.

During the analysis activity, but after the results are compiled and analysis and trend evaluation have occurred, it is recommended that internal meetings be held within IT to review the results and collectively identify improvement opportunities. It is important to have these internal meetings before you begin presenting and using the information which is the next activity of Continual Service Improvement. The result is that IT is a key player in determining how the results and any actions items are presented to the business.

This puts IT in a better position to formulate a plan of presenting the results and any action items to the business and to senior IT management. Throughout this publication the terms 'service' and 'service management' have been used extensively. IT is too often focused on managing the various systems used by the business, often (but incorrectly) equating service and system. A service is actually made up of systems. Therefore if IT wants to be perceived as a key player, then IT must move from a systems-based organization to a service-based organization. This transition will force the improvement of communication between the different IT silos that exist in many IT organizations.

Performing proper analysis on the data also places the business in a position to make strategic, tactical and operational decisions about whether there is a need for service improvement. Unfortunately, the analysis activity is often not done. Whether it is due to a lack of resources with the right skills and/or simply a lack of time is unclear. What is clear is that without proper analysis, errors will continue to occur and mistakes will continue to be repeated. There will be little improvement.

Data analysis transforms the information into knowledge of the events that are affecting the organization. As an example, a sub-activity of Capacity Management is workload management. This can be viewed as analysing the data to determine which customers use what resource, how they use the resource, when they use the resource and how this impacts the overall performance of the resource. You will also be able to see if there is a trend on the usage of the resource over a period of time. From an incremental improvement process this could lead to some focus on demand management, or influencing the behaviour of customers.

Consideration must be given to the skills required to analyse from both a technical viewpoint and from an interpretation viewpoint.

When analysing data, it is important to seek answers to questions such as:

■ Are operations running according to plan? This could be a project plan, financial plan, availability, capacity or even IT Service Continuity Management plan

■ Are targets defined in SLAs or the Service Catalogue being met?

■ Are there underlying structural problems that can be identified?

■ Are corrective actions required?

■ Are there any trends? If so then what are the trends showing? Are they positive trends or negative trends?

■ What is leading to or causing the trends?

Reviewing trends over a period of time is another important task. It is not good enough to see a snapshot of a data point at a specific moment in time, but to look at the data points over a period of time. How did we do this month compared to last month, this quarter compared to last quarter, this year compared to last year?

8.6.6 Step 6 – Presenting and using the information

The sixth step is to take our knowledge and present it, that is, turn it into wisdom by utilizing reports, monitors, action plans, reviews, evaluations and opportunities. Consider the target audience; make sure that you identify exceptions to the service, benefits that have been revealed, or can be expected. Data gathering occurs at the operational level of an organization. Format this data into knowledge that all levels can appreciate and gain insight into their needs and expectations.

This stage involves presenting the information in a format that is understandable, at the right level, provides value, notes exceptions to service, identifies benefits that were revealed during the time period, and allows those receiving the information to make strategic, tactical and operational decisions. In other words, presenting the information in the manner that makes it the most useful for the target audience.

Creating reports and presenting information is an activity that is done in most organizations to some extent or another; however it often is not done well. For many organizations this activity is simply taking the gathered raw data (often straight from the tool) and reporting this same data to everyone. There has been no processing and analysis of the data.

There are usually three distinct audiences:

- **The business** – Their real need is to understand whether IT delivered the service they promised at the levels they promised and if not, what corrective actions are being implemented to improve the situation
- **Senior (IT) management** – This group is often focused on the results surrounding CSFs and KPIs such as, customer satisfaction, actual vs. plan, costing and revenue targets. Information provided at this level helps determine strategic and tactical improvements on a larger scale. Senior (IT) management often wants this type of information provided in the form of a Balanced Scorecard or IT scorecard format to see the big picture at one glance
- **Internal IT** – This group is often interested in KPIs and activity metrics that help them plan, coordinate, schedule and identify incremental improvement opportunities.

Now more than ever, IT must invest the time to understand specific business goals and translate IT metrics to reflect an impact against these goals. Businesses invest in tools and services that affect productivity, and support should be one of those services. The major challenge, and one that can be met, is to effectively communicate the

business benefits of a well-run IT support group. The starting point is a new perspective on goals, measures, and reporting, and how IT actions affect business results. You will then be prepared to answer the question: 'How does IT help to generate value for your company?'

Although most reports tend to concentrate on areas where things are not going as well as hoped for, do not forget to report on the good news as well. A report showing improvement trends is IT services' best marketing vehicle. It is vitally important that reports show whether CSI has actually improved the overall service provision and if it has not, the actions taken to rectify the situation.

8.6.7 Step 7 – Implementing corrective action

Use the knowledge gained to optimize, improve and correct services. Managers need to identify issues and present solutions. Explain how the corrective actions to be taken will improve the service.

CSI identifies many opportunities for improvement however organizations cannot afford to implement all of them. Based on goals, objectives and types of service breaches, an organization needs to prioritize improvement activities. Improvement initiatives can also be externally driven by regulatory requirements, changes in competition, or even political decisions.

After a decision to improve a service and/or service management process is made, then the Service Lifecycle continues. A new Service Strategy may be defined, Service Design builds the changes, Service Transition implements the changes into production and then Service Operation manages the day-to-day operations of the service and/or service management processes. Keep in mind that CSI activities continue through each phase of the Service Lifecycle.

Each Service Lifecycle phase requires resources to build or modify the services and/or service management processes, potential new technology or modifications to existing technology, potential changes to KPIs and other metrics and possibly even new or modified OLAs/UCs to support SLAs. Communication, training and documentation are required to transition a new/improved service, tool or service management process into production.

8.6.8 Monitoring and data collection throughout the Service Lifecycle

Service Strategy is responsible for monitoring the progress of strategies, standards, policies and architectural decisions that have been made and implemented.

Service Design monitors and gathers data associated with creating and modifying (design efforts of) services and service management processes. This part of the Service Lifecycle also measures against the effectiveness and ability to measure CSFs and KPIs that were defined through gathering business requirements. Service Design also defines what should be measured. This would include monitoring project schedules, progress to project milestones, and project results against goals and objectives.

Service Transition develops the monitoring procedures and criteria to be used during and after implementation. Service Transition monitors and gathers data on the actual release into production of services and service management processes. It is the responsibility of Service Transition to ensure that the services and service management processes are embedded in a way that can be managed and maintained according to the strategies and design efforts. Service Transition develops the monitoring procedures and criteria to be used during and after implementation.

Service Operation is responsible for the actual monitoring of services in the production environment. Service Operation plays a large part in the processing activity. Service Operation provides input into what can be measured and processed into logical groupings as well as doing the actual processing of the data. Service Operation would also be responsible for taking the component data and processing it in a format that will provide a better end-to-end perspective of the service achievements.

8.6.9 Role of other processes in monitoring and data collection

Service Level Management

SLM plays a key role in the data-gathering activity as SLM is responsible for not only defining business requirements but also IT's capabilities to achieve them.

- One of the first items in defining IT's capabilities is to identify what monitoring and data collection activities are currently taking place
- SLM then needs to look at what is happening with the monitoring data. Is the monitoring taking place only at a component level and, if so, is anyone looking at multiple components to provide an end-to-end service performance perspective?
- SLM should also identify who gets the data, whether any analysis takes place on the data before it is presented, and if any trend evaluation is undertaken to understand the performance over a period of time. This information will be helpful in following CSI activities
- Through the negotiation process with the business, SLM would define what to measure and which aspects to report. This would in turn drive the monitoring and data collection requirements. If there is no capability to monitor and/or collect data on an item then it should not appear in the SLA. SLM should be a part of the review process to monitor results
- SLM is responsible for developing and getting agreement on OLAs and UCs that require internal or external monitoring.

Availability and Capacity Management

■ Provide significant input into existing monitoring and data collection capabilities, tool requirements to meet new data collection requirements and ensure the Availability and Capacity Plans are updated to reflect new or modified monitoring and data collection requirements

■ Are accountable for the actual infrastructure monitoring and data collection activities that take place. Therefore roles and responsibilities need to be defined and the roles filled with properly skilled and trained staff

■ Are accountable for ensuring tools are in place to gather data

■ Are accountable for ensuring that the actual monitoring and data collection activities are consistently performed.

Incident Management and Service Desk

■ Incident Management can define monitoring requirements to support event and incident detection through automation and also has the ability to automatically open Incident tickets and/or auto-escalate Incident tickets

■ Event and Incident monitoring can identify abnormal situations and conditions which helps with predicting and pre-empting situations and conditions thereby avoiding possible service and component failures

■ Monitor response times, repair times, resolution times and Incident escalations

■ As a single point of contact it is important for the Service Desk to monitor telephony items such as call volumes, average speed of answer, call abandonment rates etc., so that immediate action can be taken when there is an increase in calls to the Service Desk. This would also apply to those Service Desks who provide support via e-mail and via the web.

Security Management

Security Management contributes to monitoring and data collection in the following manner:

■ Defines security monitoring and data collection requirements

■ Monitors, verifies and tracks the levels of security according to the organizational security policies and guidelines

■ Assists in determining effects of security measures on data monitoring and collection from the perspectives of confidentiality (accessible only to those who should), integrity (data is accurate and not corrupted or not corruptible) and availability (data is available when needed).

Financial Management

Financial Management is responsible for monitoring and collecting data associated with the actual expenditures vs. budget and is able to provide input on questions such as: Are costing or revenue targets on track? Financial Management should also monitor the ongoing cost per service etc.

In addition Financial Management will provide the necessary templates to assist CSI to create the budget and expenditure reports for the various improvement initiatives as well as providing the means to compute the ROI of the improvements.

8.6.10 Metrics and measurement

In general, a metric is a scale of measurement defined in terms of a standard, i.e. in terms of a well-defined unit. The quantification of an event through the process of measurement relies on the existence of an explicit or implicit metric (see Table 8.1), which is the standard to which measurements are referenced.

Table 8.1 Service metric examples

Measure	Metric	Quality goal	Lower limit	Upper limit
Schedule	% variation against revised plan	Within 7.5% of estimate	Not to be less than 7.5% of estimate	Not to exceed 7.5% of estimate
Effort	% variation against revised plan	Within 10% of estimate	Not to be less than 10% of estimate	Not to exceed 10% of estimate
Cost	% variation against revised plan	Within 10% of estimate	Not to be less than 10% of estimate	Not to exceed 10% of estimate
Defects	% variation against planned defect	Within 10% of estimate	Not to be less than 10% of estimate	Not to exceed 10% of estimate
Productivity	% variation against productivity goal	Within 10% of estimate	Not to be less than 10% of estimate	Not to exceed 10% of estimate
Customer satisfaction	Customer satisfaction survey result	Greater than 8.9 on the range of 1 to 10	Not to be less than 8.9 on the range of 1 to 10	

Metrics are a system of parameters or ways of quantitative assessment of a process that is to be measured, along with the processes to carry out such measurement. Metrics define what is to be measured. Metrics are usually specialized by the subject area, in which case they are valid only within a certain domain and cannot be directly benchmarked or interpreted outside it. Generic metrics, however, can be aggregated across subject areas or business units of an enterprise.

8.6.11 Interpreting metrics

When beginning to interpret the results it is important to know the data elements that make up the results, the purpose of producing the results and the expected normal ranges of the results.

Simply looking at some results and declaring a trend is dangerous. Figure 8.3 shows a trend that the Service Desk is opening fewer incident tickets over the last few months. One could believe that this is because there are fewer Incidents or perhaps it is because the customers are not happy with the service that is being provided, so they go elsewhere for their support needs. Perhaps the organization has implemented a self-help knowledge base and some customers are now using this service instead of contacting the Service Desk. Some investigation is required to understand what is driving these metrics.

Figure 8.3 Number of incident tickets opened over time

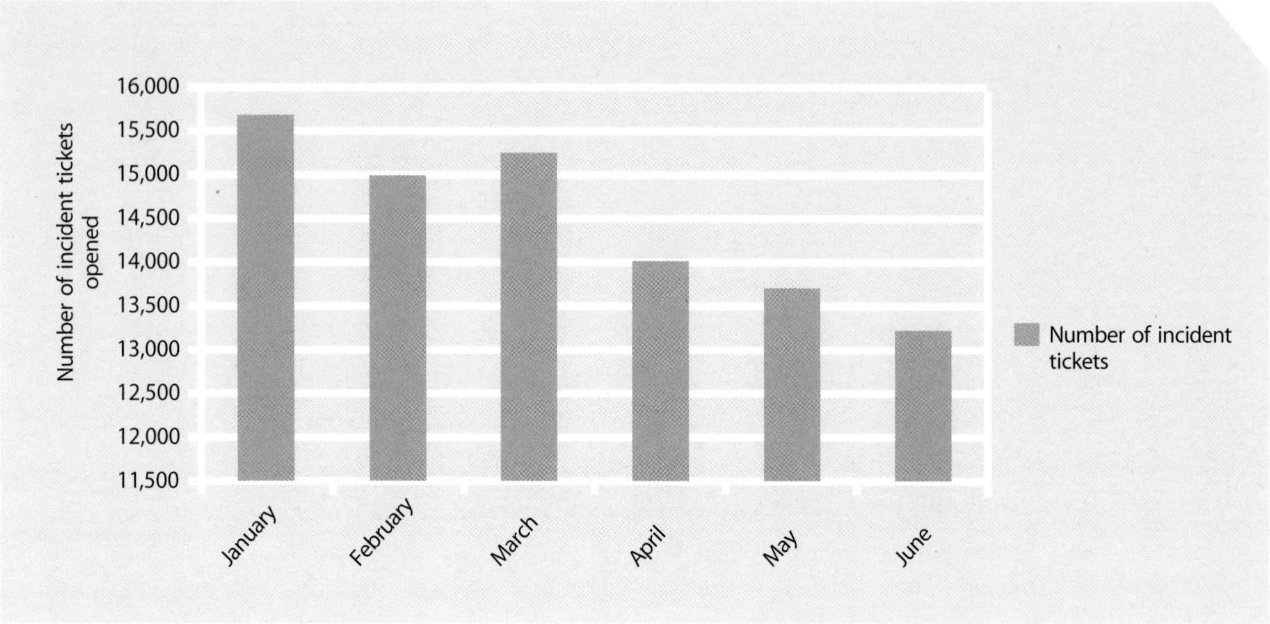

8.7 SERVICE REPORTING

A significant amount of data is collated and monitored by IT in the daily delivery of quality service to the business; however, only a small subset is of real interest and importance to the business. (Figure 8.4 shows the process.) The majority of data and its meaning are more suited to the internal management needs of IT.

The business likes to see a historical representation of the past period's performance that portrays their experience; however, it is more concerned with those historical events that continue to be a threat going forward, and how IT intend to militate against such threats.

It is not satisfactory simply to present reports which depict adherence (or otherwise) to SLAs, which in themselves are prone to statistical ambiguity. IT needs to build an actionable approach to reporting, i.e. this is what happened, this is what we did, this is how we will ensure it doesn't impact you again, and this is how we are working to improve the delivery of IT services generally.

Figure 8.4 Service reporting process

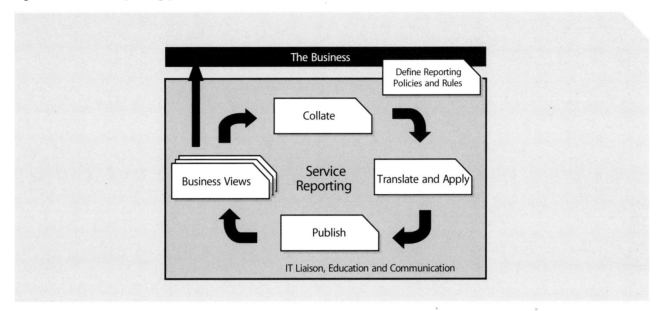

Complementary
guidance

9

9 Complementary guidance

9.1 ITIL AND OTHER FRAMEWORKS, PRACTICES AND STANDARDS

The IT industry has developed a number of frameworks, method and standards to manage a growing number of needs. Organizations can face uncertainty in understanding which framework, method or standard of practice they need in order to excel at managing IT services. Some frameworks were developed to address regulatory and legal compliance, others to streamline or re-engineer practices and most have origins in financial and manufacturing industries.

ITIL and many of these frameworks have a solid harmony and can co-exist within an organization to meet a range of service management needs.

Following are some of the more commonly known frameworks and standards that have synergy with ITIL.

9.1.1 COBIT

COBIT® stands for Control OBjectives for Information and related Technology. Originally created in 1995 as an IS audit framework, COBIT has matured to become an overall IT management framework. COBIT processes and principles are often used by IT and SOX auditors. COBIT is governed by the IT Governance Institute.

9.1.2 ISO/IEC 20000

ISO/IEC 20000:2005 promotes the adoption of an integrated process approach to effectively deliver managed services to meet business and customer requirements. For an organization to function effectively it has to identify and manage numerous linked activities. Coordinated integration and implementation of the service management processes provides ongoing control, greater efficiency and opportunities for continual improvement.

ISO 20000 is based on the ITIL service management processes.

9.1.3 ISO/IEC 15504

Also known as SPICE – Software Process Improvement and Capability dEtermination – it provides a framework for the assessment of process capability. This framework can be used by organizations involved in planning, managing, monitoring, controlling and improving the acquisition, supply, development, operation, evolution and support of products and services. It is also intended for use by assessors in the performance of process assessment, and by organizations involved in the development of process reference models, process assessment models or process assessment processes.

9.1.4 ISO/IEC 19770:2006

Developed to enable an organization to prove that it is performing software asset management (SAM) to a standard sufficient to satisfy corporate governance requirements and ensure effective support for IT service management overall. It is intended to align closely to, and to support, ISO/IEC 20000. Good practice in SAM should result in several benefits, and certifiable good practice should allow management and other organizations to place reliance on the adequacy of these processes. The expected benefits should be achieved with a high degree of confidence.

9.1.5 Management of Risk

Management of Risk (M_o_R®) provides an alternative generic framework for the management of risk across all parts of an organization – strategic, programme, project and operational. It incorporates all the activities required to identify and control the exposure to any type of risk, positive or negative, which may have an impact on the achievement of your organization's business objectives.

M_o_R provides a framework that is tried, tested and effective to help you eliminate or manage the risks involved in reaching your goals. M_o_R adopts a systematic application of principles, approach and processes to the task of identifying, assessing and then planning and implementing risk responses.

9.1.6 Project management

PMBOK® (Project Management Body of Knowledge) is owned and authored by the Project Management Institute (PMI).

The Project Management Body of Knowledge is the sum of knowledge within the profession of project management. As with other professions such as law, medicine and accounting, the body of knowledge rests with the practitioners and academics who apply and advance it. The complete Project Management Body of Knowledge includes proven traditional practices that are widely applied, as well as innovative practices that are emerging in the profession, including published and unpublished material. As a result, the Project Management Body of Knowledge is constantly evolving. (*Introduction to PMBOK*, 2004)

PRINCE2™ (PRoject IN Controlled Environments, v2) is a structured project management method owned by the OGC. Structured project management means managing the project in a logical, organized way, following defined steps. A structured project management method is the written description of this logical, organized approach.

9.1.7 CMMI

CMMi (Capability Maturity Model Integrated) was created by SEI (Software Engineering Institute) at Carnegie Mellon University in 1991. In the beginning CMM was a model for demonstrating the maturity of software development processes in the belief that more mature development processes led to better software. The basic Software CMM model has grown and been revised. CMM is now the de facto standard for measuring the maturity of any process. Organizations can be assessed against the CMM model using SCAMPI (Standard CMMI Appraisal Method for Process Improvement).

9.1.8 Six Sigma

The fundamental objective of the Six Sigma methodology is the implementation of a measurement-based strategy that focuses on process improvement and variation reduction through the application of Six Sigma improvement projects. This is accomplished through the use of two Six Sigma sub-methodologies: DMAIC and DMADV. The Six Sigma DMAIC process (define, measure, analyse, improve, control) is an improvement system for existing processes falling below specification and looking for incremental improvement. The Six Sigma DMADV process (define, measure, analyse, design, verify) is an improvement system used to develop new processes or products at Six Sigma quality levels. It can also be employed if a current process requires more than just incremental improvement.

The ITIL Service Management Model

10

10 The ITIL Service Management Model

Through the previous chapters we have learned the basics of the ITIL Service Lifecycle. This chapter helps to bring a visual perspective to what we have learned. The basic concept of using Service Management Models to implement and manage services inherently offers numerous perspectives. Depending on your organizational context, your interpretation of these will have adaptive nuances.

The ITIL Service Management Model has numerous levels of granularity. For the purposes of learning the basics, this section will take you through the basic constructs and elements, and offer a look at how the Service Management Model is applied to designing a service. The ITIL Service Lifecycle relies on processes to execute the activities involved in service management.

The elements within the Service Management Model will vary in depth, adaptation and interpretation among various service organizations depending on circumstance, culture and structure. The Service Management Model is designed to be adaptive and organizations can customize the design and use of ITIL model elements to meet their unique needs. On its own, without any adaptation, the Service Management Model is entirely complete and usable, but many organizations find that they can enhance their service capabilities by incorporating their own best practices into a hybrid structure. Care should be taken, however, when adapting the Service Management Model not to customize it to the point that service management technologies in the consumer market are no longer able to support your requirements.

Another important concept within the Service Management Model is that not all of the elements are purely processes. While many elements fit the typical characteristics of a 'process', many do not. Elements such

as Availability and Capacity Management do not fit squarely into a process profile, but are critical elements of service management that function across the lifecycle and must be managed in a formal way.

10.1 MODEL ELEMENT TYPES

The ITIL Service Management Model is comprised of two element types: Service Lifecycle governance elements and Service Lifecycle operational elements (Figure 10.1).

Figure 10.1 Service Management Model element types

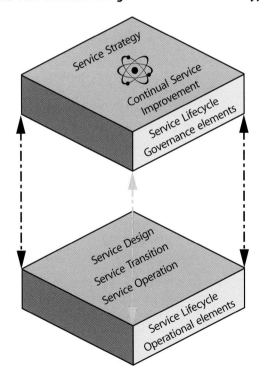

Service Lifecycle governance elements exert influence throughout the Service Lifecycle and gain feedback from

Figure 10.2 Service Lifecycle governance and operational elements

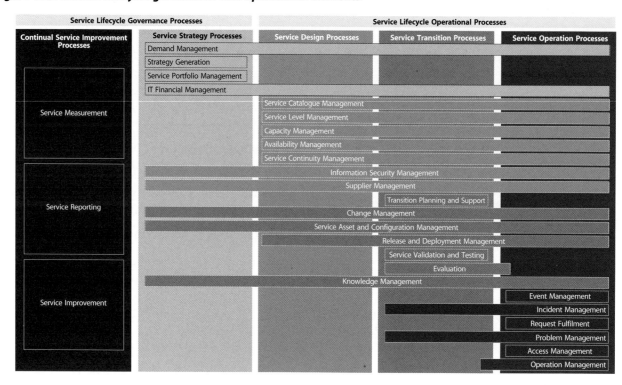

all stages of the lifecycle. They reside predominantly in Service Strategy and Continual Service Improvement.

The lifecycle structure of ITIL leverages process and activity elements throughout various stages of the lifecycle and Figure 10.2 illustrates the reach of each of the governance and operational elements across the lifecycle.

The illustrations that follow are an excerpt of the full ITIL integrated Service Management Model which is available on the ITIL Live™ web portal (www.itil-live-portal.com).

A particular scenario has been chosen to illustrate the flow and integration of the Service Management Model and how the lifecycle flows from the inception of a service to its retirement. The scenario involves a business outcome that will require a new service to be offered by a Service

Provider. In this scenario the Service Provider could be Type I, II or III (refer to section 4.3 for a description of Service Provider types).

Not all of the Service Management Model elements are shown in their entirety in this scenario, but can be referenced from the web portal in their entire depth and application. The use of this scenario is intended to help you gain an understanding of the basic practice and process elements used across the ITIL Service Lifecycle. The specific sub-process activities and work instructions are not shown here, but again, can be obtained from the ITIL web portal.

10.2 BASIC ELEMENTS

As a Service Provider, the interactions you will have in the development and delivery of services to the business will depend on the type of Service Provider you are.

Type I

Figure 10.3 Typical Type I Service Provider interactions

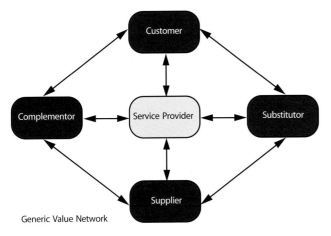

Generic Value Network

As discussed in earlier sections of this publication, a Type I Service Provider (Figure 10.3) is most often the point of focus for the business customer and all IT service needs are managed by the Service Provider using a value network of partnerships.

Type II

Figure 10.4 Type II Service Provider interactions

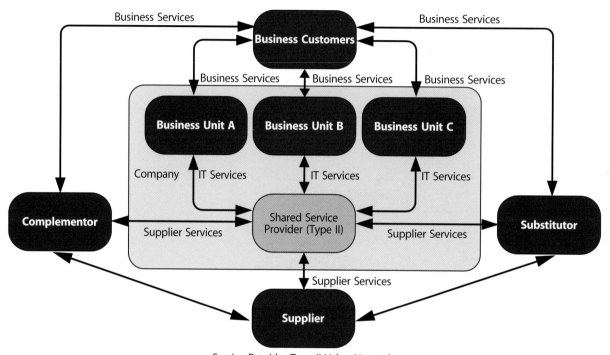

Service Provider Type II Value Network

A Type II Service Provider (Figure 10.4) will often be part of a shared Service Management Model and will provide services to a number of business customers and manage the interactions with the business customers and an external value network.

A Type III Service Provider (Figure 10.5) is most often an organization external to the business and interacts with the value network on behalf of the business customer.

Regardless of the Service Provider type, each will require the use of a range of Service Management Model process and practice elements to manage services effectively and measure the value provided to the business customer.

Figure 10.6 outlines the main process elements across the Service Lifecycle model. They are depicted with a logical flow pattern; however, they are not always executed in a linear fashion and so this should be taken into account.

Type III

Figure 10.5 Type III Service Provider interactions

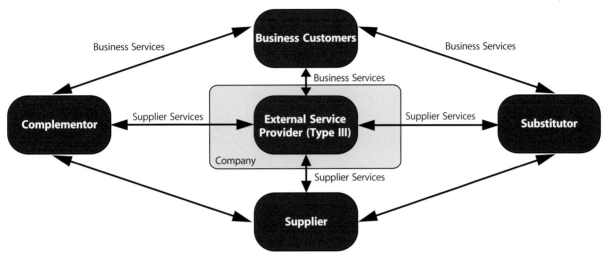

Service Provider Type III Value Network

Each of the start and termination nodes depicts an input that triggers the process or an output that triggers another process.

As an example, Figure 10.6 illustrates that the trigger for the Service Strategy processes is a desired business strategy. The termination of the Service Strategy processes is the chartering of a service and the supply of a Service Level Package, which then triggers the Service Design processes, and so on.

Within each process element, a number of main practice elements accompany each process and are carried out during the lifecycle. Figure 10.7 illustrates these.

Each of the elements shown is comprised of a variety of activities. These are not described here in detail but provided to illustrate the main practice activities an organization would expect to execute during the Service Lifecycle. Details about each of these can be found in the ITIL Service Management core lifecycle publications and on the ITIL Live™ web portal (www.itil-live-portal.com).

Figure 10.6 Basic Service Management Model process elements

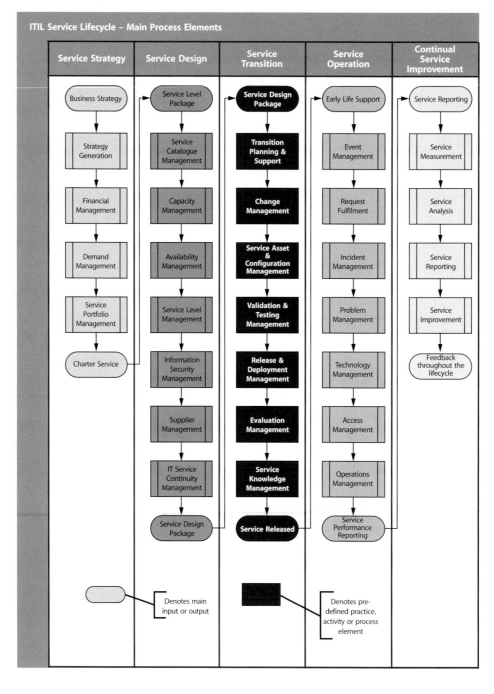

Figure 10.7 ITIL Service Lifecycle main practice elements

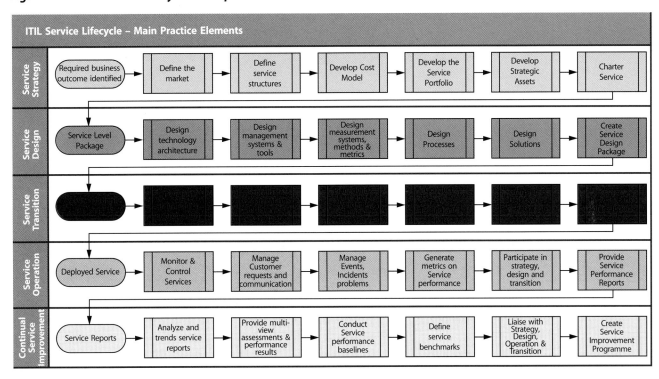

10.3 CREATING A SERVICE

The next series of workflow diagrams will take you through the practices, processes and activities of creating a service. As in the earlier diagrams, these are only depicted at the top level of workflow, but they will provide a solid understanding of the elements required.

10.4 STRATEGY GENERATION

When a business identifies a needed outcome, Service Strategy must define a number of supporting elements to deliver it. First, the perspectives, positions, plans and patterns of actions that help define the market spaces that the service will thrive in to deliver business value must be evaluated (see Figure 10.8, taken from the Service Strategy

publication). This is achieved through a strategic assessment, establishing objectives and a resulting service strategy. In our chosen scenario – creating a service – not all of these must be executed each and every time.

Assuming we have a Service Portfolio in place, the creation of a service must be subject to an evaluation of the existing services and provider capabilities to determine the best course of action.

Figure 10.9 illustrates the breadth of a Service Portfolio and the elements that need to be assessed to decide on the course of action.

Figure 10.8 Forming and formulating a Service Strategy

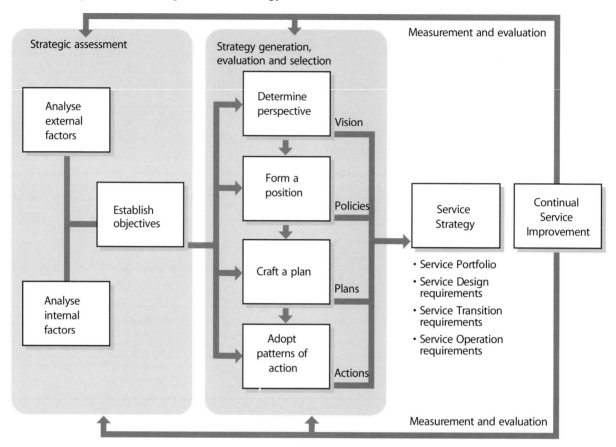

Figure 10.9 The Service Portfolio

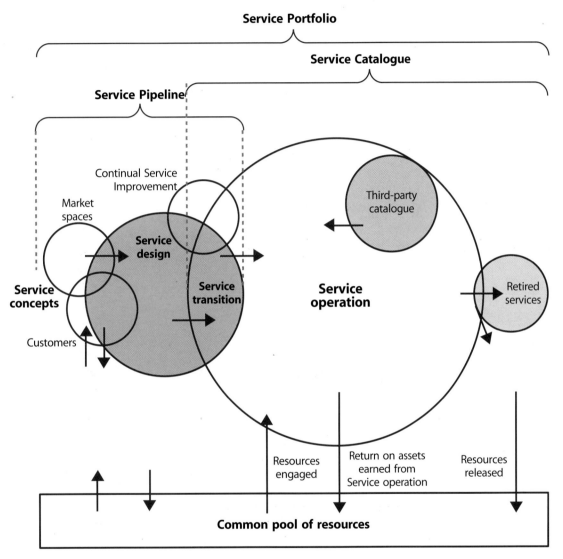

Area of circle is proportional to resources currently engaged in the lifecycle phase (Service Portfolio and Financial Management)

10.5 DECIDING THE COURSE OF ACTION TO CREATE A NEW SERVICE

10.5.1 Stage 1 – Service Strategy elements

In Figure 10.10, Service Strategy evaluates the Service Portfolio to determine if existing capabilities are in place to create the service and deliver the desired business outcomes. Note that other parts of the ITIL Service Lifecycle are involved during the assessment. For example Service Design will evaluate the existing Service Catalogue to determine if live services can be tagged to deliver the required business outcomes. Service Transition becomes involved when the new service is designed either from existing capabilities in the Service Portfolio or Catalogue, or added to them, and moves to the transition stage of the Service Lifecycle.

If during this assessment the business decides that the options available cannot be committed to at the time, Continual Service Improvement will review this periodically to determine if a future time is appropriate to charter and create the service or if there are external catalysts that might make it feasible to proceed at a particular point in time as part of a service improvement programme.

10.5.2 Stage 2 – Design the solution

In this stage, all parts of the Service Lifecycle are involved (Figure 10.11). Each provides input as part of the requirements-gathering stage to ensure that a full service-focused view is understood and leveraged when designing the service. Examples of the benefits in involving all parts of the Service Provider network are:

Figure 10.10 Stage 1 – Service Strategy elements

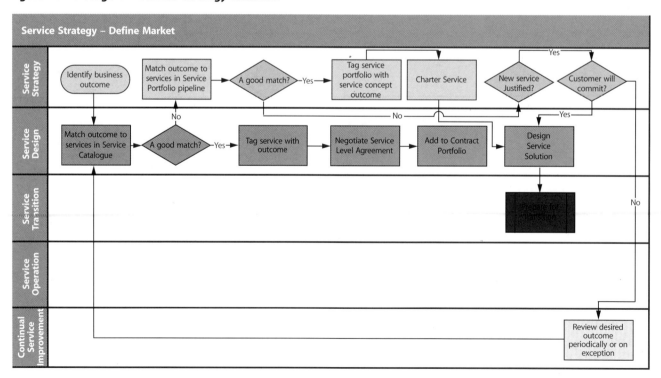

Figure 10.11 Stage 2 – Design service solution

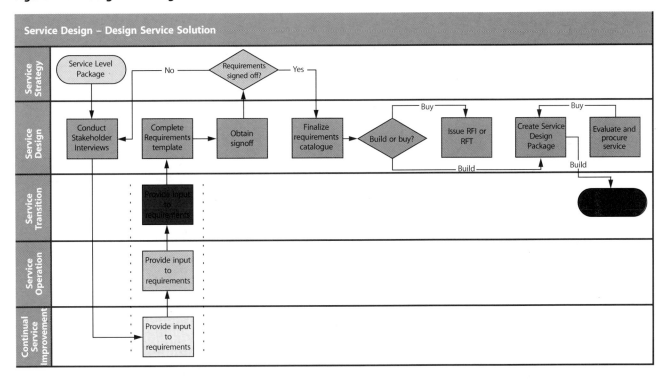

- Ability to re-use existing technology and resources in the operation and support of the new services
- Understanding the impact across the Service Provider network of introducing a new service
- Ensuring that the new Service Design is consistent with the capabilities planned and future investment strategy of the organization.

It is important to note that the Service Design stage of the lifecycle will also consider design activities that ensure Availability, Capacity, Security, Service Continuity etc. This is done during the solution design as part of the five aspects of Service Design (refer to the Service Design core publication). The detailed Service Management Model elements for these are available on the ITIL Live Web portal (www.itil-live-portal.com).

A full description of these elements and the guidance on executing them can be found in the Service Design core publication.

10.5.3 Stage 3 – Transition the service

For a service being built, once the Service Design Package (SDP) has been created during the Service Design stage, the service can be planned, built, tested and deployed. During the Service Transition stage the elements executed draw from key Service Transition processes:

- Transition Planning and Support
- Change Management
- Service Asset and Configuration Management
- Service Validation and Testing Management
- Release and Deployment Management.

Figure 10.12 Stage 3 – Transition the service

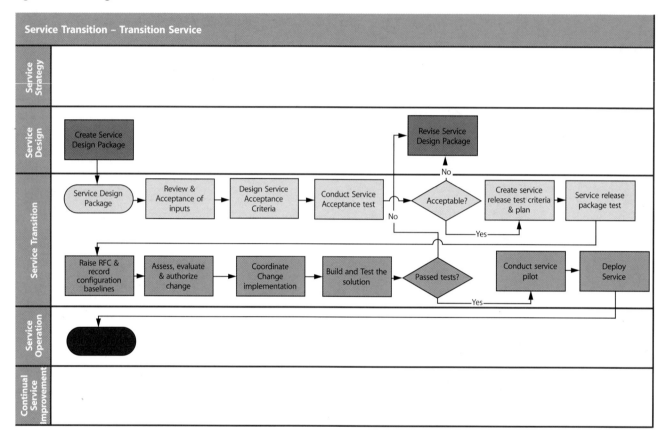

The process workflows for these can be found both in the Service Transition core publication and the ITIL Live web portal (www.itil-live-portal.com).

Figure 10.14 shows an example of the Change Management process as it would be executed in this scenario. It would be included as part of the elements shown in Figure 10.13, which are an extract from the 'Transition the service' workflow in Figure 10.12.

The full Change Management process flow for these elements (Figure 10.14) is taken from the Service Transition publication.

Now that the scenario has reached the stage of going into live operation, there are many interactions and information flows that are being passed through the various stages of the ITIL Service Lifecycle. Figure 10.15 depicts some of those interactions from a view during the transition stage of the lifecycle. Note the assortment of data and information passing between stages by this point in the creation of the service.

Figure 10.13 Change Management elements

Figure 10.14 Normal Change Management process

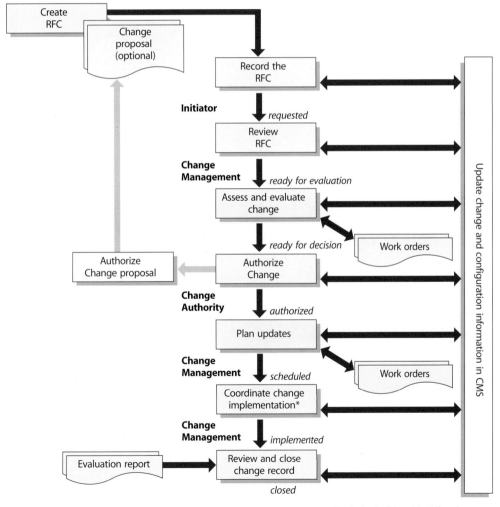

*Includes build and test the change

Figure 10.15 Information flows at the Service Transition stage

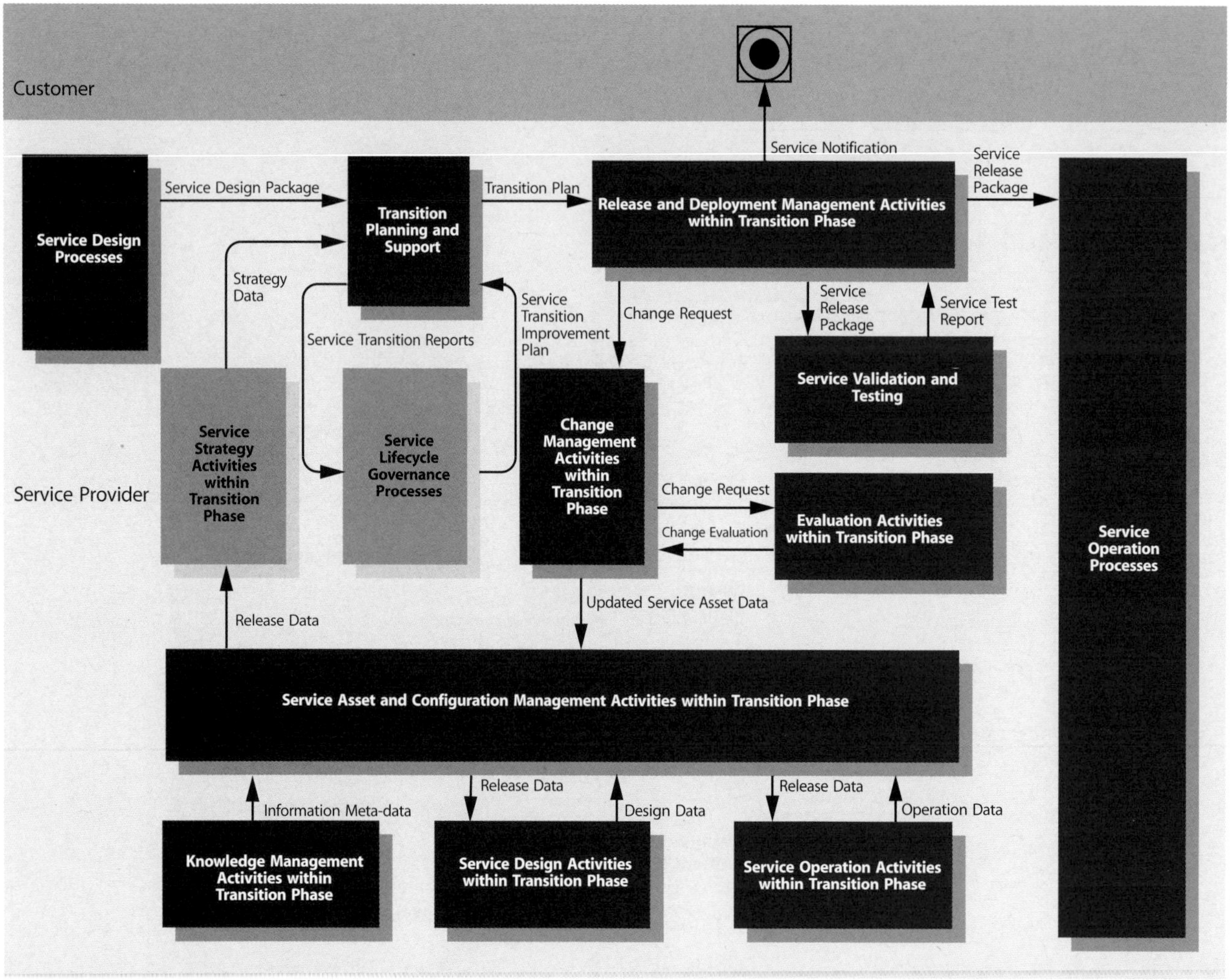

10.5.4 Stage 4 – Operate the service

In our scenario we have now deployed the new service and have accepted it into live operation. But the work from Strategy, Design and Transition is not done.

Early life support is a critical part of ensuring that what we have planned, built, tested and installed is producing the predicted results and meeting the business outcomes we started with.

Beyond early life support, the service becomes 'business as usual' and is continuously monitored and controlled, becoming part of the overall service value to the business customer.

Figure 10.16 Stage 4 – Operate the service

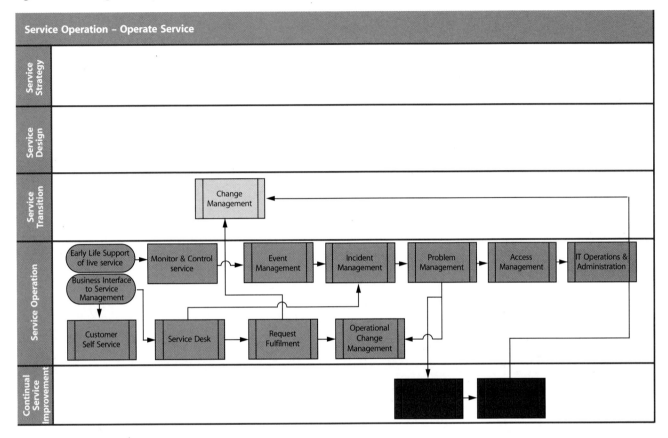

The workflow in Figure 10.16 depicts the high-level activities within Service Operation. The details of each process element and activity can be found in the Service Operation core publication and the ITIL Live™ web portal (www.itil-live-portal.com).

During early life support Service Transition and Service Operation work together. As is often the case, a number of issues with a new service may be uncovered. Depending upon the nature of these, information should be recorded either as events, incidents or known errors, and passed along the workflow accordingly. Service Strategy, Service Design and Continual Service Improvement should be provided with feedback on the performance of the new service, any issues that are revealed, how the business customer is adapting to use of the new service, etc.

It is at this stage that the measurement systems and metrics created at the design stage begin to be generated and accumulated for service reporting. It is also at this stage that the quality and value of the new service are realized since the business is now fully engaged in its use.

A few examples of the full process workflows in Service Operation are given in Figures 10.17 and 10.18. The full integrated Service Management Model and process flows can be obtained on the ITIL Live web portal.

Figure 10.17 The Event Management process

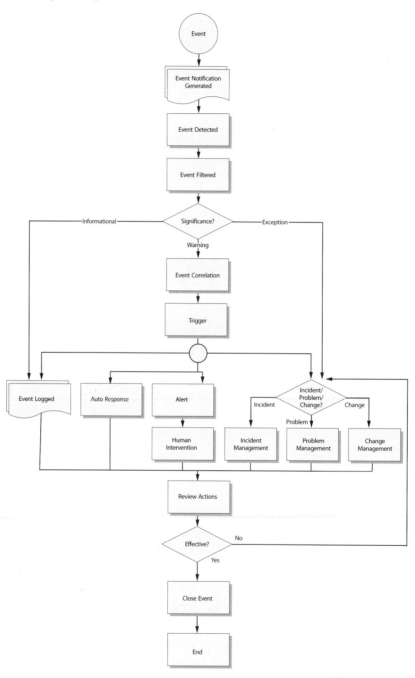

Figure 10.18 The Incident Management process flow

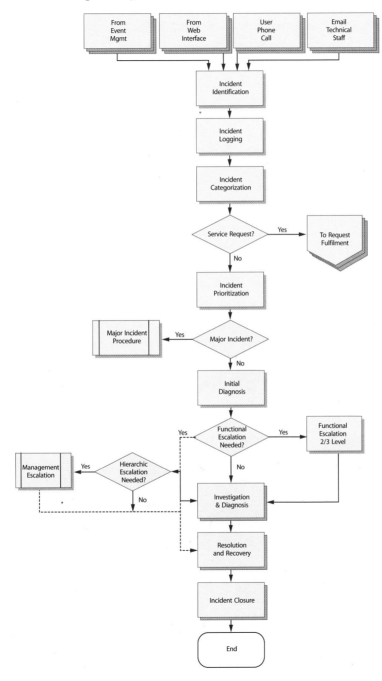

The new service is now in full operation and much more information is being exchanged within the ITIL Service Lifecycle. An example of this is provided in Figure 10.19.

10.5.5 Stage 5 – Continual Service Improvement

Even a new designed service will undergo improvements over time. There are many reasons for this. Business outcomes change as business needs evolve. New technologies become available that are sought after to improve services. Competitive forces demand rapid change capability for both business outcomes and Service Providers.

Whatever the reason behind the need for change, the Continual Service Improvement stage offers the means to cast an eye over the performance, utility and warrant of the new service on an ongoing basis.

Figure 10.20 illustrates some of the main elements and processes involved in service improvement.

The Continual Service Improvement core publication documents the full process elements. With a new service, the activities revolve around ensuring that business value and expected outcomes are being achieved, and identifying where there are opportunities to improve further. Continual Service Improvement feeds back to every stage in the Service Lifecycle.

Figure 10.19 Information flow in the Service Operation stage

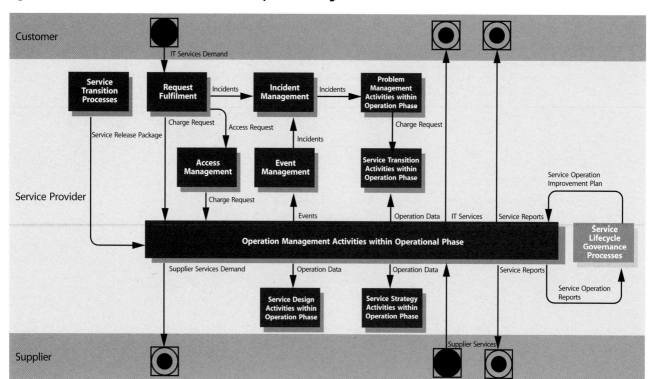

Figure 10.20 Stage 5 – Continual Service Improvement

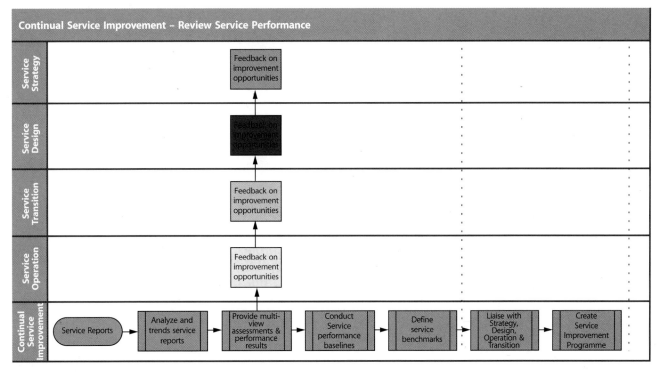

Figure 10.21 shows the information flow within the process elements of Continual Service Improvement.

These five stages form part of a larger, integrated Service Management Model and show how they would be applied for the creation of a new service. Organizations should think of the broader picture of the ebb, flow and interactions within the Service Lifecycle.

Figure 10.22 shows the high-level integrated flow between lifecycle stages.

If we think of the main elements involved in the creation of a new service as layers through the lifecycle (Figure 10.23), we see the interactions and dependencies needed to ensure that business outcomes and business value are met.

Readers are encouraged to learn more about the integrated ITIL Service Management Model by exploring the core ITIL Service Management publications and visiting the ITIL Live™ web portal (www.itil-live-portal.com).

Figure 10.21 Information flow within Continual Service Improvement

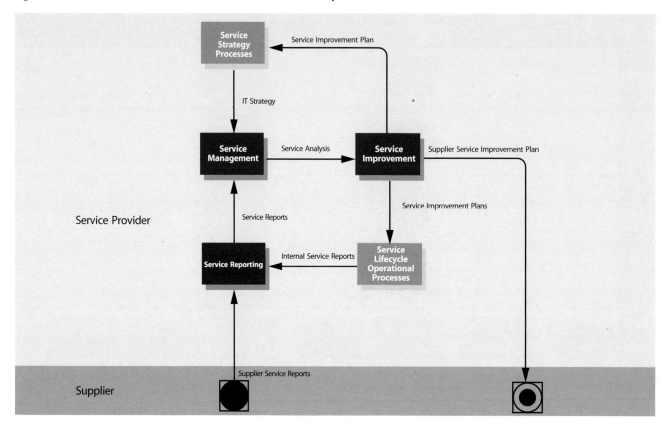

Figure 10.22 Integrated lifecycle elements flow

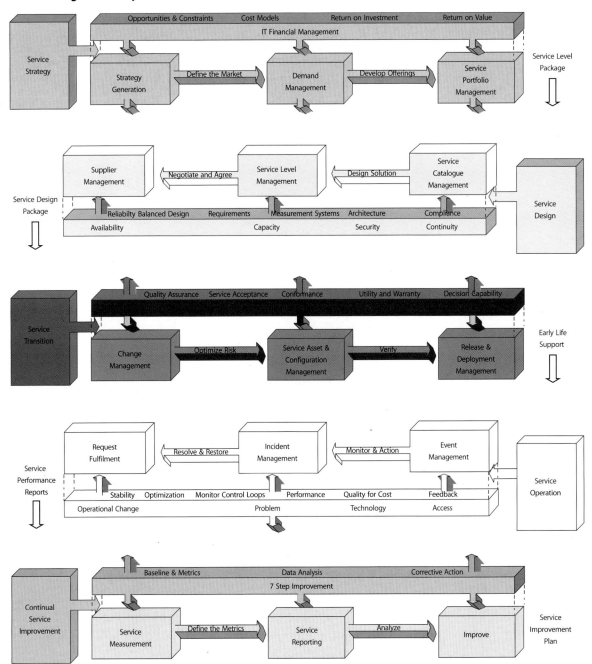

Figure 10.23 Layered view of the main elements in the Service Lifecycle

Acronyms

Acronyms

ACD	Automatic Call Distribution	CSI	Continual Service Improvement
AM	Availability Management	CSIP	Continual Service Improvement Plan
AMIS	Availability Management Information System	CSP	Core Service Package
ASP	Application Service Provider	CTI	Computer Telephony Integration
BCM	Business Capacity Management	DIKW	Data-to-Information-to-Knowledge-to-Wisdom
BCM	Business Continuity Management	ELS	Early Life Support
BCP	Business Continuity Plan	eSCM-CL	eSourcing Capability Model for Client Organizations
BIA	Business Impact Analysis		
BRM	Business Relationship Manager	eSCM-SP	eSourcing Capability Model for Service Providers
BSI	British Standards Institution		
BSM	Business Service Management	FMEA	Failure Modes and Effects Analysis
CAB	Change Advisory Board	FTA	Fault Tree Analysis
CAB/EC	Change Advisory Board/Emergency Committee	IRR	Internal Rate of Return
		ISG	IT Steering Group
CAPEX	Capital Expenditure	ISM	Information Security Management
CCM	Component Capacity Management	ISMS	Information Security Management System
CFIA	Component Failure Impact Analysis	ISO	International Organization for Standardization
CI	Configuration Item		
CMDB	Configuration Management Database	ISP	Internet Service Provider
CMIS	Capacity Management Information System	IT	Information Technology
CMM	Capability Maturity Model	ITSCM	IT Service Continuity Management
CMMI	Capability Maturity Model Integration	ITSM	IT Service Management
CMS	Configuration Management System	itSMF	IT Service Management Forum
COTS	Commercial off the Shelf	IVR	Interactive Voice Response
CSF	Critical Success Factor	KEDB	Known Error Database

KPI	Key Performance Indicator	SDP	Service Design Package
LOS	Line of Service	SFA	Service Failure Analysis
M_o_R	Management of Risk	SIP	Service Improvement Plan
MTBF	Mean Time Between Failures	SKMS	Service Knowledge Management System
MTBSI	Mean Time Between Service Incidents	SLA	Service Level Agreement
MTRS	Mean Time to Restore Service	SLM	Service Level Management
MTTR	Mean Time to Repair	SLP	Service Level Package
NPV	Net Present Value	SLR	Service Level Requirement
OGC	Office of Government Commerce	SMO	Service Maintenance Objective
OLA	Operational Level Agreement	SoC	Separation of Concerns
OPEX	Operational Expenditure	SOP	Standard Operating Procedures
OPSI	Office of Public Sector Information	SOR	Statement of requirements
PBA	Pattern of Business Activity	SPI	Service Provider Interface
PFS	Prerequisite for Success	SPM	Service Portfolio Management
PIR	Post-Implementation Review	SPO	Service Provisioning Optimization
PSA	Projected Service Availability	SPOF	Single Point of Failure
QA	Quality Assurance	TCO	Total Cost of Ownership
QMS	Quality Management System	TCU	Total Cost of Utilization
RCA	Root Cause Analysis	TO	Technical Observation
RFC	Request for Change	TOR	Terms of Reference
ROI	Return on Investment	TQM	Total Quality Management
RPO	Recovery Point Objective	UC	Underpinning Contract
RTO	Recovery Time Objective	UP	User Profile
SAC	Service Acceptance Criteria	VBF	Vital Business Function
SACM	Service Asset and Configuration Management	VOI	Value on Investment
SCD	Supplier and Contract Database	WIP	Work in Progress
SCM	Service Capacity Management		

Glossary

Glossary

The publication names included in parentheses after the name of a term identify where a reader can find more information about that term. This is either because the term is primarily used by that publication or because additional useful information about that term can be found there. Terms without a publication name associated with them may be used generally by several publications, or may not be defined in any greater detail than can be found in the glossary, i.e. we only point readers to somewhere they can expect to expand on their knowledge or to see a greater context. Terms with multiple publication names are expanded on in multiple publications.

Where the definition of a term includes another term, those related terms are given initial capitals. This is designed to help the reader with their understanding by pointing them to additional definitions that are all part of the original term they were interested in. The form *'See also* Term X, Term Y' is used at the end of a definition where an important related term is not used with the text of the definition itself.

Acceptance

Formal agreement that an IT Service, Process, Plan or other Deliverable is complete, accurate, reliable and meets its specified Requirements. Acceptance is usually preceded by Evaluation or Testing and is often required before proceeding to the next stage of a Project or Process. *See also* Service Acceptance Criteria.

Access Management

(Service Operation) The Process responsible for allowing Users to make use of IT Services, data, or other Assets. Access Management helps to protect the Confidentiality, Integrity and Availability of Assets by ensuring that only authorized Users are able to access or modify the Assets. Access Management is sometimes referred to as Rights Management or Identity Management.

Account Manager

(Service Strategy) A Role that is very similar to Business Relationship Manager, but includes more commercial aspects. Most commonly used when dealing with External Customers.

Accounting

(Service Strategy) The Process responsible for identifying actual Costs of delivering IT Services, comparing these with budgeted costs, and managing variance from the Budget.

Accredited

Officially authorized to carry out a Role. For example an Accredited body may be authorized to provide training or to conduct Audits.

Active Monitoring

(Service Operation) Monitoring of a Configuration Item or an IT Service that uses automated regular checks to discover the current status. *See also* Passive Monitoring.

Activity

A set of actions designed to achieve a particular result. Activities are usually defined as part of Processes or Plans, and are documented in Procedures.

Agreed Service Time

(Service Design) A synonym for Service Hours, commonly used in formal calculations of Availability. *See also* Downtime.

Agreement

A Document that describes a formal understanding between two or more parties. An Agreement is not legally binding, unless it forms part of a Contract. *See also* Service Level Agreement, Operational Level Agreement.

Alert

(Service Operation) A warning that a threshold has been reached, something has changed, or a Failure has occurred. Alerts are often created and managed by System Management tools and are managed by the Event Management Process.

Analytical Modelling

(Service Strategy) (Service Design) (Continual Service Improvement) A technique that uses mathematical Models to predict the behaviour of a Configuration Item or IT Service. Analytical Models are commonly used in Capacity Management and Availability Management. *See also* Modelling.

Application

Software that provides Functions that are required by an IT Service. Each Application may be part of more than one IT Service. An Application runs on one or more Servers or Clients. *See also* Application Management, Application Portfolio.

Application Management

(Service Design) (Service Operation) The Function responsible for managing Applications throughout their Lifecycle.

Application Portfolio

(Service Design) A database or structured Document used to manage Applications throughout their Lifecycle. The Application Portfolio contains key Attributes of all Applications. The Application Portfolio is sometimes implemented as part of the Service Portfolio, or as part of the Configuration Management System.

Application Service Provider

(Service Design) An External Service Provider that provides IT Services using Applications running at the Service Provider's premises. Users access the Applications by network connections to the Service Provider.

Application Sizing

(Service Design) The Activity responsible for understanding the Resource Requirements needed to support a new Application, or a major Change to an existing Application. Application Sizing helps to ensure that the IT Service can meet its agreed Service Level Targets for Capacity and Performance.

Architecture

(Service Design) The structure of a System or IT Service, including the Relationships of Components to each other and to the environment they are in. Architecture also includes the Standards and Guidelines that guide the design and evolution of the System.

Assembly

(Service Transition) A Configuration Item (CI) that is made up of a number of other CIs. For example a Server CI may contain CIs for CPUs, disks, memory, etc.; an IT Service CI may contain many hardware, software and other CIs. *See also* Component CI, Build.

Assessment

Inspection and analysis to check whether a Standard or set of Guidelines is being followed, that Records are accurate, or that Efficiency and Effectiveness targets are being met. *See also* Audit.

Asset

(Service Strategy) Any Resource or Capability. Assets of a Service Provider including anything that could contribute to the delivery of a Service. Assets can be one of the following types: Management, Organization, Process, Knowledge, People, Information, Applications, Infrastructure and Financial Capital.

Asset Management

(Service Transition) Asset Management is the Process responsible for tracking and reporting the value and ownership of financial Assets throughout their Lifecycle. Asset Management is part of an overall Service Asset and Configuration Management Process. *See also* Asset Register.

Asset Register

(Service Transition) A list of Assets that includes their ownership and value. Asset Management maintains the Asset Register.

Attribute

(Service Transition) A piece of information about a Configuration Item. Examples are: name, location, version number and Cost. Attributes of CIs are recorded in the Configuration Management Database (CMDB). *See also* Relationship.

Audit

Formal inspection and verification to check whether a Standard or set of Guidelines is being followed, that Records are accurate, or that Efficiency and Effectiveness targets are being met. An Audit may be carried out by internal or external groups. *See also* Certification, Assessment.

Authority Matrix

See RACI.

Automatic Call Distribution

(Service Operation) Use of Information Technology to direct an incoming telephone call to the most appropriate person in the shortest possible time. ACD is sometimes called Automated Call Distribution.

Availability

(Service Design) Ability of a Configuration Item or IT Service to perform its agreed Function when required. Availability is determined by Reliability, Maintainability, Serviceability, Performance and Security. Availability is usually calculated as a percentage. This calculation is often based on Agreed Service Time and Downtime. It is Best Practice to calculate Availability using measurements of the Business output of the IT Service.

Availability Management

(Service Design) The Process responsible for defining, analysing, Planning, measuring and improving all aspects of the Availability of IT services. Availability Management is responsible for ensuring that all IT Infrastructure, Processes, Tools, Roles etc. are appropriate for the agreed Service Level Targets for Availability.

Availability Management Information System

(Service Design) A virtual repository of all Availability Management data, usually stored in multiple physical locations.

Availability Plan

(Service Design) A Plan to ensure that existing and future Availability Requirements for IT Services can be provided Cost Effectively.

Back-out

See Remediation.

Backup

(Service Design) (Service Operation) Copying data to protect against loss of Integrity or Availability of the original.

Balanced Scorecard

(Continual Service Improvement) A management tool developed by Drs Robert Kaplan (Harvard Business School) and David Norton. A Balanced Scorecard enables a Strategy to be broken down into Key Performance Indicators. Performance against the KPIs is used to demonstrate how well the Strategy is being achieved. A Balanced Scorecard has four major areas, each of which has a small number of KPIs. The same four areas are considered at different levels of detail throughout the Organization.

Baseline

(Continual Service Improvement) A Benchmark used as a reference point. For example:

- An ITSM Baseline can be used as a starting point to measure the effect of a Service Improvement Plan
- A Performance Baseline can be used to measure changes in Performance over the lifetime of an IT Service
- A Configuration Management Baseline can be used to enable the IT Infrastructure to be restored to a known Configuration if a Change or Release fails.

Benchmark

(Continual Service Improvement) The recorded state of something at a specific point in time. A Benchmark can be created for a Configuration, a Process or any other set of data. For example, a benchmark can be used in:

- Continual Service Improvement, to establish the current state for managing improvements
- Capacity Management, to document performance characteristics during normal operations.

See also Benchmarking, Baseline.

Benchmarking

(Continual Service Improvement) Comparing a Benchmark with a Baseline or with Best Practice. The term Benchmarking is also used to mean creating a series of Benchmarks over time, and comparing the results to measure progress or improvement.

Best Practice

Proven Activities or Processes that have been successfully used by multiple Organizations. ITIL is an example of Best Practice.

Brainstorming

(Service Operation) A technique that helps a team to generate ideas. Ideas are not reviewed during the Brainstorming session, but at a later stage. Brainstorming is often used by Problem Management to identify possible causes.

British Standards Institution

The UK National Standards body, responsible for creating and maintaining British Standards. *See* www.bsi-global.com for more information. *See also* ISO.

Budget

A list of all the money an Organization or Business Unit plans to receive, and plans to pay out, over a specified period of time. *See also* Budgeting, Planning.

Budgeting

The Activity of predicting and controlling the spending of money. Consists of a periodic negotiation cycle to set future Budgets (usually annual) and the day-to-day monitoring and adjusting of current Budgets.

Build

(Service Transition) The Activity of assembling a number of Configuration Items to create part of an IT Service. The term Build is also used to refer to a Release that is authorized for distribution. For example server Build or laptop Build. *See also* Configuration Baseline.

Build Environment

(Service Transition) A controlled Environment where Applications, IT Services and other Builds are assembled prior to being moved into a Test or Live Environment.

Business

(Service Strategy) An overall corporate entity or Organization formed of a number of Business Units. In the context of ITSM, the term Business includes public sector and not-for-profit organizations, as well as companies. An IT Service Provider provides IT Services to a Customer within a Business. The IT Service Provider may be part of the same Business as its Customer (Internal Service Provider), or part of another Business (External Service Provider).

Business Capacity Management (BCM)

(Service Design) In the context of ITSM, Business Capacity Management is the Activity responsible for understanding future Business Requirements for use in the Capacity Plan. *See also* Service Capacity Management.

Business Case

(Service Strategy) Justification for a significant item of expenditure. Includes information about Costs, benefits, options, issues, Risks and possible problems. *See also* Cost Benefit Analysis.

Business Continuity Management

(Service Design) The Business Process responsible for managing Risks that could seriously affect the Business. BCM safeguards the interests of key stakeholders, reputation, brand and value-creating activities. The BCM Process involves reducing Risks to an acceptable level and planning for the recovery of Business Processes should a disruption to the Business occur. BCM sets the Objectives, Scope and Requirements for IT Service Continuity Management.

Business Continuity Plan

(Service Design) A Plan defining the steps required to Restore Business Processes following a disruption. The Plan will also identify the triggers for Invocation, people to be involved, communications etc. IT Service Continuity Plans form a significant part of Business Continuity Plans.

Business Customer

(Service Strategy) A recipient of a product or a Service from the Business. For example, if the Business is a car manufacturer then the Business Customer is someone who buys a car.

Business Impact Analysis

(Service Strategy) BIA is the Activity in Business Continuity Management that identifies Vital Business Functions and their dependencies. These dependencies may include Suppliers, people, other Business Processes, IT Services etc.

BIA defines the recovery requirements for IT Services. These requirements include Recovery Time Objectives, Recovery Point Objectives and minimum Service Level Targets for each IT Service.

Business Objective

(Service Strategy) The Objective of a Business Process, or of the Business as a whole. Business Objectives support the Business Vision, provide guidance for the IT Strategy and are often supported by IT Services.

Business Operations

(Service Strategy) The day-to-day execution, monitoring and management of Business Processes.

Business Perspective

(Continual Service Improvement) An understanding of the Service Provider and IT Services from the point of view of the Business, and an understanding of the Business from the point of view of the Service Provider.

Business Process

A Process that is owned and carried out by the Business. A Business Process contributes to the delivery of a product or Service to a Business Customer. For example, a retailer may have a purchasing Process that helps to deliver Services to its Business Customers. Many Business Processes rely on IT Services.

Business Relationship Management

(Service Strategy) The Process or Function responsible for maintaining a Relationship with the Business. Business Relationship Management usually includes:

- Managing personal Relationships with Business managers
- Providing input to Service Portfolio Management

- Ensuring that the IT Service Provider is satisfying the Business needs of the Customers.

This Process has strong links with Service Level Management.

Business Relationship Manager

(Service Strategy) A Role responsible for maintaining the Relationship with one or more Customers. This Role is often combined with the Service Level Manager Role. *See also* Account Manager.

Business Service

An IT Service that directly supports a Business Process, as opposed to an Infrastructure Service, which is used internally by the IT Service Provider and is not usually visible to the Business.

The term Business Service is also used to mean a Service that is delivered to Business Customers by Business Units. For example, delivery of financial services to Customers of a bank, or goods to the Customers of a retail store. Successful delivery of Business Services often depends on one or more IT Services.

Business Service Management

(Service Strategy) (Service Design) An approach to the management of IT Services that considers the Business Processes supported and the Business value provided.

This term also means the management of Business Services delivered to Business Customers.

Business Unit

(Service Strategy) A segment of the Business that has its own Plans, Metrics, income and Costs. Each Business Unit owns Assets and uses these to create value for Customers in the form of goods and Services.

Call

(Service Operation) A telephone call to the Service Desk from a User. A Call could result in an Incident or a Service Request being logged.

Call Centre

(Service Operation) An Organization or Business Unit that handles large numbers of incoming and outgoing telephone calls. *See also* Service Desk.

Call Type

(Service Operation) A Category that is used to distinguish incoming requests to a Service Desk. Common call types are Incident, Service Request and Complaint.

Capability

(Service Strategy) The ability of an Organization, person, Process, Application, Configuration Item or IT Service to carry out an Activity. Capabilities are intangible Assets of an Organization. *See also* Resource.

Capability Maturity Model

(Continual Service Improvement) The Capability Maturity Model for Software (also known as the CMM and SW-CMM) is a model used to identify Best Practices to help increase Process Maturity. CMM was developed at the Software Engineering Institute (SEI) of Carnegie Mellon University, US. In 2000, the SW-CMM was upgraded to CMMI® (Capability Maturity Model Integration). The SEI no longer maintains the SW-CMM model, its associated appraisal methods or training materials.

Capability Maturity Model Integration

(Continual Service Improvement) Capability Maturity Model® Integration (CMMI) is a process improvement approach developed by the Software Engineering Institute (SEI) of Carnegie Melon University, US. CMMI provides organizations with the essential elements of effective processes. It can be used to guide process improvement across a project, a division or an entire organization. CMMI helps integrate traditionally separate organizational functions, set process improvement goals and priorities, provide guidance for quality processes, and provide a point of reference for appraising current processes. *See* www.sei.cmu.edu/cmmi for more information. *See also* CMM, Maturity.

Capacity

(Service Design) The maximum Throughput that a Configuration Item or IT Service can deliver whilst meeting agreed Service Level Targets. For some types of CI, Capacity may be the size or volume, for example a disk drive.

Capacity Management

(Service Design) The Process responsible for ensuring that the Capacity of IT Services and the IT Infrastructure is able to deliver agreed Service Level Targets in a Cost Effective and timely manner. Capacity Management considers all Resources required to deliver the IT Service, and plans for short-, medium- and long-term Business Requirements.

Capacity Management Information System

(Service Design) A virtual repository of all Capacity Management data, usually stored in multiple physical locations.

Capacity Plan

(Service Design) A Capacity Plan is used to manage the Resources required to deliver IT Services. The Plan contains scenarios for different predictions of Business demand, and costed options to deliver the agreed Service Level Targets.

Capacity Planning

(Service Design) The Activity within Capacity Management responsible for creating a Capacity Plan.

Capital Expenditure

(Service Strategy) The cost of purchasing something that will become a financial Asset, for example computer equipment and buildings. The value of the Asset is Depreciated over multiple accounting periods.

Capital Item

(Service Strategy) Synonym for an Asset that is of interest to Financial Management because it is above an agreed financial value.

Capitalization

(Service Strategy) Identifying major Cost as Capital, even though no Asset is purchased. This is done to spread the impact of the Cost over multiple accounting periods. The most common example of this is software development, or purchase of a software licence.

Category

A named group of things that have something in common. Categories are used to group similar things together. For example, Cost Types are used to group similar types of Cost. Incident Categories are used to group similar types of Incident, CI Types are used to group similar types of Configuration Item.

Certification

Issuing a certificate to confirm Compliance to a Standard. Certification includes a formal Audit by an independent and Accredited body. The term Certification is also used to mean awarding a certificate to verify that a person has achieved a qualification.

Change

(Service Transition) The addition, modification or removal of anything that could have an effect on IT Services. The Scope should include all IT Services, Configuration Items, Processes, Documentation etc.

Change Advisory Board

(Service Transition) A group of people that advises the Change Manager in the assessment, prioritization and scheduling of Changes. This board is usually made up of representatives from all areas within the IT Service Provider, representatives from the Business and Third Parties such as Suppliers.

Change Case

(Service Operation) A technique used to predict the impact of proposed Changes. Change Cases use specific scenarios to clarify the scope of proposed Changes and to help with Cost Benefit Analysis. *See also* Use Case.

Change History

(Service Transition) Information about all changes made to a Configuration Item during its life. Change History consists of all those Change Records that apply to the CI.

Change Management

(Service Transition) The Process responsible for controlling the Lifecycle of all Changes. The primary objective of Change Management is to enable beneficial Changes to be made, with minimum disruption to IT Services.

Change Model

(Service Transition) A repeatable way of dealing with a particular Category of Change. A Change Model defines specific pre-defined steps that will be followed for a change of this Category. Change Models may be very simple, with no requirement for approval (e.g. Password

Reset) or may be very complex with many steps that require approval (e.g. major software release). *See also* Standard Change, Change Advisory Board.

Change Record

(Service Transition) A Record containing the details of a Change. Each Change Record documents the Lifecycle of a single Change. A Change Record is created for every Request for Change that is received, even those that are subsequently rejected. Change Records should reference the Configuration Items that are affected by the Change. Change Records are stored in the Configuration Management System.

Change Request

See Request for Change.

Change Schedule

(Service Transition) A Document that lists all approved Changes and their planned implementation dates. A Change Schedule is sometimes called a Forward Schedule of Change, even though it also contains information about Changes that have already been implemented.

Change Window

(Service Transition) A regular, agreed time when Changes or Releases may be implemented with minimal impact on Services. Change Windows are usually documented in SLAs.

Charging

(Service Strategy) Requiring payment for IT Services. Charging for IT Services is optional, and many Organizations choose to treat their IT Service Provider as a Cost Centre.

Chronological Analysis

(Service Operation) A technique used to help identify possible causes of Problems. All available data about the Problem is collected and sorted by date and time to provide a detailed timeline. This can make it possible to identify which Events may have been triggered by others.

CI Type

(Service Transition) A Category that is used to Classify CIs. The CI Type identifies the required Attributes and Relationships for a Configuration Record. Common CI Types include: Hardware, Document, User etc.

Classification

The act of assigning a Category to something. Classification is used to ensure consistent management and reporting. CIs, Incidents, Problems, Changes etc. are usually classified.

Client

A generic term that means a Customer, the Business or a Business Customer. For example, Client Manager may be used as a synonym for Account Manager.

The term client is also used to mean:

- A computer that is used directly by a User, for example a PC, handheld computer or workstation
- The part of a client-server application that the User directly interfaces with. For example an e-mail Client.

Closed

(Service Operation) The final Status in the Lifecycle of an Incident, Problem, Change etc. When the Status is Closed, no further action is taken.

Closure

(Service Operation) The act of changing the Status of an Incident, Problem, Change, etc. to Closed.

COBIT

(Continual Service Improvement) Control Objectives for Information and related Technology (COBIT) provides guidance and Best Practice for the management of IT Processes. COBIT is published by the IT Governance Institute. *See* www.isaca.org for more information.

Code of Practice

A Guideline published by a public body or a Standards Organization, such as ISO or BSI. Many Standards consist of a Code of Practice and a Specification. The Code of Practice describes recommended Best Practice.

Cold Standby

See Gradual Recovery.

Commercial off the Shelf

(Service Design) Application software or Middleware that can be purchased from a Third Party.

Compliance

Ensuring that a Standard or set of Guidelines is followed, or that proper, consistent accounting or other practices are being employed.

Component

A general term that is used to mean one part of something more complex. For example, a computer System may be a component of an IT Service; an Application may be a Component of a Release Unit. Components that need to be managed should be Configuration Items.

Component Capacity Management

(Service Design) (Continual Service Improvement) The Process responsible for understanding the Capacity, Utilization and Performance of Configuration Items. Data is collected, recorded and analysed for use in the Capacity Plan. *See also* Service Capacity Management.

Component CI

(Service Transition) A Configuration Item that is part of an Assembly. For example, a CPU or memory CI may be part of a Server CI.

Component Failure Impact Analysis

(Service Design) A technique that helps to identify the impact of CI failure on IT Services. A matrix is created with IT Services on one edge and CIs on the other. This enables the identification of critical CIs (that could cause the failure of multiple IT Services) and of fragile IT Services (that have multiple Single Points of Failure).

Computer Telephony Integration

(Service Operation) Computer Telephony Integration (CTI) is a general term covering any kind of integration between computers and telephone Systems. It is most commonly used to refer to Systems where an Application displays detailed screens relating to incoming or outgoing telephone calls. *See also* Automatic Call Distribution, Interactive Voice Response.

Concurrency

A measure of the number of Users engaged in the same Operation at the same time.

Confidentiality

(Service Design) A security principle that requires that data should only be accessed by authorized people.

Configuration

(Service Transition) A generic term, used to describe a group of Configuration Items that work together to deliver an IT Service, or a recognizable part of an IT Service. Configuration is also used to describe the parameter settings for one or more CIs.

Configuration Baseline

(Service Transition) A Baseline of a Configuration that has been formally agreed and is managed through the Change Management process. A Configuration Baseline is used as a basis for future Builds, Releases and Changes.

Configuration Control

(Service Transition) The Activity responsible for ensuring that adding, modifying or removing a CI is properly managed, for example by submitting a Request for Change or Service Request.

Configuration Identification

(Service Transition) The Activity responsible for collecting information about Configuration Items and their Relationships, and loading this information into the CMDB. Configuration Identification is also responsible for labelling the CIs themselves, so that the corresponding Configuration Records can be found.

Configuration Item

(Service Transition) Any Component that needs to be managed in order to deliver an IT Service. Information about each CI is recorded in a Configuration Record within the Configuration Management System and is maintained throughout its Lifecycle by Configuration Management. CIs are under the control of Change Management. CIs typically include IT Services, hardware, software, buildings, people and formal documentation such as Process documentation and SLAs.

Configuration Management

(Service Transition) The Process responsible for maintaining information about Configuration Items required to deliver an IT Service, including their Relationships. This information is managed throughout the Lifecycle of the CI. Configuration Management is part of an overall Service Asset and Configuration Management Process.

Configuration Management Database

(Service Transition) A database used to store Configuration Records throughout their Lifecycle. The Configuration Management System maintains one or more CMDBs, and each CMDB stores Attributes of CIs, and Relationships with other CIs.

Configuration Management System

(Service Transition) A set of tools and databases that are used to manage an IT Service Provider's Configuration data. The CMS also includes information about Incidents, Problems, Known Errors, Changes and Releases; and may contain data about employees, Suppliers, locations, Business Units, Customers and Users. The CMS includes tools for collecting, storing, managing, updating and presenting data about all Configuration Items and their Relationships. The CMS is maintained by Configuration Management and is used by all IT Service Management Processes. *See also* Configuration Management Database.

Configuration Record

(Service Transition) A Record containing the details of a Configuration Item. Each Configuration Record documents the Lifecycle of a single CI. Configuration Records are stored in a Configuration Management Database.

Configuration Structure

(Service Transition) The hierarchy and other Relationships between all the Configuration Items that comprise a Configuration.

Continual Service Improvement

(Continual Service Improvement) A stage in the Lifecycle of an IT Service and the title of one of the Core ITIL publications. Continual Service Improvement is responsible for managing improvements to IT Service Management Processes and IT Services. The Performance of the IT Service Provider is continually measured and improvements are made to Processes, IT Services and IT Infrastructure in order to increase Efficiency, Effectiveness and Cost Effectiveness. *See also* Plan-Do-Check-Act.

Continuous Availability

(Service Design) An approach or design to achieve 100% Availability. A Continuously Available IT Service has no planned or unplanned Downtime.

Continuous Operation

(Service Design) An approach or design to eliminate planned Downtime of an IT Service. Note that individual Configuration Items may be down even though the IT Service is Available.

Contract

A legally binding Agreement between two or more parties.

Contract Portfolio

(Service Strategy) A database or structured Document used to manage Service Contracts or Agreements between an IT Service Provider and their Customers. Each IT Service delivered to a Customer should have a Contract or other Agreement that is listed in the Contract Portfolio. *See* Service Portfolio, Service Catalogue.

Control

A means of managing a Risk, ensuring that a Business Objective is achieved, or ensuring that a Process is followed. Example Controls include Policies, Procedures, Roles, RAID, door locks etc. A Control is sometimes called a Countermeasure or safeguard. Control also means to manage the utilization or behaviour of a Configuration Item, System or IT Service.

Control Objectives for Information and related Technology

See COBIT.

Control Perspective

(Service Strategy) An approach to the management of IT Services, Processes, Functions, Assets etc. There can be several different Control Perspectives on the same IT Service, Process etc., allowing different individuals or teams to focus on what is important and relevant to their specific Role. Example Control Perspectives include Reactive and Proactive management within IT Operations, or a Lifecycle view for an Application Project team.

Control Processes

The ISO/IEC 20000 Process group that includes Change Management and Configuration Management.

Core Service

(Service Strategy) An IT Service that delivers basic Outcomes desired by one or more Customers. *See also* Supporting Service, Core Service Package.

Core Service Package

(Service Strategy) A detailed description of a Core Service that may be shared by two or more Service Level Packages. *See also* Service Package.

Cost

The amount of money spent on a specific Activity, IT Service or Business Unit. Costs consist of real cost (money), notional cost such as people's time, and Depreciation.

Cost Benefit Analysis

An Activity that analyses and compares the costs and the benefits involved in one or more alternative courses of action. *See also* Business Case, Net Present Value, Internal Rate of Return, Return on Investment, Value on Investment.

Cost Centre

(Service Strategy) A Business Unit or Project to which costs are assigned. A Cost Centre does not charge for Services provided. An IT Service Provider can be run as a Cost Centre or a Profit Centre.

Cost Effectiveness

A measure of the balance between the Effectiveness and Cost of a Service, Process or activity. A Cost Effective Process is one that achieves its Objectives at minimum Cost. *See also* KPI, Return on Investment, Value for Money.

Cost Element

(Service Strategy) The middle level of category to which Costs are assigned in Budgeting and Accounting. The highest-level category is Cost Type. For example a Cost Type of 'people' could have cost elements of payroll, staff benefits, expenses, training, overtime etc. Cost Elements can be further broken down to give Cost Units. For example the Cost Element 'expenses' could include Cost Units of Hotels, Transport, Meals etc.

Cost Management

(Service Strategy) A general term that is used to refer to Budgeting and Accounting, sometimes used as a synonym for Financial Management.

Cost Type

(Service Strategy) The highest level of category to which Costs are assigned in Budgeting and Accounting. For example hardware, software, people, accommodation, external and Transfer. *See also* Cost Element, Cost Unit.

Cost Unit

(Service Strategy) The lowest level of category to which Costs are assigned, Cost Units are usually things that can be easily counted (e.g. staff numbers, software licences) or things easily measured (e.g. CPU usage, electricity consumed). Cost Units are included within Cost Elements. For example a Cost Element of 'expenses' could include Cost Units of hotels, transport, meals etc. *See also* Cost Type.

Countermeasure

Can be used to refer to any type of Control. The term Countermeasure is most often used when referring to measures that increase Resilience, Fault Tolerance or Reliability of an IT Service.

Course Corrections

Changes made to a Plan or Activity that has already started to ensure that it will meet its Objectives. Course corrections are made as a result of Monitoring progress.

CRAMM

A methodology and tool for analysing and managing Risks. CRAMM was developed by the UK Government, but is now privately owned. *See* www.cramm.com for further information.

Crisis Management

(IT Service Continuity Management) Crisis Management is the Process responsible for managing the wider implications of Business Continuity. A Crisis Management team is responsible for Strategic issues such as managing media relations and shareholder confidence, and decides when to invoke Business Continuity Plans.

Critical Success Factor

Something that must happen if a Process, Project, Plan or IT Service is to succeed. KPIs are used to measure the achievement of each CSF. For example a CSF of 'protect IT Services when making Changes' could be measured by KPIs such as 'percentage reduction of unsuccessful Changes', 'percentage reduction in Changes causing Incidents' etc.

Culture

A set of values that is shared by a group of people, including expectations about how people should behave, their ideas, beliefs and practices. *See also* Vision.

Customer

Someone who buys goods or Services. The Customer of an IT Service Provider is the person or group that defines and agrees the Service Level Targets. The term Customers is also sometimes informally used to mean Users, for example 'this is a Customer-focused Organization'.

Customer Portfolio

(Service Strategy) A database or structured Document used to record all Customers of the IT Service Provider. The Customer Portfolio is the Business Relationship Manager's view of the Customers who receive Services from the IT Service Provider. *See also* Contract Portfolio, Service Portfolio.

Dashboard

(Service Operation) A graphical representation of overall IT Service Performance and Availability. Dashboard images may be updated in real-time, and can also be included in management reports and web pages. Dashboards can be used to support Service Level Management, Event Management or Incident Diagnosis.

Data-to-Information-to-Knowledge-to-Wisdom

A way of understanding the relationships between data, information, knowledge and wisdom. DIKW shows how each of these builds on the others.

Definitive Media Library

(Service Transition) One or more locations in which the definitive and approved versions of all software Configuration Items are securely stored. The DML may also contain associated CIs such as licences and documentation. The DML is a single logical storage area even if there are multiple locations. All software in the DML is under the control of Change and Release Management and is recorded in the Configuration Management System. Only software from the DML is acceptable for use in a Release.

Deliverable

Something that must be provided to meet a commitment in a Service Level Agreement or a Contract. Deliverable is also used in a more informal way to mean a planned output of any Process.

Demand Management

Activities that understand and influence Customer demand for Services and the provision of Capacity to meet these demands. At a Strategic level Demand Management can involve analysis of Patterns of Business Activity and User Profiles. At a tactical level it can involve use of Differential Charging to encourage Customers to use IT Services at less busy times. *See also* Capacity Management.

Deming Cycle

See Plan-Do-Check-Act.

Dependency

The direct or indirect reliance of one Process or Activity on another.

Deployment

(Service Transition) The Activity responsible for movement of new or changed hardware, software, documentation, Process etc. to the Live Environment. Deployment is part of the Release and Deployment Management Process. *See also* Rollout.

Depreciation

(Service Strategy) A measure of the reduction in value of an Asset over its life. This is based on wearing out, consumption or other reduction in the useful economic value.

Design

(Service Design) An Activity or Process that identifies Requirements and then defines a solution that is able to meet these Requirements. *See also* Service Design.

Detection

(Service Operation) A stage in the Incident Lifecycle. Detection results in the Incident becoming known to the Service Provider. Detection can be automatic, or can be the result of a user logging an Incident.

Development

(Service Design) The Process responsible for creating or modifying an IT Service or Application. Also used to mean the Role or group that carries out Development work.

Development Environment

(Service Design) An Environment used to create or modify IT Services or Applications. Development Environments are not typically subjected to the same degree of control as Test Environments or Live Environments. *See also* Development.

Diagnosis

(Service Operation) A stage in the Incident and Problem Lifecycles. The purpose of Diagnosis is to identify a Workaround for an Incident or the Root Cause of a Problem.

Diagnostic Script

(Service Operation) A structured set of questions used by Service Desk staff to ensure they ask the correct questions, and to help them Classify, Resolve and assign Incidents. Diagnostic Scripts may also be made available to Users to help them diagnose and resolve their own Incidents.

Differential Charging

A technique used to support Demand Management by charging different amounts for the same IT Service Function at different times.

Direct Cost

(Service Strategy) A cost of providing an IT Service which can be allocated in full to a specific Customer, Cost Centre, Project etc. For example, the cost of providing non-shared servers or software licences. *See also* Indirect Cost.

Directory Service

(Service Operation) An Application that manages information about IT Infrastructure available on a network, and corresponding User access Rights.

Do Nothing

(Service Design) A Recovery Option. The Service Provider formally agrees with the Customer that Recovery of this IT Service will not be performed.

Document

Information in readable form. A Document may be paper or electronic. For example, a Policy statement, Service Level Agreement, Incident Record, diagram of computer room layout. *See also* Record.

Downtime

(Service Design) (Service Operation) The time when a Configuration Item or IT Service is not Available during its Agreed Service Time. The Availability of an IT Service is often calculated from Agreed Service Time and Downtime.

Driver

Something that influences Strategy, Objectives or Requirements. For example, new legislation or the actions of competitors.

Early Life Support

(Service Transition) Support provided for a new or Changed IT Service for a period of time after it is Released. During Early Life Support the IT Service Provider may review the KPIs, Service Levels and Monitoring Thresholds, and provide additional Resources for Incident and Problem Management.

Economies of scale

(Service Strategy) The reduction in average Cost that is possible from increasing the usage of an IT Service or Asset. *See also* Economies of scope.

Economies of scope

(Service Strategy) The reduction in Cost that is allocated to an IT Service by using an existing Asset for an additional purpose. For example, delivering a new IT Service from existing IT Infrastructure. *See also* Economies of scale.

Effectiveness

(Continual Service Improvement) A measure of whether the Objectives of a Process, Service or Activity have been achieved. An Effective Process or activity is one that achieves its agreed Objectives. *See also* KPI.

Efficiency

(Continual Service Improvement) A measure of whether the right amount of resources have been used to deliver a Process, Service or Activity. An Efficient Process achieves its Objectives with the minimum amount of time, money, people or other resources. *See also* KPI.

Emergency Change

(Service Transition) A Change that must be introduced as soon as possible. For example, to resolve a Major Incident or implement a Security patch. The Change Management Process will normally have a specific Procedure for handling Emergency Changes. *See also* Emergency Change Advisory Board (ECAB).

Emergency Change Advisory Board

(Service Transition) A sub-set of the Change Advisory Board that makes decisions about high-impact Emergency Changes. Membership of the ECAB may be decided at the time a meeting is called, and depends on the nature of the Emergency Change.

Environment

(Service Transition) A subset of the IT Infrastructure that is used for a particular purpose. For example: Live Environment, Test Environment, Build Environment. It is possible for multiple Environments to share a Configuration Item, for example Test and Live Environments may use different partitions on a single mainframe computer. Also used in the term Physical Environment to mean the accommodation, air conditioning, power system etc.

Environment is also used as a generic term to mean the external conditions that influence or affect something.

Error

(Service Operation) A design flaw or malfunction that causes a Failure of one or more Configuration Items or IT Services. A mistake made by a person or a faulty Process that affects a CI or IT Service is also an Error.

Escalation

(Service Operation) An Activity that obtains additional Resources when these are needed to meet Service Level Targets or Customer expectations. Escalation may be needed within any IT Service Management Process, but is most commonly associated with Incident Management, Problem Management and the management of Customer complaints. There are two types of Escalation, Functional Escalation and Hierarchic Escalation.

eSourcing Capability Model for Client Organizations

(Service Strategy) A framework to help Organizations guide their analysis and decisions on Service Sourcing Models and Strategies. eSCM-CL was developed by Carnegie Mellon University, US. *See also* eSourcing Capability Model for Service Providers.

eSourcing Capability Model for Service Providers

(Service Strategy) A framework to help IT Service Providers develop their IT Service Management Capabilities from a Service Sourcing perspective. eSCM-SP was developed by Carnegie Mellon University, US. *See also* eSourcing Capability Model for Client Organizations.

Estimation

The use of experience to provide an approximate value for a Metric or Cost. Estimation is also used in Capacity and Availability Management as the cheapest and least accurate Modelling method.

Evaluation

(Service Transition) The Process responsible for assessing a new or Changed IT Service to ensure that Risks have been managed and to help determine whether to proceed with the Change.

Evaluation is also used to mean comparing an actual Outcome with the intended Outcome, or comparing one alternative with another.

Event

(Service Operation) A change of state that has significance for the management of a Configuration Item or IT Service.

The term Event is also used to mean an Alert or notification created by any IT Service, Configuration Item or Monitoring tool. Events typically require IT Operations personnel to take actions, and often lead to Incidents being logged.

Event Management

(Service Operation) The Process responsible for managing Events throughout their Lifecycle. Event Management is one of the main Activities of IT Operations.

Exception Report

A Document containing details of one or more KPIs or other important targets that have exceeded defined thresholds. Examples include SLA targets being missed or about to be missed, and a Performance Metric indicating a potential Capacity problem.

Expanded Incident Lifecycle

(Availability Management) Detailed stages in the Lifecycle of an Incident. The stages are Detection, Diagnosis, Repair, Recovery, Restoration. The Expanded Incident Lifecycle is used to help understand all contributions to the Impact of Incidents and to Plan how these could be controlled or reduced.

External Customer

A Customer who works for a different Business to the IT Service Provider. *See also* External Service Provider, Internal Customer.

External Metric

A Metric that is used to measure the delivery of IT Service to a Customer. External Metrics are usually defined in SLAs and reported to Customers. *See also* Internal Metric.

External Service Provider

(Service Strategy) An IT Service Provider that is part of a different Organization to its Customer. An IT Service Provider may have both Internal Customers and External Customers. *See also* Type III Service Provider.

External Sourcing

See Outsourcing.

Facilities Management

(Service Operation) The Function responsible for managing the physical Environment where the IT Infrastructure is located. Facilities Management includes all aspects of managing the physical Environment, for example power and cooling, building Access Management, and environmental Monitoring.

Failure

(Service Operation) Loss of ability to Operate to Specification, or to deliver the required output. The term Failure may be used when referring to IT Services, Processes, Activities, Configuration Items etc. A Failure often causes an Incident.

Failure Modes and Effects Analysis

An approach to assessing the potential Impact of Failures. FMEA involves analysing what would happen after Failure of each Configuration Item, all the way up to the effect on the Business. FMEA is often used in Information Security Management and in IT Service Continuity Planning.

Fast Recovery

(Service Design) A Recovery Option that is also known as Hot Standby. Provision is made to Recover the IT Service in a short period of time: typically less than 24 hours. Immediate Recovery typically uses a dedicated Fixed Facility with computer Systems, and software configured ready to run the IT Services. Immediate Recovery may take up to 24 hours if there is a need to Restore data from Backups.

Fault

See Error.

Fault Tolerance

(Service Design) The ability of an IT Service or Configuration Item to continue to Operate correctly after Failure of a Component part. *See also* Resilience, Countermeasure.

Fault Tree Analysis

(Service Design) (Continual Service Improvement) A technique that can be used to determine the chain of events that leads to a Problem. Fault Tree Analysis represents a chain of events using Boolean notation in a diagram.

Financial Management

(Service Strategy) The Function and Processes responsible for managing an IT Service Provider's Budgeting, Accounting and Charging Requirements.

First-line Support

(Service Operation) The first level in a hierarchy of Support Groups involved in the resolution of Incidents. Each level contains more specialist skills, or has more time or other resources. *See also* Escalation.

Fishbone Diagram

See Ishikawa Diagram.

Fit for Purpose

An informal term used to describe a Process, Configuration Item, IT Service etc. that is capable of meeting its objectives or Service Levels. Being Fit for Purpose requires suitable design, implementation, control and maintenance.

Fixed Cost

(Service Strategy) A Cost that does not vary with IT Service usage. For example the cost of Server hardware. *See also* Variable Cost.

Fixed Facility

(Service Design) A permanent building, available for use when needed by an IT Service Continuity Plan. *See also* Recovery Option, Portable Facility.

Follow the Sun

(Service Operation) A methodology for using Service Desks and Support Groups around the world to provide seamless 24/7 Service. Calls, Incidents, Problems and Service Requests are passed between groups in different time zones.

Fulfilment

Performing Activities to meet a need or Requirement. For example, by providing a new IT Service, or meeting a Service Request.

Function

A team or group of people and the tools they use to carry out one or more Processes or Activities. For example the Service Desk.

The term Function also has two other meanings:

- An intended purpose of a Configuration Item, Person, Team, Process or IT Service. For example one Function of an e-mail Service may be to store and forward outgoing mails, one Function of a Business Process may be to dispatch goods to Customers
- To perform the intended purpose correctly, 'The computer is Functioning'.

Functional Escalation

(Service Operation) Transferring an Incident, Problem or Change to a technical team with a higher level of expertise to assist in an Escalation.

Gap Analysis

(Continual Service Improvement) An Activity that compares two sets of data and identifies the differences. Gap Analysis is commonly used to compare a set of Requirements with actual delivery. *See also* Benchmarking.

Governance

Ensuring that Policies and Strategy are actually implemented, and that required Processes are correctly followed. Governance includes defining Roles and responsibilities, measuring and reporting, and taking actions to resolve any issues identified.

Gradual Recovery

(IT Service Continuity Management) A Recovery Option that is also known as Cold Standby. Provision is made to Recover the IT Service in a period of time greater than 72 hours. Gradual Recovery typically uses a Portable or Fixed Facility that has environmental support and network cabling, but no computer Systems. The hardware and software are installed as part of the IT Service Continuity Plan.

Guideline

A Document describing Best Practice, which recommends what should be done. Compliance with a Guideline is not normally enforced. *See also* Standard.

Help Desk

(Service Operation) A point of contact for Users to log Incidents. A Help Desk is usually more technically focussed than a Service Desk and does not provide a Single Point of Contact for all interaction. The term Help Desk is often used as a synonym for Service Desk.

Hierarchic Escalation

(Service Operation) Informing or involving more senior levels of management to assist in an Escalation.

High Availability

(Service Design) An approach or design that minimizes or hides the effects of Configuration Item Failure on the users of an IT Service. High Availability solutions are designed to achieve an agreed level of Availability and make use of techniques such as Fault Tolerance, Resilience and Fast Recovery to reduce the number of Incidents, and the Impact of Incidents.

Hot Standby

See Fast Recovery or Immediate Recovery.

Identity

(Service Operation) A unique name that is used to identify a User, person or Role. The Identity is used to grant Rights to that User, person or Roles. Example Identities might be the username SmithJ or the Role 'Change manager'.

Immediate Recovery

(Service Design) A Recovery Option that is also known as Hot Standby. Provision is made to Recover the IT Service with no loss of Service. Immediate Recovery typically uses Mirroring, Load Balancing and Split Site technologies.

Impact

(Service Operation) (Service Transition) A measure of the effect of an Incident, Problem or Change on Business Processes. Impact is often based on how Service Levels will be affected. Impact and Urgency are used to assign Priority.

Incident

(Service Operation) An unplanned interruption to an IT Service or reduction in the Quality of an IT Service. Failure of a Configuration Item that has not yet affected Service is also an Incident. For example Failure of one disk from a mirror set.

Incident Management

(Service Operation) The Process responsible for managing the Lifecycle of all Incidents. The primary Objective of Incident Management is to return the IT Service to Customers as quickly as possible.

Incident Record

(Service Operation) A Record containing the details of an Incident. Each Incident record documents the Lifecycle of a single Incident.

Indirect Cost

(Service Strategy) A Cost of providing an IT Service, which cannot be allocated in full to a specific Customer. For example, the Cost of providing shared Servers or software licences. Also known as Overhead. *See also* Direct Cost.

Information Security Management

(Service Design) The Process that ensures the Confidentiality, Integrity and Availability of an Organization's Assets, information, data and IT Services. Information Security Management usually forms part of an Organizational approach to Security Management that has a wider scope than the IT Service Provider, and includes handling of paper, building access, phone calls etc. for the entire Organization.

Information Security Management System

(Service Design) The framework of Policy, Processes, Standards, Guidelines and tools that ensures an Organization can achieve its Information Security Management Objectives.

Information Security Policy

(Service Design) The Policy that governs the Organization's approach to Information Security Management.

Information Technology

The use of technology for the storage, communication or processing of information. The technology typically includes computers, telecommunications, Applications and other software. The information may include Business data, voice, images, video etc. Information Technology is often used to support Business Processes through IT Services.

Infrastructure Service

An IT Service that is not directly used by the Business, but is required by the IT Service Provider so they can provide other IT Services. For example directory services, naming services or communication services.

Insourcing

See Internal Sourcing.

Integrity

(Service Design) A security principle that ensures data and Configuration Items are modified only by authorized personnel and Activities. Integrity considers all possible causes of modification, including software and hardware Failure, environmental Events and human intervention.

Interactive Voice Response

(Service Operation) A form of Automatic Call Distribution that accepts User input, such as key presses and spoken commands, to identify the correct destination for incoming Calls.

Intermediate Recovery

(Service Design) A Recovery Option that is also known as Warm Standby. Provision is made to Recover the IT Service in a period of time between 24 and 72 hours. Intermediate Recovery typically uses a shared Portable or Fixed Facility that has Computer Systems and Network Components. The hardware and software will need to be configured, and data will need to be restored, as part of the IT Service Continuity Plan.

Internal Customer

A Customer who works for the same Business as the IT Service Provider. *See also* Internal Service Provider, External Customer.

Internal Metric

A Metric that is used within the IT Service Provider to Monitor the Efficiency, Effectiveness or Cost Effectiveness of the IT Service Provider's internal Processes. Internal Metrics are not normally reported to the Customer of the IT Service. *See also* External Metric.

Internal Rate of Return

(Service Strategy) A technique used to help make decisions about Capital Expenditure. IRR calculates a figure that allows two or more alternative investments to be compared. A larger IRR indicates a better investment. *See also* Net Present Value, Return on Investment.

Internal Service Provider

(Service Strategy) An IT Service Provider that is part of the same Organization as its Customer. An IT Service Provider may have both Internal Customers and External Customers. *See also* Type I Service Provider, Type II Service Provider.

Internal Sourcing

(Service Strategy) Using an Internal Service Provider to manage IT Services. *See also* Service Sourcing, Type I Service Provider, Type II Service Provider.

International Organization for Standardization

The International Organization for Standardization (ISO) is the world's largest developer of Standards. ISO is a non-governmental organization that is a network of the national standards institutes of 156 countries. *See* www.iso.org for further information about ISO.

International Standards Organization

See International Organization for Standardization (ISO).

Internet Service Provider

An External Service Provider that provides access to the Internet. Most ISPs also provide other IT Services such as web hosting.

Invocation

(Service Design) Initiation of the steps defined in a plan. For example initiating the IT Service Continuity Plan for one or more IT Services.

Ishikawa Diagram

(Service Operation) (Continual Service Improvement) A technique that helps a team to identify all the possible causes of a Problem. Originally devised by Kaoru Ishikawa, the output of this technique is a diagram that looks like a fishbone.

ISO 9000

A generic term that refers to a number of international Standards and Guidelines for Quality Management Systems. *See* www.iso.org for more information. *See also* ISO.

ISO 9001

An international Standard for Quality Management Systems. *See also* ISO 9000, Standard.

ISO/IEC 17799

(Continual Service Improvement) ISO Code of Practice for Information Security Management. *See also* Standard.

ISO/IEC 20000

ISO Specification and Code of Practice for IT Service Management. ISO/IEC 20000 is aligned with ITIL Best Practice.

ISO/IEC 27001

(Service Design) (Continual Service Improvement) ISO Specification for Information Security Management. The corresponding Code of Practice is ISO/IEC 17799. *See also* Standard.

IT Directorate

(Continual Service Improvement) Senior Management within a Service Provider, charged with developing and delivering IT services. Most commonly used in UK Government departments.

IT Infrastructure

All of the hardware, software, networks, facilities, etc. that are required to develop, Test, deliver, Monitor, Control or support IT Services. The term IT Infrastructure includes all of the Information Technology but not the associated people, Processes and documentation.

IT Operations

(Service Operation) Activities carried out by IT Operations Control, including Console Management, Job Scheduling, Backup and Restore, and Print and Output Management. IT Operations is also used as a synonym for Service Operation.

IT Operations Control

(Service Operation) The Function responsible for Monitoring and Control of the IT Services and IT Infrastructure. *See also* Operations Bridge.

IT Operations Management

(Service Operation) The Function within an IT Service Provider that performs the daily Activities needed to manage IT Services and the supporting IT Infrastructure. IT Operations Management includes IT Operations Control and Facilities Management.

IT Service

A Service provided to one or more Customers by an IT Service Provider. An IT Service is based on the use of Information Technology and supports the Customer's Business Processes. An IT Service is made up from a combination of people, Processes and technology and should be defined in a Service Level Agreement.

IT Service Continuity Management

(Service Design) The Process responsible for managing Risks that could seriously affect IT Services. ITSCM ensures that the IT Service Provider can always provide minimum agreed Service Levels, by reducing the Risk to an acceptable level and Planning for the Recovery of IT Services. ITSCM should be designed to support Business Continuity Management.

IT Service Continuity Plan

(Service Design) A Plan defining the steps required to Recover one or more IT Services. The Plan will also identify the triggers for Invocation, people to be involved, communications etc. The IT Service Continuity Plan should be part of a Business Continuity Plan.

IT Service Management

The implementation and management of Quality IT Services that meet the needs of the Business. IT Service Management is performed by IT Service Providers through an appropriate mix of people, Process and Information Technology. *See also* Service Management.

IT Service Management Forum

The IT Service Management Forum is an independent Organization dedicated to promoting a professional approach to IT Service Management. The itSMF is a not-for-profit membership Organization with representation in many countries around the world (itSMF Chapters). The itSMF and its membership contribute to the development of ITIL and associated IT Service Management Standards. *See* www.itsmf.com for more information.

IT Service Provider

(Service Strategy) A Service Provider that provides IT Services to Internal Customers or External Customers.

IT Steering Group

A formal group that is responsible for ensuring that Business and IT Service Provider Strategies and Plans are closely aligned. An IT Steering Group includes senior representatives from the Business and the IT Service Provider.

ITIL

A set of Best Practice guidance for IT Service Management. ITIL is owned by the OGC and consists of a series of publications giving guidance on the provision of Quality IT Services, and on the Processes and facilities needed to support them. *See* www.itil.co.uk for more information.

Job Description

A Document that defines the Roles, responsibilities, skills and knowledge required by a particular person. One Job Description can include multiple Roles, for example the Roles of Configuration Manager and Change Manager may be carried out by one person.

Job Scheduling

(Service Operation) Planning and managing the execution of software tasks that are required as part of an IT Service. Job Scheduling is carried out by IT Operations Management, and is often automated using software tools that run batch or online tasks at specific times of the day, week, month or year.

Kano Model

(Service Strategy) A Model developed by Noriaki Kano that is used to help understand Customer preferences. The Kano Model considers Attributes of an IT Service grouped into areas such as Basic Factors, Excitement Factors, Performance Factors, etc.

Kepner & Tregoe Analysis

(Service Operation) (Continual Service Improvement) A structured approach to Problem solving. The Problem is analysed in terms of what, where, when and extent. Possible causes are identified. The most probable cause is tested. The true cause is verified.

Key Performance Indicator

(Service Design) (Continual Service Improvement) A Metric that is used to help manage a Process, IT Service or Activity. Many Metrics may be measured, but only the most important of these are defined as KPIs and used to actively manage and report on the Process, IT Service or Activity. KPIs should be selected to ensure that Efficiency, Effectiveness and Cost Effectiveness are all managed. *See also* Critical Success Factor.

Knowledge Base

(Service Transition) A logical database containing the data used by the Service Knowledge Management System.

Knowledge Management

(Service Transition) The Process responsible for gathering, analysing, storing and sharing knowledge and information within an Organization. The primary purpose of Knowledge Management is to improve Efficiency by reducing the need to rediscover knowledge. *See also* Data-to-Information-to-Knowledge-to-Wisdom.

Known Error

(Service Operation) A Problem that has a documented Root Cause and a Workaround. Known Errors are created and managed throughout their Lifecycle by Problem Management. Known Errors may also be identified by Development or Suppliers.

Known Error Database

(Service Operation) A database containing all Known Error Records. This database is created by Problem Management and used by Incident and Problem Management. The Known Error Database is part of the Service Knowledge Management System.

Known Error Record

(Service Operation) A Record containing the details of a Known Error. Each Known Error Record documents the Lifecycle of a Known Error, including the Status, Root Cause and Workaround. In some implementations a Known Error is documented using additional fields in a Problem Record.

Lifecycle

The various stages in the life of an IT Service, Configuration Item, Incident, Problem, Change etc. The Lifecycle defines the Categories for Status and the Status transitions that are permitted. For example:

- The Lifecycle of an Application includes Requirements, Design, Build, Deploy, Operate, Optimize

- The Expanded Incident Lifecycle includes Detect, Respond, Diagnose, Repair, Recover, Restore
- The Lifecycle of a Server may include: Ordered, Received, In Test, Live, Disposed etc.

Line of Service

(Service Strategy) A Core Service or Supporting Service that has multiple Service Level Packages. A line of Service is managed by a Product Manager and each Service Level Package is designed to support a particular market segment.

Live

(Service Transition) Refers to an IT Service or Configuration Item that is being used to deliver Service to a Customer.

Live Environment

(Service Transition) A controlled Environment containing Live Configuration Items used to deliver IT Services to Customers.

Maintainability

(Service Design) A measure of how quickly and Effectively a Configuration Item or IT Service can be restored to normal working after a Failure. Maintainability is often measured and reported as MTRS.

Maintainability is also used in the context of Software or IT Service Development to mean ability to be Changed or Repaired easily.

Major Incident

(Service Operation) The highest Category of Impact for an Incident. A Major Incident results in significant disruption to the Business.

Managed Services

(Service Strategy) A perspective on IT Services that emphasizes the fact that they are managed. The term Managed Services is also used as a synonym for Outsourced IT Services.

Management Information

Information that is used to support decision-making by managers. Management Information is often generated automatically by tools supporting the various IT Service Management Processes. Management Information often includes the values of KPIs such as 'Percentage of Changes leading to Incidents', or 'first-time fix rate'.

Management of Risk

The OGC methodology for managing Risks. M_o_R includes all the Activities required to identify and Control the exposure to Risk, which may have an impact on the achievement of an Organization's Business Objectives. *See* www.m-o-r.org for more details.

Management System

The framework of Policy, Processes and Functions that ensures an Organization can achieve its Objectives.

Manual Workaround

A Workaround that requires manual intervention. Manual Workaround is also used as the name of a Recovery Option in which The Business Process Operates without the use of IT Services. This is a temporary measure and is usually combined with another Recovery Option.

Marginal Cost

(Service Strategy) The Cost of continuing to provide the IT Service. Marginal Cost does not include investment already made, for example the cost of developing new software and delivering training.

Market Space

(Service Strategy) All opportunities that an IT Service Provider could exploit to meet business needs of Customers. The Market Space identifies the possible IT Services that an IT Service Provider may wish to consider delivering.

Maturity

(Continual Service Improvement) A measure of the Reliability, Efficiency and Effectiveness of a Process, Function, Organization etc. The most mature Processes and Functions are formally aligned to Business Objectives and Strategy, and are supported by a framework for continual improvement.

Maturity Level

A named level in a Maturity model such as the Carnegie Mellon Capability Maturity Model Integration.

Mean Time Between Failures

(Service Design) A Metric for measuring and reporting Reliability. MTBF is the average time that a Configuration Item or IT Service can perform its agreed Function without interruption. This is measured from when the CI or IT Service starts working, until it next fails.

Mean Time Between Service Incidents

(Service Design) A Metric used for measuring and reporting Reliability. MTBSI is the mean time from when a System or IT Service fails, until it next fails. MTBSI is equal to MTBF + MTRS.

Mean Time To Repair

The average time taken to repair a Configuration Item or IT Service after a Failure. MTTR is measured from when the CI or IT Service fails until it is repaired. MTTR does not include the time required to Recover or Restore. MTTR is sometimes incorrectly used to mean Mean Time to Restore Service.

Mean Time to Restore Service

The average time taken to restore a Configuration Item or IT Service after a Failure. MTRS is measured from when the CI or IT Service fails until it is fully restored and delivering its normal functionality. *See also* Maintainability, Mean Time to Repair.

Metric

(Continual Service Improvement) Something that is measured and reported to help manage a Process, IT Service or Activity. *See also* KPI.

Middleware

(Service Design) Software that connects two or more software Components or Applications. Middleware is usually purchased from a Supplier, rather than developed within the IT Service Provider. *See also* Off the Shelf.

Mission Statement

The Mission Statement of an Organization is a short but complete description of the overall purpose and intentions of that Organization. It states what is to be achieved, but not how this should be done.

Model

A representation of a System, Process, IT Service, Configuration Item etc. that is used to help understand or predict future behaviour.

Modelling

A technique that is used to predict the future behaviour of a System, Process, IT Service, Configuration Item etc. Modelling is commonly used in Financial Management, Capacity Management and Availability Management.

Monitor Control Loop

(Service Operation) Monitoring the output of a Task, Process, IT Service or Configuration Item; comparing this output to a predefined Norm; and taking appropriate action based on this comparison.

Monitoring

(Service Operation) Repeated observation of a Configuration Item, IT Service or Process to detect Events and to ensure that the current status is known.

Near-Shore

(Service Strategy) Provision of Services from a country near the country where the Customer is based. This can be the provision of an IT Service, or of supporting Functions such as Service Desk. *See also* On-shore, Off-shore.

Net Present Value

(Service Strategy) A technique used to help make decisions about Capital Expenditure. NPV compares cash inflows with cash outflows. Positive NPV indicates that an investment is worthwhile. *See also* Internal Rate of Return, Return on Investment.

Notional Charging

(Service Strategy) An approach to Charging for IT Services. Charges to Customers are calculated and Customers are informed of the charge, but no money is actually transferred. Notional Charging is sometimes introduced to ensure that Customers are aware of the Costs they incur, or as a stage during the introduction of real Charging.

Objective

The defined purpose or aim of a Process, an Activity or an Organization as a whole. Objectives are usually expressed as measurable targets. The term Objective is also informally used to mean a Requirement. *See also* Outcome.

Off the Shelf

See Commercial Off the Shelf.

Office of Government Commerce

OGC owns the ITIL brand (copyright and trademark). OGC is a UK Government department that supports the delivery of the government's procurement agenda through its work in collaborative procurement and in raising levels of procurement skills and capability with departments. It also provides support for complex public sector projects.

Office of Public Sector Information

OPSI licenses the Crown Copyright material used in the ITIL publications. OPSI is a UK Government department that provides online access to UK legislation, licenses the re-use of Crown Copyright material, manages the Information Fair Trader Scheme, maintains the Government's Information Asset Register and provides advice and guidance on official publishing and Crown Copyright.

Off-shore

(Service Strategy) Provision of Services from a location outside the country where the Customer is based, often in a different continent. This can be the provision of an IT Service, or of supporting Functions such as Service Desk. *See also* On-shore, Near-shore.

On-shore

(Service Strategy) Provision of Services from a location within the country where the Customer is based. *See also* Off-shore, Near-shore.

Operate

To perform as expected. A Process or Configuration Item is said to Operate if it is delivering the Required outputs. Operate also means to perform one or more Operations. For example, to Operate a computer is to do the day-to-day Operations needed for it to perform as expected.

Operation

(Service Operation) Day-to-day management of an IT Service, System, or other Configuration Item. Operation is also used to mean any pre-defined Activity or Transaction. For example loading a magnetic tape, accepting money at a point of sale, or reading data from a disk drive.

Operational

The lowest of three levels of Planning and delivery (Strategic, Tactical, Operational). Operational Activities include the day-to-day or short-term Planning or delivery of a Business Process or IT Service Management Process. The term Operational is also a synonym for Live.

Operational Cost

Cost resulting from running the IT Services. Often repeating payments. For example staff costs, hardware maintenance and electricity (also known as 'current expenditure' or 'revenue expenditure'). *See also* Capital Expenditure.

Operational Expenditure

See Operational Cost.

Operational Level Agreement

(Service Design) (Continual Service Improvement) An Agreement between an IT Service Provider and another part of the same Organization. An OLA supports the IT Service Provider's delivery of IT Services to Customers. The OLA defines the goods or Services to be provided and the responsibilities of both parties. For example there could be an OLA:

- Between the IT Service Provider and a procurement department to obtain hardware in agreed times
- Between the Service Desk and a Support Group to provide Incident Resolution in agreed times.

See also Service Level Agreement.

Operations Bridge

(Service Operation) A physical location where IT Services and IT Infrastructure are monitored and managed.

Operations Control

See IT Operations Control.

Operations Management

See IT Operations Management.

Opportunity Cost

(Service Strategy) A Cost that is used in deciding between investment choices. Opportunity Cost represents the revenue that would have been generated by using the Resources in a different way. For example the Opportunity Cost of purchasing a new Server may include not carrying out a Service Improvement activity that the money could have been spent on. Opportunity cost analysis is used as part of decision-making processes, but is not treated as an actual Cost in any financial statement.

Optimize

Review, Plan and request Changes, in order to obtain the maximum Efficiency and Effectiveness from a Process, Configuration Item, Application etc.

Organization

A company, legal entity or other institution. Examples of Organizations that are not companies include International Standards Organization or itSMF. The term Organization is sometimes used to refer to any entity that has People, Resources and Budgets. For example a Project or Business Unit.

Outcome

The result of carrying out an Activity; following a Process; delivering an IT Service etc. The term Outcome is used to refer to intended results, as well as to actual results. *See also* Objective.

Outsourcing

(Service Strategy) Using an External Service Provider to manage IT Services. *See also* Service Sourcing, Type III Service Provider.

Overhead

See Indirect cost

Pain Value Analysis

(Service Operation) A technique used to help identify the Business Impact of one or more Problems. A formula is used to calculate Pain Value based on the number of Users affected, the duration of the Downtime, the Impact on each User, and the cost to the Business (if known).

Pareto Principle

(Service Operation) A technique used to prioritize Activities. The Pareto Principle says that 80% of the value of any activity is created with 20% of the effort. Pareto Analysis is also used in Problem Management to prioritize possible Problem causes for investigation.

Partnership

A relationship between two Organizations that involves working closely together for common goals or mutual benefit. The IT Service Provider should have a Partnership with the Business, and with Third Parties who are critical to the delivery of IT Services. *See also* Value Network.

Passive Monitoring

(Service Operation) Monitoring of a Configuration Item, an IT Service or a Process that relies on an Alert or notification to discover the current status. *See also* Active Monitoring.

Pattern of Business Activity

(Service Strategy) A Workload profile of one or more Business Activities. Patterns of Business Activity are used to help the IT Service Provider understand and plan for different levels of Business Activity. *See also* User Profile.

Percentage utilization

(Service Design) The amount of time that a Component is busy over a given period of time. For example, if a CPU is busy for 1,800 seconds in a one-hour period, its utilization is 50%.

Performance

A measure of what is achieved or delivered by a System, person, team, Process or IT Service.

Performance Anatomy

(Service Strategy) An approach to Organizational Culture that integrates, and actively manages, leadership and strategy, people development, technology enablement, performance management and innovation.

Performance Management

(Continual Service Improvement) The Process responsible for day-to-day Capacity Management Activities. These include monitoring, threshold detection, Performance analysis and Tuning, and implementing changes related to Performance and Capacity.

Pilot

(Service Transition) A limited Deployment of an IT Service, a Release or a Process to the Live Environment. A pilot is used to reduce Risk and to gain User feedback and Acceptance. *See also* Test, Evaluation.

Plan

A detailed proposal that describes the Activities and Resources needed to achieve an Objective. For example a Plan to implement a new IT Service or Process. ISO/IEC 20000 requires a Plan for the management of each IT Service Management Process.

Plan-Do-Check-Act

(Continual Service Improvement) A four-stage cycle for Process management, attributed to Edward Deming. Plan-Do-Check-Act is also called the Deming Cycle.

PLAN: Design or revise Processes that support the IT Services.

DO: Implement the Plan and manage the Processes.

CHECK: Measure the Processes and IT Services, compare with Objectives and produce reports.

ACT: Plan and implement Changes to improve the Processes.

Planned Downtime

(Service Design) Agreed time when an IT Service will not be available. Planned Downtime is often used for maintenance, upgrades and testing. *See also* Change Window, Downtime.

Planning

An Activity responsible for creating one or more Plans. For example, Capacity Planning.

PMBOK

A Project management Standard maintained and published by the Project Management Institute. PMBOK stands for Project Management Body of Knowledge. *See* www.pmi.org for more information. *See also* PRINCE2.

Policy

Formally documented management expectations and intentions. Policies are used to direct decisions, and to ensure consistent and appropriate development and implementation of Processes, Standards, Roles, Activities, IT Infrastructure etc.

Portable Facility

(Service Design) A prefabricated building, or a large vehicle, provided by a Third Party and moved to a site when needed by an IT Service Continuity Plan. *See also* Recovery Option, Fixed Facility.

Post-Implementation Review

A Review that takes place after a Change or a Project has been implemented. A PIR determines if the Change or Project was successful, and identifies opportunities for improvement.

Practice

A way of working, or a way in which work must be done. Practices can include Activities, Processes, Functions, Standards and Guidelines. *See also* Best Practice.

Prerequisite for Success

An Activity that needs to be completed, or a condition that needs to be met, to enable successful implementation of a Plan or Process. A PFS is often an output from one Process that is a required input to another Process.

Pricing

(Service Strategy) Pricing is the Activity for establishing how much Customers will be Charged.

PRINCE2

The standard UK government methodology for Project management. *See* www.ogc.gov.uk/prince2 for more information. *See also* PMBOK.

Priority

(Service Transition) (Service Operation) A Category used to identify the relative importance of an Incident, Problem or Change. Priority is based on Impact and Urgency, and is used to identify required times for actions to be taken. For example the SLA may state that Priority 2 Incidents must be resolved within 12 hours.

Proactive Monitoring

(Service Operation) Monitoring that looks for patterns of Events to predict possible future Failures. *See also* Reactive Monitoring.

Proactive Problem Management

(Service Operation) Part of the Problem Management Process. The Objective of Proactive Problem Management is to identify Problems that might otherwise be missed. Proactive Problem Management analyses Incident Records, and uses data collected by other IT Service Management Processes to identify trends or significant problems.

Problem

(Service Operation) A cause of one or more Incidents. The cause is not usually known at the time a Problem Record is created, and the Problem Management Process is responsible for further investigation.

Problem Management

(Service Operation) The Process responsible for managing the Lifecycle of all Problems. The primary objectives of Problem Management are to prevent Incidents from happening, and to minimize the Impact of Incidents that cannot be prevented.

Problem Record

(Service Operation) A Record containing the details of a Problem. Each Problem Record documents the Lifecycle of a single Problem.

Procedure

A Document containing steps that specify how to achieve an Activity. Procedures are defined as part of Processes. *See also* Work Instruction.

Process

A structured set of Activities designed to accomplish a specific Objective. A Process takes one or more defined inputs and turns them into defined outputs. A Process may include any of the Roles, responsibilities, tools and management Controls required to reliably deliver the outputs. A Process may define Policies, Standards, Guidelines, Activities and Work Instructions if they are needed.

Process Control

The Activity of planning and regulating a Process, with the Objective of performing the Process in an Effective, Efficient and consistent manner.

Process Manager

A Role responsible for Operational management of a Process. The Process Manager's responsibilities include Planning and coordination of all Activities required to carry out, monitor and report on the Process. There may be several Process Managers for one Process, for example regional Change Managers or IT Service Continuity Managers for each data centre. The Process Manager Role is often assigned to the person who carries out the Process Owner Role, but the two Roles may be separate in larger Organizations.

Process Owner

A Role responsible for ensuring that a Process is Fit for Purpose. The Process Owner's responsibilities include sponsorship, Design, Change Management and continual improvement of the Process and its Metrics. This Role is often assigned to the same person who carries out the Process Manager Role, but the two Roles may be separate in larger Organizations.

Production Environment

See Live Environment.

Profit Centre

(Service Strategy) A Business Unit that charges for Services provided. A Profit Centre can be created with the objective of making a profit, recovering Costs, or running at a loss. An IT Service Provider can be run as a Cost Centre or a Profit Centre.

Pro-forma

A template, or example Document containing example data that will be replaced with the real values when these are available.

Programme

A number of Projects and Activities that are planned and managed together to achieve an overall set of related Objectives and other Outcomes.

Project

A temporary Organization, with people and other Assets required to achieve an Objective or other Outcome. Each Project has a Lifecycle that typically includes initiation, Planning, execution, Closure etc. Projects are usually managed using a formal methodology such as PRINCE2.

Projected Service Outage

(Service Transition) A Document that identifies the effect of planned Changes, maintenance Activities and Test Plans on agreed Service Levels.

PRojects IN Controlled Environments

See PRINCE2

Qualification

(Service Transition) An Activity that ensures that IT Infrastructure is appropriate, and correctly configured, to support an Application or IT Service. See also Validation.

Quality

The ability of a product, Service, or Process to provide the intended value. For example, a hardware Component can be considered to be of high Quality if it performs as expected and delivers the required Reliability. Process Quality also requires an ability to monitor Effectiveness and Efficiency, and to improve them if necessary. See also Quality Management System.

Quality Assurance

(Service Transition) The Process responsible for ensuring that the Quality of a product, Service or Process will provide its intended Value.

Quality Management System

(Continual Service Improvement) The set of Processes responsible for ensuring that all work carried out by an Organization is of a suitable Quality to reliably meet Business Objectives or Service Levels. See also ISO 9000.

Quick Win

(Continual Service Improvement) An improvement Activity that is expected to provide a Return on Investment in a short period of time with relatively small Cost and effort. See also Pareto Principle.

RACI

(Service Design) (Continual Service Improvement) A Model used to help define Roles and Responsibilities. RACI stands for Responsible, Accountable, Consulted and Informed.

Reactive Monitoring

(Service Operation) Monitoring that takes action in response to an Event. For example submitting a batch job when the previous job completes, or logging an Incident when an Error occurs. See also Proactive Monitoring.

Reciprocal Arrangement

(Service Design) A Recovery Option. An agreement between two Organizations to share resources in an emergency. For example, Computer Room space or use of a mainframe.

Record

A Document containing the results or other output from a Process or Activity. Records are evidence of the fact that an activity took place and may be paper or electronic. For example, an Audit report, an Incident Record, or the minutes of a meeting.

Recovery

(Service Design) (Service Operation) Returning a Configuration Item or an IT Service to a working state. Recovery of an IT Service often includes recovering data to a known consistent state. After Recovery, further steps may be needed before the IT Service can be made available to the Users (Restoration).

Recovery Option

(Service Design) A Strategy for responding to an interruption to Service. Commonly used Strategies are Do Nothing, Manual Workaround, Reciprocal Arrangement, Gradual Recovery, Intermediate Recovery, Fast Recovery, Immediate Recovery. Recovery Options may make use of dedicated facilities, or Third Party facilities shared by multiple Businesses.

Recovery Point Objective

(Service Operation) The maximum amount of data that may be lost when Service is Restored after an interruption. Recovery Point Objective is expressed as a length of time before the Failure. For example a Recovery Point Objective of one day may be supported by daily Backups, and up to 24 hours of data may be lost. Recovery Point Objectives for each IT Service should be negotiated, agreed and documented, and used as requirements for Service Design and IT Service Continuity Plans.

Recovery Time Objective

(Service Operation) The maximum time allowed for recovery of an IT Service following an interruption. The Service Level to be provided may be less than normal Service Level Targets. Recovery Time Objectives for each IT Service should be negotiated, agreed and documented. *See also* Business Impact Analysis.

Redundancy

See Fault Tolerance.

The term Redundant also has a generic meaning of obsolete, or no longer needed.

Relationship

A connection or interaction between two people or things. In Business Relationship Management it is the interaction between the IT Service Provider and the Business. In Configuration Management it is a link between two Configuration Items that identifies a dependency or connection between them. For example Applications may be linked to the Servers they run on, IT Services have many links to all the CIs that contribute to that IT Service.

Relationship Processes

The ISO/IEC 20000 Process group that includes Business Relationship Management and Supplier Management.

Release

(Service Transition) A collection of hardware, software, documentation, Processes or other Components required to implement one or more approved Changes to IT Services. The contents of each Release are managed, tested and deployed as a single entity.

Release and Deployment Management

(Service Transition) The Process responsible for both Release Management and Deployment.

Release Identification

(Service Transition) A naming convention used to uniquely identify a Release. The Release Identification typically includes a reference to the Configuration Item and a version number. For example Microsoft Office 2003 SR2.

Release Management

(Service Transition) The Process responsible for Planning, scheduling and controlling the movement of Releases to Test and Live Environments. The primary Objective of Release Management is to ensure that the integrity of the Live Environment is protected and that the correct

Components are released. Release Management is part of the Release and Deployment Management Process.

Release Process

The name used by ISO/IEC 20000 for the Process group that includes Release Management. This group does not include any other Processes.

Release Process is also used as a synonym for Release Management Process.

Release Record

(Service Transition) A Record in the CMDB that defines the content of a Release. A Release Record has Relationships with all Configuration Items that are affected by the Release.

Release Unit

(Service Transition) Components of an IT Service that are normally Released together. A Release Unit typically includes sufficient components to perform a useful Function. For example one Release Unit could be a Desktop PC, including Hardware, Software, Licences, Documentation etc. A different Release Unit may be the complete Payroll Application, including IT Operations Procedures and user training.

Release Window

See Change Window.

Reliability

(Service Design) (Continual Service Improvement) A measure of how long a Configuration Item or IT Service can perform its agreed Function without interruption. Usually measured as MTBF or MTBSI. The term Reliability can also be used to state how likely it is that a Process, Function etc. will deliver its required outputs. See also Availability.

Remediation

(Service Transition) Recovery to a known state after a failed Change or Release.

Repair

(Service Operation) The replacement or correction of a failed Configuration Item.

Request for Change

(Service Transition) A formal proposal for a Change to be made. An RFC includes details of the proposed Change, and may be recorded on paper or electronically. The term RFC is often misused to mean a Change Record, or the Change itself.

Request Fulfilment

(Service Operation) The Process responsible for managing the Lifecycle of all Service Requests.

Requirement

(Service Design) A formal statement of what is needed. For example, a Service Level Requirement, a Project Requirement or the required Deliverables for a Process. See also Statement of requirements.

Resilience

(Service Design) The ability of a Configuration Item or IT Service to resist Failure or to Recover quickly following a Failure. For example an armoured cable will resist failure when put under stress. See also Fault Tolerance.

Resolution

(Service Operation) Action taken to repair the Root Cause of an Incident or Problem, or to implement a Workaround. In ISO/IEC 20000, Resolution Processes is the Process group that includes Incident and Problem Management.

Resolution Processes

The ISO/IEC 20000 Process group that includes Incident Management and Problem Management.

Resource

(Service Strategy) A generic term that includes IT Infrastructure, people, money or anything else that might help to deliver an IT Service. Resources are considered to be Assets of an Organization. *See also* Capability, Service Asset.

Response Time

A measure of the time taken to complete an Operation or Transaction. Used in Capacity Management as a measure of IT Infrastructure Performance, and in Incident Management as a measure of the time taken to answer the phone, or to start Diagnosis.

Responsiveness

A measurement of the time taken to respond to something. This could be Response Time of a Transaction, or the speed with which an IT Service Provider responds to an Incident or Request for Change etc.

Restoration of Service

See Restore.

Restore

(Service Operation) Taking action to return an IT Service to the Users after Repair and Recovery from an Incident. This is the primary Objective of Incident Management.

Retire

(Service Transition) Permanent removal of an IT Service, or other Configuration Item, from the Live Environment. Retired is a stage in the Lifecycle of many Configuration Items.

Return on Investment (ROI)

(Service Strategy) (Continual Service Improvement) A measurement of the expected benefit of an investment. In the simplest sense it is the net profit of an investment divided by the net worth of the assets invested. *See also* Net Present Value, Value on Investment.

Return to Normal

(Service Design) The phase of an IT Service Continuity Plan during which full normal operations are resumed. For example, if an alternative data centre has been in use, then this phase will bring the primary data centre back into operation, and restore the ability to invoke IT Service Continuity Plans again.

Review

An evaluation of a Change, Problem, Process, Project etc. Reviews are typically carried out at predefined points in the Lifecycle, and especially after Closure. The purpose of a Review is to ensure that all Deliverables have been provided, and to identify opportunities for improvement. *See also* Post-Implementation Review.

Rights

(Service Operation) Entitlements, or permissions, granted to a User or Role. For example the Right to modify particular data, or to authorize a Change.

Risk

A possible event that could cause harm or loss, or affect the ability to achieve Objectives. A Risk is measured by the probability of a Threat, the Vulnerability of the Asset to that Threat, and the Impact it would have if it occurred.

Risk Assessment

The initial steps of Risk Management. Analysing the value of Assets to the business, identifying Threats to those

Assets, and evaluating how Vulnerable each Asset is to those Threats. Risk Assessment can be quantitative (based on numerical data) or qualitative.

Risk Management

The Process responsible for identifying, assessing and controlling Risks. *See also* Risk Assessment.

Role

A set of responsibilities, Activities and authorities granted to a person or team. A Role is defined in a Process. One person or team may have multiple Roles, for example the Roles of Configuration Manager and Change Manager may be carried out by a single person.

Rollout

(Service Transition) *See* Deployment.

Most often used to refer to complex or phased Deployments or Deployments to multiple locations.

Root Cause

(Service Operation) The underlying or original cause of an Incident or Problem.

Root Cause Analysis

(Service Operation) An Activity that identifies the Root Cause of an Incident or Problem. RCA typically concentrates on IT Infrastructure failures.

Running Costs

See Operational Costs.

Scalability

The ability of an IT Service, Process, Configuration Item etc. to perform its agreed Function when the Workload or Scope changes.

Scope

The boundary, or extent, to which a Process, Procedure, Certification, Contract etc. applies. For example the Scope of Change Management may include all Live IT Services and related Configuration Items, the Scope of an ISO/IEC 20000 Certificate may include all IT Services delivered out of a named data centre.

Second-line Support

(Service Operation) The second level in a hierarchy of Support Groups involved in the resolution of Incidents and investigation of Problems. Each level contains more specialist skills, or has more time or other resources.

Security

See Information Security Management.

Security Management

See Information Security Management.

Security Policy

See Information Security Policy.

Separation of Concerns

(Service Strategy) An approach to Designing a solution or IT Service that divides the problem into pieces that can be solved independently. This approach separates 'what' is to be done from 'how' it is to be done.

Server

(Service Operation) A computer that is connected to a network and provides software Functions that are used by other Computers.

Service

Delivering something of value to a Customer that is not goods (physical things with material value). Examples of

Services include banking, legal support or e-mail. Service is also used as a synonym for IT Service.

Service Acceptance Criteria

(Service Transition) A set of criteria used to ensure that an IT Service meets its functionality and Quality Requirements and that the IT Service Provider is ready to Operate the new IT Service when it has been Deployed. *See also* Acceptance.

Service Analytics

(Service Strategy) A technique used in the assessment of the Business Impact of Incidents. Service Analytics Models the dependencies between Configuration Items, and the dependencies of IT Services on Configuration Items.

Service Asset

Any Capability or Resource of a Service Provider. *See also* Asset.

Service Asset and Configuration Management

(Service Transition) The Process responsible for both Configuration Management and Asset Management.

Service Capacity Management

(Service Design) (Continual Service Improvement) The Activity responsible for understanding the Performance and Capacity of IT Services. The Resources used by each IT Service and the pattern of usage over time are collected, recorded, and analysed for use in the Capacity Plan. *See also* Business Capacity Management, Resource Capacity Management.

Service Catalogue

(Service Design) A database or structured Document with information about all Live IT Services, including those available for Deployment. The Service Catalogue is the only part of the Service Portfolio published to Customers, and is used to support the sale and delivery of IT Services. The Service Catalogue includes information about deliverables, prices, contact points, ordering and request Processes. *See also* Contract Portfolio.

Service Continuity Management

See IT Service Continuity Management.

Service Contract

(Service Strategy) A Contract to deliver one or more IT Services. The term Service Contract is also used to mean any Agreement to deliver IT Services, whether this is a legal Contract or an SLA. *See also* Contract Portfolio.

Service Culture

A Customer-oriented Culture. The major Objectives of a Service Culture are Customer satisfaction and helping Customers to achieve their Business Objectives.

Service Design

(Service Design) A stage in the Lifecycle of an IT Service. Service Design includes a number of Processes and Functions and is the title of one of the Core ITIL publications. *See also* Design.

Service Design Package

(Service Design) Document(s) defining all aspects of an IT Service and its Requirements through each stage of its Lifecycle. A Service Design Package is produced for each new IT Service, major Change or IT Service Retirement.

Service Desk

(Service Operation) The Single Point of Contact between the Service Provider and the Users. A typical Service Desk manages Incidents and Service Requests, and also handles communication with the Users.

Service Failure Analysis

(Service Design) An Activity that identifies underlying causes of one or more IT Service interruptions. SFA identifies opportunities to improve the IT Service Provider's Processes and tools, and not just the IT Infrastructure. SFA is a time-constrained, project-like activity, rather than an ongoing process of analysis.

Service Hours

(Service Design) (Continual Service Improvement) An agreed time period when a particular IT Service should be available. For example, 'Monday-Friday 08:00 to 17:00 except public holidays'. Service Hours should be defined in a Service Level Agreement.

Service Improvement Plan

(Continual Service Improvement) A formal Plan to implement improvements to a Process or IT Service.

Service Knowledge Management System

(Service Transition) A set of tools and databases that are used to manage knowledge and information. The SMKS includes the Configuration Management System, as well as other tools and databases. The SKMS stores, manages, updates and presents all information that an IT Service Provider needs to manage the full Lifecycle of IT Services.

Service Level

Measured and reported achievement against one or more Service Level Targets. The term Service Level is sometimes used informally to mean Service Level Target.

Service Level Agreement

(Service Design) (Continual Service Improvement) An Agreement between an IT Service Provider and a Customer. The SLA describes the IT Service, documents Service Level Targets and specifies the responsibilities of the IT Service Provider and the Customer. A single SLA may cover multiple IT Services or multiple Customers. *See also* Operational Level Agreement.

Service Level Management

(Service Design) (Continual Service Improvement) The Process responsible for negotiating Service Level Agreements, and ensuring that these are met. SLM is responsible for ensuring that all IT Service Management Processes, Operational Level Agreements and Underpinning Contracts are appropriate for the agreed Service Level Targets. SLM monitors and reports on Service Levels, and holds regular Customer reviews.

Service Level Package

(Service Strategy) A defined level of Utility and Warranty for a particular Service Package. Each SLP is designed to meet the needs of a particular Pattern of Business Activity. *See also* Line of Service.

Service Level Requirement

(Service Design) (Continual Service Improvement) A Customer Requirement for an aspect of an IT Service. SLRs are based on Business Objectives and are used to negotiate agreed Service Level Targets.

Service Level Target

(Service Design) (Continual Service Improvement) A commitment that is documented in a Service Level Agreement. Service Level Targets are based on Service Level Requirements, and are needed to ensure that the IT Service design is Fit for Purpose. Service Level Targets should be measurable, and are usually based on KPIs.

Service Maintenance Objective

(Service Operation) The expected time that a Configuration Item will be unavailable due to planned maintenance Activity.

Service Management

Service Management is a set of specialized organizational capabilities for providing value to Customers in the form of services.

Service Management Lifecycle

An approach to IT Service Management that emphasizes the importance of coordination and Control across the various Functions, Processes and Systems necessary to manage the full Lifecycle of IT Services. The Service Management Lifecycle approach considers the Strategy, Design, Transition, Operation and Continuous Improvement of IT Services.

Service Manager

A manager who is responsible for managing the end-to-end Lifecycle of one or more IT Services. The term Service Manager is also used to mean any manager within the IT Service Provider. Most commonly used to refer to a Business Relationship Manager, a Process Manager, an Account Manager or a senior manager with responsibility for IT Services overall.

Service Operation

(Service Operation) A stage in the Lifecycle of an IT Service. Service Operation includes a number of Processes and Functions and is the title of one of the Core ITIL publications. *See also* Operation.

Service Owner

(Continual Service Improvement) A Role that is accountable for the delivery of a specific IT Service.

Service Package

(Service Strategy) A detailed description of an IT Service that is available to be delivered to Customers. A Service Package includes a Service Level Package and one or more Core Services and Supporting Services.

Service Pipeline

(Service Strategy) A database or structured Document listing all IT Services that are under consideration or Development, but are not yet available to Customers. The Service Pipeline provides a Business view of possible future IT Services and is part of the Service Portfolio that is not normally published to Customers.

Service Portfolio

(Service Strategy) The complete set of Services that are managed by a Service Provider. The Service Portfolio is used to manage the entire Lifecycle of all Services, and includes three Categories: Service Pipeline (proposed or in Development); Service Catalogue (Live or available for Deployment); and Retired Services. *See also* Service Portfolio Management, Contract Portfolio.

Service Portfolio Management

(Service Strategy) The Process responsible for managing the Service Portfolio. Service Portfolio Management considers Services in terms of the Business value that they provide.

Service Potential

(Service Strategy) The total possible value of the overall Capabilities and Resources of the IT Service Provider.

Service Provider

(Service Strategy) An Organization supplying Services to one or more Internal Customers or External Customers. Service Provider is often used as an abbreviation for IT Service Provider. *See also* Type I Service Provider, Type II Service Provider, Type III Service Provider.

Service Provider Interface

(Service Strategy) An interface between the IT Service Provider and a User, Customer, Business Process or a Supplier. Analysis of Service Provider Interfaces helps to coordinate end-to-end management of IT Services.

Service Provisioning Optimization

(Service Strategy) Analysing the finances and constraints of an IT Service to decide if alternative approaches to service delivery might reduce Costs or improve Quality.

Service Reporting

(Continual Service Improvement) The Process responsible for producing and delivering reports of achievement and trends against Service Levels. Service Reporting should agree the format, content and frequency of reports with Customers.

Service Request

(Service Operation) A request from a User for information, or advice, or for a Standard Change or for Access to an IT Service. For example to reset a password, or to provide standard IT Services for a new User. Service Requests are usually handled by a Service Desk, and do not require an RFC to be submitted.

Service Sourcing

(Service Strategy) The Strategy and approach for deciding whether to provide a Service internally or to outsource it to an External Service Provider. Service Sourcing also means the execution of this Strategy.

Service Sourcing includes:

- Internal Sourcing – Internal or Shared Services using Type I or Type II Service Providers
- Traditional Sourcing – Full Service Outsourcing using a Type III Service Provider

- Multi-vendor Sourcing – Prime, Consortium or Selective Outsourcing using Type III Service. Providers.

Service Strategy

(Service Strategy) The title of one of the Core ITIL publications. Service Strategy establishes an overall Strategy for IT Services and for IT Service Management.

Service Transition

(Service Transition) A stage in the Lifecycle of an IT Service. Service Transition includes a number of Processes and Functions and is the title of one of the Core ITIL publications. *See also* Transition.

Service Utility

(Service Strategy) The Functionality of an IT Service from the Customer's perspective. The Business value of an IT Service is created by the combination of Service Utility (what the Service does) and Service Warranty (how well it does it). *See also* Utility.

Service Validation and Testing

(Service Transition) The Process responsible for Validation and Testing of a new or Changed IT Service. Service Validation and Testing ensures that the IT Service matches its Design Specification and will meet the needs of the Business.

Service Valuation

(Service Strategy) A measurement of the total Cost of delivering an IT Service, and the total value to the Business of that IT Service. Service Valuation is used to help the Business and the IT Service Provider agree on the value of the IT Service.

Service Warranty

(Service Strategy) Assurance that an IT Service will meet agreed Requirements. This may be a formal Agreement such as a Service Level Agreement or Contract, or may be a marketing message or brand image. The Business value of an IT Service is created by the combination of Service Utility (what the Service does) and Service Warranty (how well it does it). *See also* Warranty.

Serviceability

(Service Design) (Continual Service Improvement) The ability of a Third-Party Supplier to meet the terms of its Contract. This Contract will include agreed levels of Reliability, Maintainability or Availability for a Configuration Item.

Shift

(Service Operation) A group or team of people who carry out a specific Role for a fixed period of time. For example there could be four shifts of IT Operations Control personnel to support an IT Service that is used 24 hours a day.

Simulation modelling

(Service Design) (Continual Service Improvement) A technique that creates a detailed model to predict the behaviour of a Configuration Item or IT Service. Simulation models can be very accurate but are expensive and time consuming to create. A simulation model is often created by using the actual Configuration Items that are being modelled, with artificial Workloads or Transactions. They are used in Capacity Management when accurate results are important. A simulation model is sometimes called a Performance Benchmark.

Single Point of Contact

(Service Operation) Providing a single consistent way to communicate with an Organization or Business Unit. For example, a Single Point of Contact for an IT Service Provider is usually called a Service Desk.

Single Point of Failure

(Service Design) Any Configuration Item that can cause an Incident when it fails, and for which a Countermeasure has not been implemented. A SPOF may be a person, or a step in a Process or Activity, as well as a Component of the IT Infrastructure. *See also* Failure.

SLAM Chart

(Continual Service Improvement) A Service Level Agreement Monitoring Chart is used to help monitor and report achievements against Service Level Targets. A SLAM Chart is typically colour coded to show whether each agreed Service Level Target has been met, missed, or nearly missed during each of the previous 12 months.

SMART

(Service Design) (Continual Service Improvement) An acronym for helping to remember that targets in Service Level Agreements and Project Plans should be Specific, Measurable, Achievable, Relevant and Timely.

Snapshot

(Service Transition) The current state of a Configuration as captured by a discovery tool. Also used as a synonym for Benchmark. *See also* Baseline.

Source

See Service Sourcing.

Specification

A formal definition of Requirements. A Specification may be used to define technical or Operational Requirements, and may be internal or external. Many public Standards consist of a Code of Practice and a Specification. The Specification defines the Standard against which an Organization can be Audited.

Stakeholder

All people who have an interest in an Organization, Project, IT Service etc. Stakeholders may be interested in the Activities, targets, Resources or Deliverables. Stakeholders may include Customers, Partners, employees, shareholders, owners etc.

Standard

A mandatory Requirement. Examples include ISO/IEC 20000 (an international Standard), an internal security standard for Unix configuration, or a government standard for how financial Records should be maintained. The term Standard is also used to refer to a Code of Practice or Specification published by a Standards Organization such as ISO or BSI. *See also* Guideline.

Standard Change

(Service Transition) A pre-approved Change that is low Risk, relatively common and follows a Procedure or Work Instruction. For example, password reset or provision of standard equipment to a new employee. RFCs are not required to implement a Standard Change, and they are logged and tracked using a different mechanism, such as a Service Request. *See also* Change Model.

Standard Operating Procedures

(Service Operation) Procedures used by IT Operations Management.

Standby

(Service Design) Used to refer to Resources that are not required to deliver the Live IT Services, but are available to support IT Service Continuity Plans. For example a Standby data centre may be maintained to support Hot Standby, Warm Standby or Cold Standby arrangements.

Statement of requirements

(Service Design) A Document containing all Requirements for a product purchase, or a new or changed IT Service. *See also* Terms of Reference.

Status

The name of a required field in many types of Record. It shows the current stage in the Lifecycle of the associated Configuration Item, Incident, Problem etc.

Status Accounting

(Service Transition) The Activity responsible for recording and reporting the Lifecycle of each Configuration Item.

Storage Management

(Service Operation) The Process responsible for managing the storage and maintenance of data throughout its Lifecycle.

Strategic

(Service Strategy) The highest of three levels of Planning and delivery (Strategic, Tactical, Operational). Strategic Activities include Objective setting and long-term Planning to achieve the overall Vision.

Strategy

(Service Strategy) A Strategic Plan designed to achieve defined Objectives.

Super User

(Service Operation) A User who helps other Users, and assists in communication with the Service Desk or other parts of the IT Service Provider. Super Users typically provide support for minor Incidents and training.

Supplier

(Service Strategy) (Service Design) A Third Party responsible for supplying goods or Services that are required to deliver IT services. Examples of suppliers include commodity hardware and software vendors, network and telecom providers, and outsourcing Organizations. *See also* Underpinning Contract, Supply Chain.

Supplier and Contract Database

(Service Design) A database or structured Document used to manage Supplier Contracts throughout their Lifecycle. The SCD contains key Attributes of all Contracts with Suppliers, and should be part of the SMKS.

Supplier Management

(Service Design) The Process responsible for ensuring that all Contracts with Suppliers support the needs of the Business, and that all Suppliers meet their contractual commitments.

Supply Chain

(Service Strategy) The Activities in a Value Chain carried out by Suppliers. A Supply Chain typically involves multiple Suppliers, each adding value to the product or Service.

Support Group

(Service Operation) A group of people with technical skills. Support Groups provide the Technical Support needed by all of the IT Service Management Processes. *See also* Technical Management.

Support Hours

(Service Design) (Service Operation) The times or hours when support is available to the Users. Typically these are the hours when the Service Desk is available. Support Hours should be defined in a Service Level Agreement, and may be different from Service Hours. For example, Service Hours may be 24 hours a day, but the Support Hours may be 07:00 to 19:00.

Supporting Service

(Service Strategy) A Service that enables or enhances a Core Service. For example, a Directory Service or a Backup Service. *See also* Service Package.

SWOT Analysis

(Continual Service Improvement) A technique that reviews and analyses the internal strengths and weaknesses of an Organization and of the external opportunities and threats that it faces. SWOT stands for Strengths, Weaknesses, Opportunities and Threats.

System

A number of related things that work together to achieve an overall Objective. For example:

- A computer System including hardware, software and Applications
- A management System, including multiple Processes that are planned and managed together. For example, a Quality Management System
- A Database Management System or Operating System that includes many software modules that are designed to perform a set of related Functions.

System Management

The part of IT Service Management that focuses on the management of IT Infrastructure rather than Process.

Tactical

The middle of three levels of Planning and delivery (Strategic, Tactical, Operational). Tactical Activities include the medium-term Plans required to achieve specific Objectives, typically over a period of weeks to months.

Tag

(Service Strategy) A short code used to identify a Category. For example tags EC1, EC2, EC3 etc. might be used to identify different Customer outcomes when analysing and comparing Strategies. The term Tag is also used to refer to the activity of assigning Tags to things.

Technical Management

(Service Operation) The Function responsible for providing technical skills in support of IT Services and management of the IT Infrastructure. Technical Management defines the Roles of Support Groups, as well as the tools, Processes and Procedures required.

Technical Observation

(Continual Service Improvement) A technique used in Service Improvement, Problem investigation and Availability Management. Technical support staff meet to monitor the behaviour and Performance of an IT Service and make recommendations for improvement.

Technical Service

See Infrastructure Service.

Technical Support

See Technical Management.

Tension Metrics

(Continual Service Improvement) A set of related Metrics, in which improvements to one Metric have a negative effect on another. Tension Metrics are designed to ensure that an appropriate balance is achieved.

Terms of Reference

(Service Design) A Document specifying the Requirements, Scope, Deliverables, Resources and schedule for a Project or Activity.

Test

(Service Transition) An Activity that verifies that a Configuration Item, IT Service, Process etc. meets its Specification or agreed Requirements. *See also* Service Validation and Testing, Acceptance.

Test Environment

(Service Transition) A controlled Environment used to Test Configuration Items, Builds, IT Services, Processes etc.

Third Party

A person, group or Business that is not part of the Service Level Agreement for an IT Service, but is required to ensure successful delivery of that IT Service. For example, a software Supplier, a hardware maintenance company, or a facilities department. Requirements for Third Parties are typically specified in Underpinning Contracts or Operational Level Agreements.

Third-line Support

(Service Operation) The third level in a hierarchy of Support Groups involved in the resolution of Incidents and investigation of Problems. Each level contains more specialist skills, or has more time or other resources.

Threat

Anything that might exploit a Vulnerability. Any potential cause of an Incident can be considered to be a Threat. For example a fire is a Threat that could exploit the Vulnerability of flammable floor coverings. This term is commonly used in Information Security Management and

IT Service Continuity Management, but also applies to other areas such as Problem and Availability Management.

Threshold

The value of a Metric that should cause an Alert to be generated, or management action to be taken. For example 'Priority 1 Incident not solved within four hours', 'more than five soft disk errors in an hour', or 'more than 10 failed changes in a month'.

Throughput

(Service Design) A measure of the number of Transactions, or other Operations, performed in a fixed time. For example, 5,000 e-mails sent per hour, or 200 disk I/Os per second.

Total Cost of Ownership

(Service Strategy) A methodology used to help make investment decisions. TCO assesses the full Lifecycle Cost of owning a Configuration Item, not just the initial Cost or purchase price. *See also* Total Cost of Utilization.

Total Cost of Utilization

(Service Strategy) A methodology used to help make investment and Service Sourcing decisions. TCU assesses the full Lifecycle Cost to the Customer of using an IT Service. *See also* Total Cost of Ownership.

Total Quality Management

(Continual Service Improvement) A methodology for managing continual Improvement by using a Quality Management System. TQM establishes a Culture involving all people in the Organization in a Process of continual monitoring and improvement.

Transaction

A discrete Function performed by an IT Service. For example transferring money from one bank account to another. A single Transaction may involve numerous additions, deletions and modifications of data. Either all of these complete successfully or none of them is carried out.

Transition

(Service Transition) A change in state, corresponding to a movement of an IT Service or other Configuration Item from one Lifecycle status to the next.

Transition Planning and Support

(Service Transition) The Process responsible for Planning all Service Transition Processes and coordinating the resources that they require. These Service Transition Processes are Change Management, Service Asset and Configuration Management, Release and Deployment Management, Service Validation and Testing, Evaluation and Knowledge Management.

Trend Analysis

(Continual Service Improvement) Analysis of data to identify time-related patterns. Trend Analysis is used in Problem Management to identify common Failures or fragile Configuration Items, and in Capacity Management as a Modelling tool to predict future behaviour. It is also used as a management tool for identifying deficiencies in IT Service Management Processes.

Tuning

The Activity responsible for Planning changes to make the most efficient use of Resources. Tuning is part of Performance Management, which also includes Performance monitoring and implementation of the required Changes.

Type I Service Provider

(Service Strategy) An Internal Service Provider that is embedded within a Business Unit. There may be several Type I Service Providers within an Organization.

Type II Service Provider

(Service Strategy) An Internal Service Provider that provides shared IT Services to more than one Business Unit.

Type III Service Provider

(Service Strategy) A Service Provider that provides IT Services to External Customers.

Underpinning Contract

(Service Design) A Contract between an IT Service Provider and a Third Party. The Third Party provides goods or Services that support delivery of an IT Service to a Customer. The Underpinning Contract defines targets and responsibilities that are required to meet agreed Service Level Targets in an SLA.

Unit Cost

(Service Strategy) The Cost to the IT Service Provider of providing a single Component of an IT Service. For example the Cost of a single desktop PC, or of a single Transaction.

Urgency

(Service Transition) (Service Design) A measure of how long it will be until an Incident, Problem or Change has a significant Impact on the Business. For example a high Impact Incident may have low Urgency, if the Impact will not affect the Business until the end of the financial year. Impact and Urgency are used to assign Priority.

Usability

(Service Design) The ease with which an Application, product, or IT Service can be used. Usability Requirements are often included in a Statement of requirements.

Use Case

(Service Design) A technique used to define required functionality and Objectives, and to design Tests. Use Cases define realistic scenarios that describe interactions between Users and an IT Service or other System. *See also* Change Case.

User

A person who uses the IT Service on a day-to-day basis. Users are distinct from Customers, as some Customers do not use the IT Service directly.

User Profile

(Service Strategy) A pattern of User demand for IT Services. Each User Profile includes one or more Patterns of Business Activity.

Utility

(Service Strategy) Functionality offered by a Product or Service to meet a particular need. Utility is often summarized as 'what it does'. *See also* Service Utility.

Validation

(Service Transition) An Activity that ensures a new or changed IT Service, Process, Plan or other Deliverable meets the needs of the Business. Validation ensures that Business Requirements are met even though these may have changed since the original design. *See also* Verification, Acceptance, Qualification, Service Validation and Testing.

Value Chain

(Service Strategy) A sequence of Processes that creates a product or Service that is of value to a Customer. Each step of the sequence builds on the previous steps and contributes to the overall product or Service. *See also* Value Network.

Value for Money

An informal measure of Cost Effectiveness. Value for Money is often based on a comparison with the Cost of alternatives. *See also* Cost Benefit Analysis.

Value Network

(Service Strategy) A complex set of relationships between two or more groups or organizations. Value is generated through exchange of knowledge, information, goods or Services. *See also* Value Chain, Partnership.

Value on Investment

(Continual Service Improvement) A measurement of the expected benefit of an investment. VOI considers both financial and intangible benefits. *See also* Return on Investment.

Variable Cost

(Service Strategy) A Cost that depends on how much the IT Service is used, how many products are produced, the number and type of Users, or something else that cannot be fixed in advance. *See also* Variable Cost Dynamics.

Variable Cost Dynamics

(Service Strategy) A technique used to understand how overall Costs are affected by the many complex variable elements that contribute to the provision of IT Services.

Variance

The difference between a planned value and the actual measured value. Commonly used in Financial Management, Capacity Management and Service Level Management, but could apply in any area where Plans are in place.

Verification

(Service Transition) An Activity that ensures a new or changed IT Service, Process, Plan or other Deliverable is complete, accurate, reliable and matches its design specification. *See also* Validation, Acceptance, Service Validation and Testing.

Verification and Audit

(Service Transition) The Activities responsible for ensuring that information in the CMDB is accurate and that all Configuration Items have been identified and recorded in the CMDB. Verification includes routine checks that are part of other processes. For example, verifying the serial number of a desktop PC when a User logs an Incident. Audit is a periodic, formal check.

Version

(Service Transition) A Version is used to identify a specific Baseline of a Configuration Item. Versions typically use a naming convention that enables the sequence or date of each Baseline to be identified. For example Payroll Application Version 3 contains updated functionality from Version 2.

Vision

A description of what the Organization intends to become in the future. A Vision is created by senior management and is used to help influence Culture and Strategic Planning.

Vital Business Function

(Service Design) A Function of a Business Process that is critical to the success of the Business. Vital Business Functions are an important consideration of Business Continuity Management, IT Service Continuity Management and Availability Management.

Vulnerability

A weakness that could be exploited by a Threat. For example an open firewall port, a password that is never changed, or a flammable carpet. A missing Control is also considered to be a Vulnerability.

Warm Standby

See Intermediate Recovery.

Warranty

(Service Strategy) A promise or guarantee that a product or Service will meet its agreed Requirements. *See also* Service Validation and Testing, Service Warranty.

Work in Progress

A Status that means Activities have started but are not yet complete. It is commonly used as a Status for Incidents, Problems, Changes etc.

Work Instruction

A Document containing detailed instructions that specify exactly what steps to follow to carry out an Activity. A Work Instruction contains much more detail than a Procedure and is only created if very detailed instructions are needed.

Workaround

(Service Operation) Reducing or eliminating the Impact of an Incident or Problem for which a full Resolution is not yet available. For example by restarting a failed Configuration Item. Workarounds for Problems are documented in Known Error Records. Workarounds for Incidents that do not have associated Problem Records are documented in the Incident Record.

Workload

The Resources required to deliver an identifiable part of an IT Service. Workloads may be categorized by Users, groups of Users or Functions within the IT Service. This is used to assist in analysing and managing the Capacity, Performance and Utilization of Configuration Items and IT Services. The term Workload is sometimes used as a synonym for Throughput.

Index

Index